Also by David Horovitz

A Little Too Close to God: The Thrills and Panic of a Life in Israel

Shalom, Friend: The Life and Legacy of Yitzhak Rabin
(editor, and coauthor with *The Jerusalem Report* staff)

Still Life with Bombers

Still Life with Bombers

Israel in the Age of Terrorism

David Horovitz

Alfred A. Knopf New York 2004

This Is a Borzoi Book Published by Alfred A. Knopf

Published in the United States by Alfred A. Knopf,
a division of Random House, Inc., New York, and simultaneously
in Canada by Random House of Canada Limited, Toronto.
Distributed by Random House, Inc., New York.
www.aaknopf.com

Knopf, Borzoi Books and the colophon
are registered trademarks of Random House, Inc.

ISBN 1-4000-4067-1

Manufactured in the United States of America
First Edition

For Lisa, Josh, Adam and Kayla

Pray for the peace of Jerusalem;
Those who love you shall prosper.
Peace be within your walls . . .

—*Psalm 122*

Things to do today:

1. Get Up
2. Survive
3. Go to Bed

—*refrigerator magnet sold at Magnetron,*
Downtown Disney, Orlando, Florida

Contents

Preface

Early in the sunny afternoon of September 19, 2002, a young Palestinian man boarded a crowded bus in the center of Tel Aviv and detonated the explosive device he was carrying. Yoni Jesner, a nineteen-year-old from Glasgow, Scotland, was one of the six innocent victims of the crime. Yoni's family agreed to donate his organs, and one of his kidneys was transplanted into the body of a seven-year-old Arab girl, Yasmin Abu Ramila.

Yoni had been studying at a yeshiva south of Jerusalem and planned to stay on for another year. He then intended to head to London, where he would take up his deferred place at medical school. After qualifying, he wanted to build his life in Israel as a doctor. On the day those plans were blown away, he had been on his way to see his uncle, who was on vacation at a Tel Aviv hotel.

Three months later, a colleague of mine at work, Adi Covitz, also originally from Scotland, showed me an e-mail she had received. Headed "Yoni's Words of Wisdom for Life," it was a transcript of two pages in Yoni's handwriting that had been found on his body. Written for himself, as a kind of personal behavioral code, some of these thoughts are simply straightforward and sensible: "Sleep before a test or exam." "Always buy presents at least one week in advance." Some of them are the sweet thoughts of a nineteen-year-old: "Don't wear your trousers too high up."

"Don't slag off [put down] past girlfriends in front of prospective ones—very off-putting." And some of them are wise and gracious: "Don't make out that something is very obvious, or people will be scared to ask questions." "Don't be scared to get up and dance. You'll get the hang of it." I know I wasn't making lists like that when I was his age.

Three days after he was killed, Yoni's eldest brother, Ari, twenty-six, convened a press conference at a small downstairs room in the David's Citadel Hotel in Jerusalem. A lawyer living in London, Ari, short-haired, with an unobtrusive black skullcap, wearing glasses and a MARYLAND FOOTBALL T-shirt, spoke calmly and firmly, in Hebrew and in English, about the death of his brother and the way it had struck his family—his emotional turmoil betrayed only, perhaps, by the exaggerated emphasis he placed on some of his words and the way two fingers of each hand pressed down hard on either side of a microphone stand on the table in front of him.

"Yoni was torn from us at such a young age," Ari began. "He had a lot of plans for the future, but he had already achieved much in his short life, and touched and influenced many.

"We are torn apart as a family, hugely shocked," Ari continued. "It will take a long time before the events of the past few days sink in and we can start to grasp what happened."

Ari said he and Yoni had never discussed the possibility of his being killed, "but it had certainly crossed my mind, as it does everyone's in the state of Israel, living with the threat of suicide bombers. . . . But you have to go about your daily life and hope these things aren't going to happen." Ari said that he himself had studied in Israel for two years and noted that, far from deterring his family from maintaining a connection to Israel, Yoni's death had strengthened their "resolve to move here. The fact that we decided that Yoni should be buried in Jerusalem connects us even more deeply to Israel. Yoni would have wanted to stay here and be buried here. A lot of Israelis don't realize," Ari added, "that although many of us live abroad, we regard Israel as our home."

When Ari had answered a handful of questions from the twenty or so journalists crammed into the stuffy room, and the press conference was over, he came over to me—to my surprise, as we'd never met previously—and told me he appreciated the columns that I write in *The Jerusalem Report*, articles that, after the second Intifada erupted in September 2000, were largely devoted to my thoughts on the conflict: the causes, blame, solutions, the futile, relentless bloodshed. Ari said that my thinking largely reflected his own and that of his family, that I wrote the kinds of things he would want to if that was what he did for a living. He said he would be happy and interested to talk to me more about his brother and about his brother's death if I wanted.

I thanked him, tried uselessly to find some words to console him, wished him well and left. But then I went back into the room and asked Ari if I could take him up on his offer. And we tentatively arranged to meet again, which we did.

I believe in the power of the written word, and clearly Ari does, too. My encounter with him deepened my determination to write a book that could offer a sense of what it was like to live through this new-millennial round of the ancient Middle Eastern conflict, why we were plunged into it, how it was understood and misunderstood.

I have focused on the two and a half years from the Camp David summit in July 2000, when we appeared to be on the brink of a permanent Israeli-Palestinian peace treaty, to the overwhelming January 2003 election victory of Ariel Sharon and his Likud party, a ballot-box testament to Israeli despair and disillusion. It was a period of confrontation more bloody and relentlesss than any I had lived through. Seven hundred Israelis died. So, too, did almost two thousand Palestinians, many of whom were also innocent victims. The Middle East is never stagnant, and many aspects of our reality changed after that. Too many did not: The Palestinian mainstream still refused to legitimize a Jewish Israel and to concertedly confront the violent extremists who continued to bomb us. I feel sadly confident that the hostility I detail is no aberration, no final vicious flexing before our conflict is resolved. Nothing would give me more pleasure than to be wrong.

I don't claim to have many answers. I'm not even sure I'm asking the right questions. But I'm trying to do in my way what everybody needs to do in theirs if people like Yoni Jesner, with their lives ahead of them and goodness in their hearts, are to stop dying before their time.

From 1997 to late 1999, I wrote another book, *A Little Too Close to God: The Thrills and Panic of a Life in Israel.* Though not short on bitterness, pessimism and tales of violent conflict, it was, I think, fundamentally optimistic—certainly with regard to the prospects for peace in the Middle

East. I completed it just about the last time I was feeling seriously hopeful, during a brief (illusory) moment when it seemed that, after years of deadlock, the then-imminent election of Ehud Barak as Israel's prime minister might possibly reopen the door to dialogue with the Palestinians and, perhaps, a permanent peace accord, to be followed, perhaps again, by accords normalizing our relations with other hitherto implacable foes in the neighborhood. The book was published in May 2000, coinciding with Barak's landslide election victory over Benjamin Netanyahu, a juncture when such optimism was relatively widespread in Israel, among those who cared in the United States and outside our region, and among some Palestinians, Syrians and moderate Arabs elsewhere. My relative optimism was swiftly overtaken by events: After the failure of the July Camp David summit, hosted by President Clinton, between Barak and Yasser Arafat, and in the wake of a controversial visit to the Temple Mount by the then Israeli opposition leader, Ariel Sharon, that September, the second Intifada erupted, and raged on through weeks, then months, then years.

Deep within me, I share the same basic optimism I had back then—a belief in the decency and humanity of the ordinary people in this dire Middle Eastern nightmare zone. But like most of us with eyes in our head, I am much more immediately conscious than I was just a few short years ago of the evil that men are prepared to do, and especially the threat posed by the death cult that is extremist Islam. Last century, we saw how a vast regime of pure evil could organize and engineer killing on an unimaginable scale. But nowadays, the weaponry of murder is so much more sophisticated, and therefore a wide infrastructure of support is no longer a prerequisite. The readiness of just a few unspeakably callous individuals to use whatever materiel they can attain to kill those they deem their enemies, wherever they can, in as large numbers as they can, represents as potent a threat to life on this planet as man has yet manufactured.

While the year 2002, for instance, may have seen no single assault as cataclysmic as that of September 11, 2001, the murder of Daniel Pearl in January; the attack on the Ghriba synagogue in Djerba, Tunisia, in which 15 people were killed, in April; the killing of 2 people at the Los Angeles airport in July; the hostage taking by Chechen gunmen of an entire Moscow theater audience, which ended with more than 100 deaths, in October; the Bali nightclub bombing, in which 187 people were killed, that same month; the attack on Israelis in Mombasa, Kenya, in which 13 people were killed in November; and that month's 200-plus deaths in

Miss World–centered rioting in Nigeria—not to mention waves of other killings during the year in Afghanistan, Bangladesh, India, Pakistan, the Philippines and Yemen—were all instigated by Islamic extremists. And there have been so many more atrocities since then. It seems to me that our challenge—the challenge of those of us all across the world who delight in the simple pleasure of life—is twofold: to work in concert to deny these forces the weapons of mass destruction they will all too plainly use, and to woo away potential recruits from their embrace.

The second Intifada placed Israel on the front line of this struggle—targeted consistently by Islamic extremists who openly acknowledge their strategic goal of ridding the Middle East of what they describe as its "sovereign Jewish infection." The official Palestinian leadership spoke in less apocryphal, genocidal terms, but it frequently set a similar tone—delegitimizing the Jewish state in the eyes of its people through its media and its education system, and encouraging and funding the bombers—while simultaneously attempting to persuade an often gullible international community that it was seeking only the legitimate, and readily attainable, goal of independence for a new state of Palestine in East Jerusalem, the West Bank and the Gaza Strip.

Some people have told me in recent months, after hearing me lecture, or being interviewed, or reading this or that article I've written, that I have "moved to the right," which, in Israeli political terms, would mean that I have become less willing to compromise with the Palestinians. That is not true. I am as ready as I ever was to support the most dramatic territorial compromise in the cause of true peace. Without that compromise, indeed, we will not be able to maintain the democratic, predominantly Jewish nation we have struggled to preserve here since 1948. The political right in Israel flatly refuses to recognize this, and the policies it espouses offer us no future.

But in the aftermath of Camp David, I no longer believed that Yasser Arafat's Palestinian leadership was prepared for reconciliation, under any terms, with the Jewish state. Arafat knew the demographics—knew how rapidly the Palestinian population will overhaul the Jewish population between the Jordan River and the Mediterranean Sea—and concluded that there was no need to become notorious in Islamic history as the elderly ex-revolutionary who betrayed his faith and his cause to sign a binding accommodation with a Jewish nation. He may or may not have agreed with many of Israel's enemies, who believe that our country, for all its technical military might, can be swept away like a spider's web if attacked ruthlessly and cleverly enough for long enough. But he did believe—and in this he may be right—that time and weight of numbers are on the Palestinians' side, and he allowed the Islamic extremists to wreak merry hell in the interim: Today, there are a little over 5 million Jews and 4.5 million Arabs between the river and the sea; by 2020, the demographers say, there will be a substantial Arab majority. And that is why, when a genuine chance presented itself at Camp David to achieve statehood for his people on almost all of the land they purported to seek, Arafat spurned it. Only the willfully self-delusional—on the far left in Israel, in too much of Europe, in parts of the United States (including some well-meaning souls within the Jewish community)—can still look at what has unfolded here in the last few years and insist that Arafat was really a peacemaker, and that if only Israel had played its diplomatic cards more sensitively, and reined in its military forces, we could have successfully consummated the Oslo peace process.

But if Arafat was prepared to preside over month after month of killings of hundreds of innocent Israelis—provoking appalling suffering for his people, and their deaths by the hundreds, too, as Israel, often in an unconscionably heavy-handed way, tried to protect itself—those who follow him need not do the same. If I did not believe in the possibility of peace in the Middle East, and that there are vast numbers of people not only on the Israeli side but also on the Palestinian side who are determined to achieve it, I could not possibly raise my family here. How could I bring up my children in an environment where the future promised an undiluted sentence of violence and despair, with a constant fear of sudden death?

My most fervent hope is that this book—with its depiction of the untenable reality that the violence of the second Intifada dictated for us all here, and our efforts nonetheless to keep plugging away in a daily life so precious and so vulnerable—can come to be read as history, an account of a bloody bygone era, since superseded by a blessed return to sanity.

—D.H., JERUSALEM, *October 2003*

Still Life with Bombers

1.

Bethlehem, Then and Now

One day in May 2000, we strapped the kids into the backseat and drove to Bethlehem. The journey lasted all of ten minutes: out of the house, a couple of left turns and a short zip along Hebron Road, past a decaying mobile-home village hurriedly erected for Ethiopian immigrants a decade earlier, and an archaeological dig uncovering remains of a Byzantine church built sixteen hundred years ago at the spot where Mary reputedly rested en route from Galilee to her world-changing delivery. There was only one roadblock separating Jerusalem from Bethlehem—the Israeli one; the Palestinian Authority never wished to acknowledge the outer limits of areas under its control. I slowed, intending to ask the army personnel whether there was any reason not to cross into PA territory, but I didn't get the chance. Two dusty-uniformed soldiers, peering out from a roadside kiosk planted among assorted knee-high hard plastic and concrete blocks, waved us through indifferently.

There was no sense whatsoever of having entered a different neighborhood, much less a different country. For a start, we'd seen no uniformed Palestinians. The main road featured the combined Hebrew and Arabic signposting that is routine inside Israel. The houses on either side were finished in the same golden Jerusalem stone as those in the Jewish neighborhoods behind us. Many of the cars carried the registration plates of the PA (green numbers on a white background), but there were plenty with yellow Israeli plates as well, including a convoy of four-wheel-drive vehicles parked outside the restaurant where some friends had suggested we might want to eat.

Inside, the decor was simple and unremarkable. We knew we were in the fiefdom of Yasser Arafat, rather than that of then Israeli prime minister Ehud Barak, only because of the small framed photograph near the kitchen that showed the beaming, sparkly-toothed proprietor standing alongside an equally sparkly Palestinian chairman. The menu was commonplace—hummus and tahini, hamburgers and chips—although the waiters, attending to that small crowd of Israeli jeep drivers and to three or four quieter tables of Palestinian and Israeli families, were wearing immaculate white jackets, which you'd never see in an Israeli restaurant.

This day out in the nearest big city, albeit one that happened to be in quasi-Palestine, was hardly a daring foray into potentially dangerous land. Indeed, if I'd thought there was any risk at all, we wouldn't have gone. My kids were eight, six and three at the time, and I'm not the kind of dad who takes unnecessary risks with them. Or, at least, I didn't think I was that kind of dad in those relatively easygoing days.

We drove leisurely on after lunch, and Bethlehem's fuller character started to reveal itself. There were hints of its past and, as it would turn out, future potential as a war zone in the massive concrete walls that the Israeli army had constructed after gun battles a few years earlier around Rachel's Tomb. Much visited by childless mothers seeking assistance from the divine power that gave Jacob's wife her beloved Joseph and Benjamin, the area saw Israeli soldiers and Palestinian gunmen firing on one another for days in September 1996, in what became known as the "Temple Mount Tunnel Riots"—confrontations that erupted across the West Bank after Israel secretively dug out a new opening to an ancient water tunnel alongside the ultrasensitive Temple Mount in Jerusalem's Old City. Amid similar confrontations, Israel would later abandon other enclaves at less prestigious holy sites inside Palestinian territory—an ancient synagogue on the outskirts of Jericho, and a tomb, rather sketchily linked to the biblical Joseph, on the edge of Nablus. But Rachel's Tomb was too central to the Jewish narrative, too symbolic, to relinquish. So instead of pulling out, the army brought in the builders, whose bleak roughcast barriers had now given the formerly modest site the aspect of a high-security prison.

As we drove farther into the city, Israeli-planted Hebrew signposting thinned out. But the occasional grocery or hardware store advertised its name in both Arabic and Hebrew, and a few dentists had even put up what appeared to be new Hebrew signs to promote their services. For the first time in years, it seemed, Israelis were being invited to place the fate of one of the most sensitive of body parts in the hands, literally, of those who had so recently been perceived as their enemies. We stopped at a warehouse-size store to price Ping-Pong tables. At a roadside grocery, we bought British chocolate bars, scarce in Israel because of the lingering effects of Arab boycott threats against companies that traded with the Jewish state. We strolled around Manger Square, past the polished plate-glass windows of the stores selling olive-wood souvenirs, and ducked low to enter the grotto beneath the Church of the Nativity there, the reputed birthplace of Jesus. Unfazed, we drove past Deheishe refugee camp, once a major Intifada combat zone, where a towering stone sculpture showing the entire territory of pre-Israel mandatory Palestine stood in tribute to the "martyrs" who'd given their lives over the decades of struggle. And when we got lost en route to one of our destinations, Solomon's Pools, ancient reservoirs that used to be a staple of every Jewish tourist group's visit to Israel, we did what good boys and girls who grow up in London (me) and Dallas (my wife, Lisa) are told to do: We asked a policeman, in this case a machine gun–packing Palestinian policeman in a dark blue uniform, who cheerfully redirected us. He even commandeered a loitering teenager, who jumped into the car to ensure we didn't stray again, and who waved us good-bye when we'd found the historic spot, which was located next to the construction site of a substantial shopping mall.

Lisa had been mildly concerned when the youth bounded unexpectedly into the car, and she was more so when we drove farther from the main Bethlehem drag into a neighboring village called Artis, the site of an exquisite church and a backstreet art gallery. When I parked the car, we were immediately surrounded by curious young Palestinian children, who followed us to the doorway of the gallery. But Lisa's understandable concern was misplaced. The whole day passed as uneventfully as I had expected it would. We broadened our horizons and were back in Israel before dusk.

These, after all, were the months of hope and optimism, and the intermingling of our two populations. More than 100,000 Palestinian construction workers, agricultural laborers, hotel waiters and other jobholders were legally making the daily journey into Israel. Perhaps three times that number were making the same journey without the necessary work permits. Israel was thus the absolute mainstay of the Palestinian economy. And hundreds of thousands of Israelis like us were spending Saturdays shopping, eating and seeing the sights in a once Wild West Bank that had now apparently been tamed. Israel had a year earlier elected a prime minister, Barak, whose central campaign platform had been his pledge to attain a permanent peace accord with the supposedly eager Arafat. Peace with Syria, we were led to believe, was but a diplomatic finesse away, and our much-anticipated New Middle East seemed to be taking shape before our eyes. One of the Israel TV newsmagazine shows had just screened a feature about Israeli travel agencies running oversubscribed tours to Gaza, taking Israeli tourists to view firsthand the horrors of the notorious refugee camps mere minutes away: "Here we are at Jebalya, where the Intifada started in 1987." They didn't call it the "first Intifada" back then. The TV crew had filmed a middle-aged Israeli housewife calling home on her cell phone, wide-eyed at the indignities being suffered by the downtrodden Gaza populace she had just been to see, detailing the appalling overcrowding, the empty refrigerators, the sewage running down the narrow camp alleys. "You wouldn't believe it!" she exclaimed, every inch the pampered, camera-clutching Western sightseer, reeling with horrified fascination on initial exposure to the underdeveloped world.

The underlying assumption of these Gaza visits, indeed of the entire craze of visiting Palestine, was that here was a vanishing world, and that this was the last chance to espy the repressed Palestinian in his pitiful habitat, the manipulated pawn of the cynical Middle East powers now about to be liberated, freed to pluck the juicy fruits of peace. At *The Jerusalem Report,* we had just run a cover story titled "Crossing the Great Divide," which detailed that burgeoning phenomenon of Israelis weekending on the other side of the checkpoints. The article, by Peter Hirschberg, documented the lengthy traffic jams that built up every Saturday as thousands of motorists headed toward the West Bank shopping meccas, Palestinian stores where the prices for just about everything, from kitchen utensils to furniture to jeans and teddy bears, were 50 percent below Israeli costs. It noted the heavy baccarat, roulette and blackjack action at the Oasis casino, a pink-stone incongruity opposite a refugee camp in the desert outside Jericho, where daily takings were believed to commonly exceed $1 million, much of it heading into PA coffers. It listed the varied attractions that were drawing Israelis to other benevolent "hot spots": the healing waters of Nablus; the spanking new Jericho cable car, ascending to the monastery at Jesus' testing ground atop the "Mount of

Temptation"; the line of cheap jewelry stores in Gaza City's "Gold Market." Shlomo Dror, an official from the Civil Administration, the Israeli authority that had overseen years of Israeli occupation and was gradually becoming irrelevant as territory was handed over to the PA, told us that the Palestinians were doing everything to protect the Israelis and thus safeguard the growing economic interaction. "The Palestinians are feeling the impact of the peace process," he exulted. "They see that it improves the economy. This is in all our interest." Only one interviewee in the article, Eli Sarig, a pensioner from Tel Aviv, cornered on a day trip to Gaza, sounded a sour note: "One bomb and this is all over," he muttered warily. Then he added with quite remarkable prescience, "If there's no agreement on Jerusalem or the fate of the refugees, the PA might ease up on Hamas, and who will come here then?"

. . . • . . .

I know that the Palestinians with whom we came into contact on that family outing to Bethlehem, and the tens of thousands who could have come into contact with us had they chosen to, were not watching our innocent progress through their city with barely suppressed hatred and revulsion, poised with knives behind their backs to stab me, my wife, my two sons and my daughter the moment their leadership signaled for the murdering to begin. I'm not saying that their hearts genuinely lifted at the sight of our arrival, but they were profiting from our presence, "feeling the impact" of coexistence, as Shlomo Dror put it. And the construction of that shopping mall across from Solomon's Pools, like the massive contemporaneous investment in refurbishing grand but dilapidated hotels and the erection of new ones, was predicated on the firm conviction that something really had changed, that the two peoples were a long way down the road, if not to full and lasting peace, then to a considerable degree of banal and mutually beneficial reconciliation.

And yet, within just a few months of our little visit, this fragile era of interaction was spectacularly concluded, overtaken by an eruption of violence so widespread and so pervasive as to render that earlier period almost inconceivable, impossible to credit if you hadn't experienced it yourself. The Ping-Pong table catalog I brought home that day sits in a living-room cupboard like the prized relic cherished by the hero of one of those kids' fantasy stories, the only tangible proof to the brave adventurer, and to those who doubted him, that he had actually journeyed to the lost world and lived to tell the tale. By that October, Rachel's Tomb was again a focus of armed confrontation, just one of countless flash points throughout the West Bank. Palestinian gunmen had established a reign of fear in much of Bethlehem, commandeering the adjacent Christian village of Beit Jala, from which they poured bullets into Gilo, the southernmost Jerusalem neighborhood across the valley, home to many of our friends and barely five minutes from our own house. That same month, two Israeli reservists—Yosef Avrahami, thirty-eight, and Vadim Norzich, thirty-five—suffering from a fatal lack of directional sense, had blundered harmlessly toward a Palestinian police checkpoint outside Ramallah, north of Jerusalem, been captured at gunpoint, dragged to the city police station and beaten and battered to death there by a savage, bloodthirsty, baying mob. The Jericho casino had disproved its "Oasis" moniker, serving as a firing ground for Palestinian gunmen and attracting the consequent attentions of Israeli shells, which shattered its elegant facade and brought down the ceiling of the gaming hall. The brief era of the Jericho cable car was well and truly over. Cheap West Bank shopping was a thing of the past. Only a suicidal lunatic would have gone refugee-camp sight-seeing in Gaza. And it was front-page news when an amateur Israeli hang-gliding enthusiast, helpless in a wicked wind, crash-landed in Ramallah and made it out without being attacked.

In May 2002, almost two years to the day since that family outing, I spent another afternoon in Bethlehem, watching the final denouement of yet another nadir in Israeli-Palestinian relations, the six-week siege at the Church of the Nativity, in the course of which several people, including the church's own bell ringer, lost their lives. There were no happy-go-lucky Israeli families entering Christ's city that day, no customers at the restaurants, no Israeli mouths trustingly open beneath the assured hands of concerned Palestinian dentists. In the preceding weeks, in a desperate last-resort effort to thwart waves of Palestinian suicide bombers dispatched into Israel across the porous borders from Bethlehem and other West Bank population centers, the Israeli army had reoccupied this city and most others. Storefronts were reduced to rubble. Some of those expensively rebuilt hotels had been destroyed all over again. In places, the roads themselves had been ripped up by Israeli bulldozers. As in previous antiterror incursions over the last months, countless people had been killed, many of them Palestinian civilians.

As a passenger in a clear plastic–walled jeep driven by a freelance Canadian photographer who careened through the streets, I was fairly confident there would be few Palestinian gunmen foolish enough to show themselves and risk their lives in the Israeli-held city by firing on us, and I consequently was more concerned about incurring the wrath of the Israeli forces, around whose tank barrels we had to maneuver disconcertingly on a number of occasions. Abandoning the vehicle perhaps sixteen hundred feet from Manger Square, we walked through the empty streets toward the church, our footsteps echoing in the silence, watched from behind barred windows by Palestinian families kept inside by Israeli curfew orders. We passed dozens of cars casually crushed by Israeli tanks, and walked through the vegetable market with its putrid, foul-smelling produce, hurriedly abandoned when the Israelis arrived.

Reporters were being corralled by the army onto the rooftops of two buildings overlooking the church, one of them the former headquarters of the Bethlehem City Council, where I had interviewed the late longtime mayor Elias Freij in significantly better times. Now tired soldiers were snoring on the floor of his office, and barbed wire had, for some reason, been laid out to prevent access to lower levels.

In the course of the day, to the supporting waves and cheers of their relatives on other rooftops, thirty-nine Palestinian gunmen filed out of the holy site—alleged terrorists, wanted by Israel, who had fired their way into the building six weeks earlier in the accurate assumption that it constituted just about the only place in the city in which they might find refuge. Under the complicated terms of a deal it had taken all those weeks to broker, thirteen of them, the alleged Intifada heavyweights, said by Israel to have "blood on their hands," were promptly sent into exile, absorbed by various European nations. The other twenty-six were summarily dispatched to the Gaza Strip, a sort of "internal" Palestinian exile. After they had departed, in the kind of farcical hiccup that often characterizes the deflation of such moments of high political drama, we witnessed a delay caused by "international human rights activists"—mainly American and European youngsters—who had sneaked into the church days earlier to demonstrate "solidarity" with the Palestinians and who were now refusing to vacate the premises. Having spent rather too long on rooftop duty, one foreign reporter, no longer sympathetic to their cause, offered a suggestion to the army's media liaison team for resolving this unexpected final stalemate: "Tell them," he said, "that you'll kill a dolphin every hour until they come out."

When the ten protesters eventually emerged, plainclothes CIA agents entered the church to catalog the weaponry and booby-trap devices the gunmen had left behind. Dozens of monks and priests and a few nuns milled outside—members of the clergy who had suffered through the siege, resolutely honoring their religious commitment to protect the holy places come what might—embracing and waving. A handful of reporters were escorted into the building to record the squalor—the strewn bedclothes, the discarded food tins, the garbage—and to detail the battered state of the church itself. There were smashed windows, bullet marks in the walls and bullet holes in a nine-hundred-year-old fresco, and there was heavy damage to the adjacent Parish Hall, where a fire that broke out on April 8, just six days into the siege, had blackened the room and destroyed valuable Franciscan robes and parts of a new pipe organ.

Bethlehem remained a war zone for a long time after that, surrounded by Israeli troops, who moved in and pulled out as their information on terror cells dictated, imposing and lifting curfews, clashing with Palestinian gunmen. The soldiers would leave for Christmas and come back for New Year's.

Jesus' birthplace need not have become one more focus of murderous Palestinian plotting and fierce Israeli countermeasures. It could have flourished as a bastion of economic interaction between Israelis and Palestinians, and tourism from Israel, the region and around the world, the most natural of all drawing points for millions of Christians. Its lurch into violence was a direct consequence of what happened two months after my family's outing there: the unsuccessful effort at forging a permanent Israeli-Palestinian peace accord, when Arafat and Barak, hosted by President Clinton, spent two weeks in negotiations at Camp David, the presidential retreat in Maryland.

At those talks, Barak invited Arafat to establish an independent Palestinian state throughout the Gaza Strip and almost all of the West Bank, connected by a guaranteed "safe passage" route across the sovereign state of Israel, which, like it or not, happens to separate those two landmasses. But Arafat would not be wooed. And in late September 2000, Ariel Sharon made his visit to the Temple Mount and four Palestinians were killed there in the heavy rioting that followed a day later. Arafat capitalized on the feverish anti-Israeli sentiment he had fomented, most especially in the Palestinian media over previous weeks, and had schoolchildren bused to junctions adjacent to Jewish settlements in the West Bank and Gaza Strip, deploying gunmen within the crowds to fire on Israeli soldiers, who fired back, with fatal consequences. His TV stations broadcast speeches on Friday mornings from mosques, where imams urged their flocks to kill Jews everywhere. And a murderous campaign of terrorism was born—not a second installment of the popular uprising against Israeli occupation that had raged from 1987 to 1993 and caught Israel, and Arafat, quite unawares, but a documentedly deliberate terrorist assault designed to tear Israel apart and attain through violence that which Israel could never concede in negotiation.

In May 2000, Arafat had watched as the Israeli army, on Prime Minister Barak's orders, fled back to the international border from the "security zone" it had maintained in southern Lebanon for two decades. The soldiers—or rather, the politicians who dispatched them—had been battered into submission by year after year of attacks by the forces of Hezbollah, the fanatical pro-Iranian guerrilla movement that had long since embraced suicide bombing as a strategic weapon and elevated death in the cause of attacking Jews to the highest form of sacrifice. Arafat had watched and, I believe, been inspired.

Shutting itself off from the hundreds of thousands of Palestinian workers, setting up roadblocks, closing off individual cities and ordering curfews, and assassinating key bomb makers and killing no shortage of Palestinian civilians in what the generals called "collateral damage," Israel tried to defend itself against the gunmen and the dozens of suicide bombers who hurled themselves into its civilian midst. And in the process, the question of who had started this conflict and who bore the blame became increasingly irrelevant, overwhelmed by a tide of personal bereavement, mutual pain, mistrust and the desire for vengeance.

So it wasn't only Bethlehem that became a war zone, a scene of physical devastation, economic collapse, loathing and despair. That was the landscape for our two warring peoples everywhere, on either side of the emphatically reestablished dividing line. And there seemed precious little prospect of change or relief. Indeed, it was a measure of how bleak the future looked that I sometimes tried to seek some encouragement from the memory of that uneventful spring day my family spent in Bethlehem: If we could fall from unremarkable interaction to armed confrontation so fast, could we, just perhaps, reverse the tide as rapidly? But rationally, I knew that we had slipped back a generation, maybe several. Another generation of young Palestinians had been educated to hate, and that

2.

The Grisly Lottery

I awoke on October 1, 2002, to find my wife sobbing beside me. When I tried to console her, she explained that she'd checked her e-mail first thing, as always, and found a note from her sister Sharon, who lives in New York. We'd gone to sleep the previous night knowing that an as-yet-unnamed soldier had been killed in Nablus. Sharon had since learned that the twenty-one-year-old who had died, shot by a Palestinian gunman in the Casbah, was Ari Weiss, the son of Rabbi Shmuel Weiss, a charismatic, nondogmatic, open-minded Orthodox rabbi who had been the director of youth programming at the synagogue Lisa had attended when growing up in Dallas, a man she admired and respected. No wonder Lisa was crying—Rabbi Weiss, like Lisa, had moved from Dallas to Israel, made the same decision she had over where to raise his family, with unspeakable consequences. As our children slept the early-morning slumber of the innocents in their rooms down the hall, halfway between birth and military service, we reflected tearfully, for the thousandth time, on the rights and wrongs, on the fairness, of the decisions we had taken about how and where to bring them up, whether we realized the consequences, where our responsibilities lay as Zionists, as Jews, as parents.

That same day, we drove to the funeral at the military cemetery in the Weiss family's adopted hometown, Ra'ananah, northeast of Tel Aviv. The graveyard is at the end of a cul-de-sac, and as we neared it, the traffic thickened, slowed, then halted altogether. When we finally made it to the top of the bottleneck, we saw that a single policeman was responsible for the jam. He motioned us to open the window, then asked us where we were headed. To the funeral of Ari Weiss, we replied—as the realization dawned on us that even as we converged to mourn the latest victim of this conflict, we could be guaranteed no respite from terrorism; the policeman was on security duty, ensuring that nobody would take advantage of this gathering of bereft Israelis to strike at us again.

It was the first time we'd attended a soldier's funeral and, as Lisa said to me when we left an hour and forty harrowing minutes later, she prays she will never have to go through the experience again. And that nobody else will, either.

As most cemeteries are, this one was beautifully peaceful, trees and exuberantly colorful flowers bursting out from around the headstones. The harmony and calm were so distinct from the bustling city down the street, and from the mayhem that had brought us here.

We were greeted by the sight of row upon row of green berets, worn by young people in their late teens and early twenties, members of Ari Weiss's brigade. We followed them from the entrance toward the designated grave site, but we could not get near it; even though the funeral service was not scheduled to start for fifteen minutes or so, that immediate area was already crowded with hundreds of mourners.

We wound up standing on a lawn of exquisite green, below the main throng. The grounds filled up still further, but in a terrible quiet; the silence of the sweltering midafternoon was broken only by intermittent beeps as the mourners switched off their cell phones. Then, from the high ground ahead of us, another row of soldiers filed in, and there was a gasp and a groan from nearer the front as Ari's coffin swung into view, borne shoulder-high and covered in the Israeli flag. And until the service ended—as the coffin was lowered; as relatives and friends and fellow soldiers took their turns shoveling the fresh light brown soil down into the cavity; and as commanders, rabbis, military comrades, siblings and Ari's father delivered their eulogies—an awful low rhythmic wail accompanied the proceedings, the unbearable, disbelieving moan of the bereaved family, burying a young man long, long before his time.

The military eulogies were strikingly understated, and all the more affecting for that. Ari was a steadfast soldier, we heard, one who cared for his friends, even giving up his leave so that they might go home in an emergency. Barely two weeks earlier, the local rabbi said, when Ari and his unit were deployed deep inside Palestinian territory and had run short of supplies, he had telephoned his mother, Susie, his personal superwoman, for help. He sought food not just for himself but for his thirty-five comrades as well. And his mother, needless to say, came through—thanks to the generosity of the local stores and sufficient indomitability in the face of military bureaucracy as to be able to mobilize an army jeep to make the delivery into the heart of Nablus. When a reporter for *The Jerusalem Post* wrote up the story, Ari was anxious that it focus not on him, but on his mother, we were told; the accompanying picture made plain his boyish pride in her achievement. "This was a man who thought not of himself but of how he could help his friends," the rabbi said, "because he came from a family that had instilled in him the finest of compassionate values. . . . Who could have known that, just two weeks later, the wheel would turn in so terrible a way? Who could have known?"

One of Ari's two brothers stepped forward, his voice breaking, to describe him with searing honesty as both "my competition" and "my flesh," and as the peacemaker among their six siblings. A sister, audibly fighting away tears, spoke of her pride in him, and in his death in defense of the people and country of Israel.

Now Ari's father stepped forward. As he spoke, he sounded like a man reaching out for salvation. He referred to the Torah portion concerning Akedat Yitzhak, the recounting of God's supreme test of Abraham, whom he orders to slaughter his son Isaac. It was the portion that Ari had read out in synagogue on the day of his bar mitzvah ceremony eight years earlier. As Abraham raises the knife and prepares to heed the divine command without question, the Lord sends an angel to stay his arm and spare the child. "But this son has not been spared," cried Rabbi Weiss in tones, it seemed to me, less of bitterness than agonized mystification. A man whose faith appeared unshaken at the worst moment a father could ever face, the rabbi declared that he did not question God's will. That Ari had served in the army of his country was "not a punishment, but a privilege," he insisted. But, he asked, pleading, "Oh God, so many offerings, yet still no Temple—when will you finally bring the redemption? When will there be an end to the spilling of blood?"

The funeral concluded with the firing of a salvo of bullets in honor of the dead soldier—four rifles, firing three times in unison, crashingly loud and final. Whatever their intended purpose, they brought to my mind nothing so much as the gunfire that had killed Ari Weiss, the cold finality and the dizzying randomness of death. Hundreds of soldiers were at that funeral, soldiers who had not been killed. Their hundreds of families were not ruined. What quirk had determined that it would be Ari who would die, his family that would be devastated?

We made our way out of the cemetery, past the policeman on security duty and into the traffic. The words that stayed with me were perhaps the simplest that we had heard all day, from the mayor of Ra'ananah, Ze'ev Bielski, in rudimentary English: "We are sorry. We are terribly sorry. We took your son into the army. And he is not coming back."

Ari's funeral brought home to Lisa and me more starkly than any previous horror the potential price we pay for living here, a price we must weigh, day after day, against the determination not to be driven from our land, from the only place where the Jews' fate as a nation is in our own hands. And it brought home for me a related and weighty realization: that I do not have the kind of faith in a benevolent almighty power, running the world according to some unknowable master plan, that might enable me to survive this kind of unthinkable loss with any sanity-preserving acceptance. My connection to this land is not religiously inspired in so profound a way. It is a connection born of an awareness of my family's and my people's religious and historical roots, a fierce identification with the fate of my people, a desire to be part of the rebuilding of our homeland, the shaping of our modern destiny. I most certainly do believe in the existence of higher, unfathomable powers. I cannot look at the miracles that are my children and not gratefully acknowledge that infinite forces are at work in the universe. But such powers have no shape for me, no personality. Unlike the Orthodox, I do not live my life according to a framework that I believe those forces to have laid down for mankind in general or Jews in particular. So I could not cry out to the Almighty for help or succor or enlightenment in times of crisis. And I'd never internalized the size of that vacuum until the funeral of Ari Weiss.

. . . • . . .

The deployment of that security policeman at the top of the road, meanwhile, confirmed a very different realization: that nowhere in this country, absolutely nowhere, was one now immune from terrorism.

I've lived in Israel for half my life now, having moved here from London in 1983. And while there had been very few periods since then when the living was easy, nothing could compare to the hell we'd been forced to endure since the outbreak of this round of conflict. There have always been what, in retrospect, you'd have to call minor irritants about living here, however annoying they may have seemed: People can be rude and loud, and they smoke too much. The pace of life makes Manhattan seem mellow. Finances aren't easy, tax rates are high, and Lisa, a social worker, can't find work in her profession that would more than cover the consequent payments for child care. Schools are underfunded and overcrowded, teachers underpaid. Hospitals, our phenomenal hospitals, always operate under every kind of strain. There's no shortage of intra-Jewish hatreds and discriminations, and they are more intense than in Jewish communities overseas, where Jews need to be more self-effacing. There's reserve duty that can take fathers in combat units away from their homes for a month a year until they're well into their forties. The threats posed by hostile regional powers were there long before the first Intifada or the second: We may be the fourth-mightiest military power on the planet, but you can traverse the country, west to east, in twenty minutes at some points, and it's only a seven-hour drive tip to toe, and that creates vulnerability. None of the above, however, ever outweighed the incomparable pleasure of living in one's homeland, the invigoration of a common purpose among similarly energized people. And it still didn't.

But after the second Intifada started, few of our friends from abroad visited. It was sad for us, but we understood them. They hadn't chosen to live here, so why place themselves in unnecessary danger when, sooner or later, they'd be able to tour with impunity? And, of course, we could always fly out to see them. Some were baffled over why we were staying.

That the tourist streams dried up goes without saying, but the wider economic consequences were devastating, too. One in ten businesses was going bankrupt each year. My daughter, Kayla, on her sixth birthday, October 21, 2002, was walking with Lisa along Emek Refaim Street in the German Colony and passed a hairdresser. It was 5:30 p.m. and the place was empty. "Mummy, that must be a really bad hairdresser," Kayla piped up, "because there's no one in there now, and the last time we walked past there was no one in there, either." "No, honey," said her mother, "it's just that people probably don't have the money to get their hair cut that often." Left unsaid was the fact that there had been a suicide attack at Karkur Junction in northern Israel an hour earlier, in which fourteen

Israelis had been killed, and people were probably, if only briefly, disinclined to go out. "I feel like the country is dying all around us," Lisa said to me that night as we watched the horrific TV footage from the bomb site, just a couple of hours after we'd sung "Happy Birthday" to Kayla around a cake with candy stars and vanilla icing.

We were bashed to hell internationally—by politicians, diplomats and journalists—and told we were the architects of our own misfortune. And we watched the tide of hatred and venom against us spread through the region and beyond. It was hard to try to stay pragmatic, to maintain a semblance of intellectual honesty and sift the genuine and constructive criticisms from the lies and the revisionism lobbed not only from overseas but from our own extremists as well—those on one side, who proclaimed that Oslo would have worked if only we'd been smarter or better, and those on the other side, who wanted the Oslo advocates tried for treason.

It was difficult not to worry about my family's physical health, and my children's long-term psychological health, which I wanted to believe had not been overly affected thus far. They had not, mercifully, been directly exposed to any violence. I think Josh, born in 1992, could cope with my firm ban on his going out with his friends to a nearby crowded pizzeria. They quickly forgot about the earsplitting crack on November 4, 2002, that brought much of Jerusalem to a brief standstill: My son Adam, who was eight at the time, fell off his chair in school, and Josh, in the midst of drawing, said his hand went right off the page. It wasn't a bomb, but an F-16 pilot breaking the sound barrier, as well as air force regulations, setting off car alarms, panic and an investigation. But the older they got, the more aware my children would become of the horrors that surround us. When we visited the Children's Museum in Manhattan in the summer of 2002, there was an exhibit where you could play anchorperson. Josh instinctually sat at the desk, cleared his throat and began "reporting" a bombing. Already, at home or in the car, if he suspected that Lisa and I were whispering because there'd been an attack, Josh demanded details. "Tell me," he'd say. "I live here." And if his suspicions were confirmed, his first question, like all of our first questions, was "How many?"

We didn't have the radio blaring news at home. We'd rather answer the kids' questions ourselves than have the gory details fed in directly by TV. I realized how important that distance was during what should have been a treat: Ehud Ya'ari, among the best-known journalists in Israel, had invited my whole family to visit him at work at Channel 2, the main commercial TV station, where he is the Arab affairs editor. Ehud met us at the entrance to the studio complex, an ultramodern glass and stone construction around the corner from the Elvis Inn landmark—a gas station with a café crammed with Elvis memorabilia—in the hills outside Jerusalem. He led the way into the newsroom and introduced us to a few reporters and presenters. We did a circuit of the makeup room, the editing suites, the monitoring area—where Ehud receives just about every channel in the Arab world—and even met the weather forecaster, so we knew before the rest of the country that the next day would be—no surprise for late summer—hot and dry. The 6:00 p.m. news bulletin was still ten minutes away, so Ehud took us into the studio itself—dozens of lights springing down from the ceiling, impressive banks of TV screens for background, robot cameras untouched by human hand.

Then he escorted us up a spiral staircase to the control room, where the news director and his young and rather glamorous assistants would coordinate the program, cueing correspondents and film clips and switching between the cameras, watching the clock, canceling more marginal items and inserting more vital ones. And after swearing us to silence and placing us in chairs at the back of the room, Ehud popped back down the stairs to the studio, got his makeup touched up, inserted his earpiece and took his seat alongside the presenter, the unflappable Oshrat Kotler, as the digital clock counted down. The intro music rolled, the six o'clock news graphic appeared on one of the dozens of screens in the control room, the director cued Oshrat and she started to read the headlines.

And all of a sudden, this wasn't fun anymore. Because the news in Israel, even when viewed amid all the excitement and positive energy of the newsroom itself, and Israel's hippest and most modern newsroom at that, isn't entertainment for children. The news at the top of the hour concerned a major alert in northern Jerusalem, where there were roadblocks and a massive police deployment because of hard information about a suicide bomber en route. The second item dealt with the capture of a Palestinian terror cell that had trained in Iraq and had been intercepted on its return to the West Bank; it had allegedly been planning an attack at Ben-Gurion Airport. The third item, delivered by our host Ehud, related to the refusal by the then besieged Arafat to hand over the twenty alleged terrorists whom Israel said were hiding out with him in the last remaining building of what had once been his sprawling Ramallah headquarters complex. And the fourth item focused on the death of a young Palestinian boy in Nablus, a thirteen-year-old whose shooting by Israeli forces had been witnessed by a group of international human rights activists, one of whom was interviewed in the studio.

It was only about fifteen minutes before Ehud, his commentator's duties done, returned to us. The most gracious and lovable host imaginable, he even stopped off at the cafeteria to buy some sweets for the kids. Josh and Adam would chorus later that night that the experience had been "fantastic." But their attention had been fixed rigidly on the flickering screens, watching the reporters' larger-than-life faces, the footage of roadblocks in Jerusalem, soldiers on the move and the wailing relatives of the dead young Palestinian boy. I'd much rather they hadn't seen all that.

People with longer memories of Israel than I have will tell you that there were times, particularly in the early years, when the threat of war was omnipresent, and there was no certainty that if and when those hostilities began, the state would prevail. During this second Intifada conflict, by contrast, we were emphatically not under existential military threat. But our nation was at stake, nonetheless. This was terrorism as a strategic weapon—an onslaught designed to terrify all our people, destroy the economy and force mass emigration. Its orchestrators could reasonably have expected it to succeed. That it did not is testament to Israelis' remarkable resilience. The intensity of the terror attacks was unprecedented. In March 2002, for instance, 126 Israelis were killed, in the single bloodiest month for such attacks in the entire history of the modern state. And the attacks were taking place everywhere—not only throughout the disputed territories but throughout sovereign, purportedly nondisputed Israel as well: West Jerusalem, south all the way to Beersheba, north all the way to Haifa and beyond. It was safe nowhere. In fact, with the Al-Qaeda attacks in Mombasa in November 2002—the car bombing of an Israeli-owned hotel, and the near-miss missile attack on an Israeli civilian airplane—we learned that we were under threat even when overseas.

Jerusalem was among the most affected areas, and there were periods when Lisa and I mused about moving somewhere that might be a little less fraught. We have a friend who is raising her family in Zichron Ya'akov, a tranquil, leafy community on a hillside in traditional wine-making country way up north. Much more central, there's Tel Aviv, where the bombers were not striking quite as often, and the atmosphere was lighter than here in Jerusalem, and the downtown was diverse, whereas ours was decaying. We spent many weekends in Tel Aviv—strolling along ultrahip Shenkin

Street, admiring the outré outfits, the palette-stretching hair colors, the dogs, or browsing through the artists' market at Nahalat Binyamin, where you can buy precious little that is practical but almost anything that is creatively extravagant, from didgeridoos (tubular Australian Aboriginal wind instruments) to Little Prince toilet-roll holders. It was our jobs (mine in journalism and Lisa's in real estate), our friends, the fact that I've never wanted to live anywhere but here and the relative quality of the kids' school that kept us in Jerusalem.

All this, and our universal vulnerability: On a flight out of Israel once, I got talking to a gray-haired man sitting next to me. He looked like an older version of Moni Mordechai, spokesman for Rabbi Michael Melchior, a rare moderate Orthodox cleric, who was deputy foreign minister at the time. It turned out that he was indeed spokesman Mordechai's father, Ezra, and he was flying to a conference of shoe manufacturers in Düsseldorf. Our conversation twice disintegrated into schoolboy giggles, thanks to the antics of an unfortunate stewardess and her more unfortunate passengers: She upset an entire beef dinner, tomato sauce and all, down the white T-shirt and across the immaculate pants of Ezra's business partner, who was sitting on the far side of him, and sent another passenger, in a nearby row, rushing to the back of the plane with a similar tomato-based stain down the shoulder and across the front of her white blouse. But we did manage to discuss the admirable uphill efforts of Rabbi Melchior to initiate a peaceful dialogue among Middle Eastern Jewish, Christian and Muslim clerics, an effort energetically backed by such luminaries as Britain's Archbishop of Canterbury but doomed by the death threats and other pressures that gradually led to the withdrawal of the most credible Islamic participants. And I shared with the avuncular Ezra my worries about raising a family in our bloody region, and he reminded me that Tel Aviv, where he lived, was considerably less tense and bomb-blighted than my city. "You might think about moving there," he suggested. "It's really a different world." The very next day saw the bombing that killed Yoni Jesner and five others in central Tel Aviv.

The inescapable, unlimited threat of the bombers meant that to leave home in the morning was to enter a kind of grisly lottery—going out into a world in which there was absolutely no certainty that we, our children and all the other people we loved would make it home safely again at the end of the day. A cold comparison of statistics would indicate that more Israelis were actually being killed in car accidents than acts of terrorism.

But to invoke that comparison is to miss the point: When we get behind the wheels of our cars, we like to imagine—with good reason, if we are capable drivers—that provided we exercise the necessary good sense and, where required, employ the appropriate defensive measures, we will have sufficient control to ensure that we reach our destination unharmed. During this conflict, no amount of commonsense behavior and defensive tactics could provide a similar insurance against death by terrorism. It was out of our hands. As a nation, we had been stripped of a fundamental assumption enjoyed by civilized people the world over: that those with whom we come into contact in the normal course of our business and leisure share our simple appreciation of the gift of life. In fact, we had to assume precisely the opposite: that wherever we congregated in any kind of numbers—at a movie theater, in a café, at a lecture or merely in a huddle on the curbside, waiting to cross the street—somebody might be lurking there, a person whose most fervent desire was to end his or her life violently and to take as many of us as possible to our deaths as well. Many Israelis couldn't even assume that they were safe in their own houses; there were so many cases of gunmen bursting into homes in settlements and fatally shooting parents and children in their beds or cowering defenseless in the corners of their living rooms.

I don't remember reading a newspaper article positing that if anywhere in Israel was a "safe haven" from terrorism, it was the Hebrew University in Jerusalem. But that was a widespread assumption. Overseas students on programs there were explicitly told to stay on campus whenever possible; it was the safest place in town. Why? Because about two thousand of the students there are Arabs. And so it might have been reasonably believed that nobody would want to blow it up. But on July 31, 2002, the Hebrew University was blown up. A bomb was placed in one of the main cafeterias, at the Frank Sinatra Building, and nine people were killed and dozens more injured. The bomber, Muhammad Ouda, was a Palestinian painter working on campus, and he knew full well when he placed his device that he risked killing both Jews and Muslims. If all those who strive to kill and maim the innocent have forsaken their humanity, what words are left with which to revile murderers whose indifference extends to the suffering of their own kin? The bomber had even gotten to know some of the people who regularly ate in the cafeteria he targeted. The president of the university, Professor Menachem Magidor, told me that Ouda had painted the office of one of his victims, Levina Shapira, a fifty-three-year-old Jerusalem-born mother of three.

Hebrew University, it should be stressed, did not assume that it was off-limits to terrorism. It employed stringent security precautions. But who would have suspected the twenty-nine-year-old Ouda, whose father had worked at the university before him and who had no "security record"? That hardly added up to a "typical" bomber's profile. Who, before we all had to believe it, would have believed that he would have been so determined to carry out these killings that when the device failed to detonate via his remote-control cell phone on Tuesday, he would calmly retrieve it, have it "repaired," again smuggle it onto campus over the same high fence, plant it again on Wednesday and this time achieve his purpose? (Incidentally, he turned up for work the following day as usual, and was arrested only after a chance tip-off, which originated with a eyewitness who had seen him praying with Islamic radicals.)

The Hebrew University blast, I have to acknowledge, shocked me pretty thoroughly. Twenty years earlier, fresh off the plane from London, I had moved into my first Israeli home at the Resnick dormitories on that same Mount Scopus campus. I wasn't a complete newcomer; I'd vacationed in Israel many times before. But the transition from tourist to immigrant was made particularly smooth by the university experience, an introduction to Israel that was cushioned by the fact that dozens of overseas students, plenty of them English-speaking people with similar backgrounds, interests and concerns, were taking the same first tentative steps as citizens in the dorm rooms all around me. That included Lisa, whom I first met in a political science class on Mount Scopus. Among the most unfamiliar experiences was living and studying with Arabs. Initially, I was struck by the phenomenal English of the young Arab man and the two Arab women in a literature class I was taking; the markedly different smells that would emanate from the kitchen on the floor above mine when Arab students were cooking; even the unusual plastic flip-flops those students padded about in. Pretty soon, I paid no heed to any of that anymore.

I can't say that I made firm friendships with Arab students in those days, but I was certainly on casual "How are you doing?" terms with them. They were young students feeling their way, just like I was. The intermingling of Israeli Jewish, Arab and overseas students had begun years earlier, and has continued ever since, unremarked and remarkable—especially remarkable given the conflict after September 2000. Jews and Arabs live together, study together and eat together in the cafés and restaurants—like the Frank Sinatra cafeteria. Since July 31, 2002, I haven't been able to stop thinking of the dozens of times I ate my chicken schnitzel with my wife-to-be and other lifelong friends in that cafeteria, or to stop comparing that idyllic past with the reality of that terrible Wednesday afternoon—every window smashed, gashes in the plaster of the wall nearest the blast, the ceiling collapsed, an air-conditioning vent hanging drunkenly down, the floor still damp where the blood had pooled and nine more innocents lay dead, with many more fighting not to join them, youngsters with nails in their necks and shrapnel in their hearts.

I have kept up my Hebrew University connection down the years. I've lectured occasionally to Israeli students and those on the overseas program. I was involved in early 2002 in the university's first alumni reunion. A hoped-for mass gathering of ex-students from abroad proved untenable because of security concerns, but we all decided the event should go ahead anyway, however many felt able to attend—and, in the event, it attracted a healthy and inspiring crowd. A postcard from the university urging us to "hold the date" for the second "Alumni Homecoming & Solidarity Mission" was sitting in my mailbox when I came home from the Sinatra bomb site. (That mission went ahead in December 2002, attended by a small but steadfast group of overseas arrivals.)

On the night of the bombing, I watched young students from Israel, England, America, Japan, Korea, France, Russia and elsewhere tell the TV reporters that they wouldn't capitulate to the terrorists by giving up on Hebrew U. or, in the case of the foreigners, on Israel. "Yes, I still have a Russian passport," said one girl, then added slowly and earnestly, worried that the interviewer wouldn't quite understand what she was saying, "but this is my home."

One lightly injured American answered the inevitable question about what he'd told his panicked mother by saying, "That I got blown up in a bomb . . . and that Israel's great. And the bars are open late."

I don't know how resilient they'll prove in the long term. I certainly don't know if I would have been so brave twenty years ago. But those students, those idealistic, determined students, gave me some much-needed inspiration, as does the pluralistic university they attend.

. . . . • . . .

How would Americans or Britons have fared under this kind of sustained universal aggression? Americans, appallingly, have gained no little experience from September 11, 2001, anthrax in the mail and the Washington Beltway sniper. That adds up to an insight into what we were enduring, and you be the judge as to how you would cope with the daily recognition that violent death can strike anywhere at any moment—in terms of how you might reorganize your personal routine, and in terms of the demands you'd make of your leaders to put an immediate halt to the outrage, the kinds of measures you'd insist be employed to keep your loved ones safe. To my mind, the people of Israel displayed extraordinary fortitude under attack, both in the means they advocated to thwart the dozens upon dozens of bombers and in the determination to keep on living "normal" lives in what were patently abnormal, untenable circumstances.

In fact, what television footage, focusing on the bloody and unnatural rather than on the serene and mundane, did not convey across the oceans is that we *were* living something approximating normal lives. The good restaurants downtown were still packed on the weekends. And people came back to them even after they'd been blown up. Consider, for example, Jerusalem's Moment café, opposite the prime minister's official residence in Rehaviah, where a suicide bomber blew up the packed Saturday-night crowd on March 9, 2002. He killed eleven Israelis, all of whom were between the ages of twenty-two and thirty-one. Moment began rebuilding itself the very next day, and soon regained popularity. When the Sbarro franchise at the junction of Jaffa and King George streets was blown up on August 9, 2001, and fifteen people were killed—a crime notoriously celebrated with a festive replica exhibition, complete with fake pizza, mounted by the Hamas bomber's ideological peers at the Al Najah university campus in Nablus in the West Bank—the owner immediately announced that the only appropriate response was to ensure he reopened as quickly as possible. That Israelis shared his resilience was demonstrated by a rise in business in the first weeks after the reopening. Many restaurants closed down, but that was more because of the collapse of tourism and the local economic meltdown than a consequence of Israelis feeling intimidated.

Concerts and lectures were still well attended. When the artistically courageous David Mamet showed personal courage and flew in to open the July 2002 Jerusalem Film Festival, and disarmingly shrugged off the ovation by remarking that he had merely "come for the popcorn," the Sultan's Pool Amphitheater was filled to overflowing with thousands of "to hell with the risk, we're going out tonight" Israelis, even though four people had just been killed in a double suicide bombing in Tel Aviv and eight more in a bus ambush outside the West Bank settlement of Emanuel. Four months later, when my peerlessly well organized wife had prebooked seats and we turned up to see the second Harry Potter movie at the mall in Mevasseret Tsiyyon, outside Jerusalem, there were hundreds of disappointed, ticketless kids chastising their hapless parents for not having similarly anticipated the overwhelming demand—again, even though malls were prime targets for bombers and about twenty Israelis had been killed in recent days, including in a bus bombing in Jerusalem and a shooting attack in Beit She'an.

I'll never forget waiting in a soap and candle specialty store in Jerusalem's German Colony at the height of a bomber alert. Roadblocks had been up at each end of the street and policemen and soldiers were patrolling the sidewalks, but the customer ahead of me insisted that the infinitely patient salesman repackage the gift items she had just bought. The cops were deployed en masse to prevent a feared explosion, and yet here she was, complaining vigorously that she could still see the staple where he had closed off the cellophane. And then he suggested that he put a pretty sticker over it, and she grudgingly accepted that solution. Half of me wanted to scream, Lady, when we could be blown up here any minute, does it really matter that you can see the staple? But the other half, which prevailed, admired her unrelenting pedantry, her desire to have her gift just so, no matter what was going on around us—the surreal juxtaposition of the murderous and the mundane.

Lisa and I essentially took the same approach, in the same neighborhood, in late summer of 2001, when Lisa gave me what turned out to be a terrific and unusually extravagant birthday present—a wine-appreciation course. Every Wednesday evening for six weeks, no matter that the Intifada was raging and the *hatraot*—bomb warnings—were at their height, we met up with our teacher and two other genteel couples in the local wine store, where we learned to pick out and appreciate our Chardonnays and our Merlots while dutifully cleansing our palates with water between sips and spits. Sitting around a sturdy wooden table at the back of the store, while police cars patrolled the main road outside, we earnestly discussed decanting, correct serving temperatures, the merits of particular vintages and what to look for on labels. It was at once escapist—we could imagine ourselves in Chile, Australia or Italy as we tasted their products—surreal and defiantly normal.

What we had all done, though, to enable ourselves to keep on resolutely closing that front door behind us and gingerly entering the daily lottery, was construct what we liked to think were prudent frameworks to minimize the risks of our exposure. These frameworks were quite possibly entirely delusional, rendering us no safer at all. But they were, I think, what kept us hardy and sane, or at least relatively sane.

Most Jews overseas drew a redline at visiting any part of Israel during the second Intifada. But here, too, we all drew our redlines. We had friends in oft-bombed Tel Aviv who simply wouldn't visit more-bombed Jerusalem. We chose never to take the kids to visit relatives in the West Bank settlements. They, in turn, wouldn't visit friends in settlements in the Gaza Strip. As for the settlers of Gaza, I don't know where they drew their redlines.

For our family, and many others, the redlines included not using the civilian Egged and Dan bus services if at all possible. Lisa and I never let the kids take buses—so much so that boarding a bus, any bus, is an adventure for them. From the comfort of our cars, moreover, we tried to avoid driving too near a bus, especially when it was at a stop—picking up passengers or, heaven forbid, bombers—since an exploding Egged tends to spell devastation not only for those aboard but also for some of those unlucky enough to be right behind, in front of or to the side of the blast.

Sadly, to minimize our presumed vulnerability, another guideline was to employ more caution when dealing with Arabs we didn't know too well. I feel guilty just writing that. But all bets were off out here, and Jews weren't blowing up our buses and shopping centers. I made this dreadful but essential point to very good friends of ours who live in Beit Shemesh, between Jerusalem and Tel Aviv, and who deep into this second Intifada were still employing casual Palestinian laborers to finish construction work on their home. The workers were supervised by Mohammad, the contractor from Hebron who had overseen the original construction. They had no fears about Mohammad, a middle-aged family man who "wouldn't harm a fly," they said, and they always trusted him to bring similarly minded workers. So when the police would carry out routine sweeps for Palestinians working in Israel without the necessary permits and would send a patrol car into their neighborhood, our friends would shelter their illegals inside their house and tell the cops they'd seen no Palestinians about. The subterfuge put a little more bread, for a little longer, on the tables of a few more West Bank Palestinians. I, however, put a stop to that. I told them I was sure they were right to place their faith in Mohammad's decency, but how good a judge could he be of his workers' sensibilities? Maybe one of them had lost a sibling in a confrontation with Israeli troops and was now bent on revenge. Maybe one of them was being pressured by an extremist group, viciously threatened if he didn't harm some Jews. Who could know what scenarios were being played out and what the repercussions might be?

I am absolutely not saying that all Arabs had become enemies—I hope that's clear. But wariness was warranted. Even some Arabs who were Israeli citizens had been convicted of plotting attacks, and others had died carrying them out.

Another aspect of our purportedly prudent antiterror framework—to give an example from my home that will resonate with many Israeli families—saw Lisa and me engage in protracted discussions about subjects as mundane as where to do the shopping. In our case, there were three main options: the small neighborhood grocery stores, the local supermarkets and the big indoor shopping mall.

At the grocery stores, a five-minute walk from home in two or three directions, there were no security guards on the doors and so no impediment to a potential bomber. But then again, there weren't generally that many people roaming the aisles of those shops at any one time, and so there was no particular incentive for a killer to strike there.

At our nearest supermarkets in Talpiot, by contrast, armed security guards were deployed at the front entrances, rigorously plumbing into the depths of handbags and feeling awkwardly under coats and sweaters for concealed explosives. That was a deterrent for the bombers, but not a foolproof one. With large numbers of shoppers converging, supermarkets had proved popular targets. And even if the security guard was thorough and brave, there was no guarantee he'd thwart an attack, just a near certainty he'd get killed in it. In the suicide bombing of the Supersol supermarket at Kiryat Yovel, fifteen minutes away in West Jerusalem, on March 29, 2002, the guard, Haim Smadar, evidently noticed something suspicious about the teenage Palestinian girl who approached the front entrance; he blocked her way and began a body search. At which point, Ayat Akhras detonated the explosives she had strapped around her waist, killing herself, Smadar (a fifty-five-year-old father of six) and a seventeen-year-old Israeli girl, Rachel Levy, whose mother had sent her shopping for Shabbat food.

Our third shopping option, the mall in southern Jerusalem, Kanyon Malkha, was by far the most secure, theoretically. The kids, as well as Lisa and I, are all blondish or ginger-haired and so bear more resemblance to a family of Swedish diplomats than to Middle Easterners. And yet when we drove up to Malkha, we got stopped like everybody else at the entrance to the parking lot. And even after we'd answered the guard's questions in Hebrew, he'd still check the trunk of the car, inspecting the Ikea hammock I kept forgetting to take out, rummaging suspiciously amid the lengths of old kite string, bottles of semiclear liquid (cloudy old water) and bits of wiring from defunct computers. And after we'd parked, there was still the airport-style metal detector gate to negotiate at the entrance or another guard with the airport-style metal/explosive–detector stick. So when we, or anybody else, finally got into the mall, it was only natural to feel safe. But if someone with murderous intentions did somehow, despite all that security, make it into Malkha—closed-in, always jam-packed Malkha—the consequences would be all the more devastating, the death toll all the more horrific. And of course no security system is foolproof, not even in ultraexperienced Israel. In fact, certainly not in Israel, where M16-toting soldiers are routinely waved through the metal detectors, and where Arab gunmen have frequently donned stolen Israeli army uniforms when carrying out attacks.

Similarly, we had family discussions about which cinemas to see movies in, the decisive factor being the precise deployment and perceived competence of the security guards. We discussed which school trips to send the kids on. One day, we kept Adam home rather than allow him to visit a theater in the center of Jerusalem, even though his school had consulted with City Hall, draconian security measures were promised and the mayor himself had assured us that our children would be safe. The mayor legitimately had his own agenda: He did not want to see Israelis "giving in" to terrorism. He believed that perceived weakness among Jerusalemites would encourage the bombers and thus prompt further attacks. In principle, I tended to agree with him. But I'd make my own decisions about where and when to send my children out onto potentially murderous streets.

On the fairly rare occasions when we went out to a restaurant, we'd agonize over that choice, too, with the freshness of the food and breadth of the chef's imagination ranking a distant second and third to the perceived safety of the location. For a treat, we took the kids out to the restaurant at the Cinémathèque just outside central Jerusalem, deeming it to be relatively secure, even though it overlooks the ominously named Valley of Hell (its notoriety earned in the seventh century B.C., for the child sacrifices carried out there by King Manasseh). Not only was there the standard guard at the Cinémathèque's main entrance, but that entrance is reached via a long and awkwardly proportioned staircase; we figured a bomber would have to make an extra-special effort to schlepp down all those stairs, and might opt for somewhere closer to the main road. If that sounds amusing and a little flippant, it isn't meant to—the inconvenience of that staircase was something we earnestly debated, a key factor in our selection of a dining venue.

Lisa and I would go out for a coffee on a Friday morning much more often than for an evening meal. We'd choose one of the cafés on Emek Refaim, the main street of the vibrant German Colony. Kids go to school in Israel Sunday through Friday, but most of us grown-ups work Sunday through Thursday, so Friday offers a weekly opportunity for Lisa and me to spend some daytime together. And having a recreational coffee and croissant out became perforce an act of (mild) Zionist commitment, providing much-needed, if minor, economic support for one of the nation's innumerable cash-strapped businesses. But as we sipped, we'd sometimes ask ourselves if it was "fair to the kids" for us to be out in a high-risk zone—both of us in one place. One of those Emek Refaim cafés, Caffit, was targeted by a suicide bomber in March 2002, but as he tried to detonate his device, he was bustled out of the café and pinned to the ground by the security guard and a brave waiter, who had spotted him. (Café Hillel, down the road, was blown up in September 2003, with seven fatalities, including a bride who was to be married the next day.)

As we took our seats in Caffit or the adjacent Masarik, I found myself acting like a mafiosio, sitting with my back to the wall. It was not that I feared some Sicilian gangster might want to sidle up behind me to settle a generations-old dispute, but because it wasn't good enough for me that there was a guard on the door. I wanted to watch the guard in action, to make sure he was not indulging in that Israeli obsession—speaking endlessly to someone on a cell phone—and thus taking his mind off the bag- and body-searching task at hand. And I wanted to check the new arrivals myself, too: What did she have in all those canvas shopping bags? Why was he wearing that quilted jacket on a sunny morning?

If they were scrupulous, the guards could afford to make no assumptions: Old women, kids in strollers and everyone else had to be checked. My friend Irit tried to enter the Aroma café, opposite Caffit, offering her breezy Hebrew "good morning" to the guard and assuming that her authentic accent would be all the proof he'd need that she was a native-born Israeli and thus no threat. Not so fast. He blocked her path, brandished his bomb-detector stick and demanded to examine the suspicious bulge out front—she was seven months pregnant. After the guard allowed her to pass, he was apologetic but, rightly, unrepentant: Wafa Idris, the Palestinian woman who had detonated a device at the junction of King George and Jaffa streets on January 27, 2002, killing one and injuring more than one hundred, apparently kept it hidden under her sweater as she traveled in, feigning pregnancy to avoid suspicion. Her crime, as the first female bomber, meant not just minor indignity for the likes of Irit but also routine humiliation at checkpoints everywhere for all other Palestinian women.

. . . • . . .

One of our few visitors from abroad asked me how many diners an Israeli restaurant had to hold to be legally obligated to employ a security guard. The question was beside the point: If you didn't employ a guard, no one would patronize your establishment. Exceptions to this rule were rare.

Growing up in an Orthodox Jewish family, and in England, I was, until my twenties, a thoroughly conservative eater. I gradually submitted to my wife's enterprising culinary suggestions but for years drew the line at raw fish. Then I cowrote and edited a biography of the late Yitzhak Rabin; it got translated into Portuguese and I was invited to São Paulo, Brazil, to promote it. And since people eat a lot of sushi in São Paolo, I relented. It was sublime. I've been, er, hooked ever since.

A few years ago, a wonderful sushi restaurant, Sakura, opened up in Jerusalem. It's not cheap, but we'd eat there occasionally. A few months into the new violence, we sortied out again to Sakura, an inconspicuous presence in a narrow ally just behind the town center's Jaffa Road. When we reached it, there was no guard. I looked at Lisa and she looked at me. There was a pause. But since we didn't have the kids with us and we'd really been looking forward to the meal, we both said, "What the hell," and went in. So there was the exception to the rule: If you didn't have a guard, you'd better serve exceptionally good sushi.

. . . • . . .

There were attendant problems with and deficiencies in many of our purportedly protective precautions. Most of all, Israeli Jews' disconnection from Arabs was embittering and counterproductive, an extension of the antibomber collective punishments that saw roadblocks and curfews all over the West Bank. And for all the national and personal precautions, there was never going to be 100 percent bomber protection. We might watch the security guard at the door of a café like hawks to make sure he was doing his job. He might be the most efficient deterrent out there. But this was Israel, where it was a safe bet that many, probably most or quite possibly all of the kitchen staff were Arabs—albeit probably "Israeli" Arabs, part of our 1.2 million–strong Arab minority with Israeli ID papers, rather than the physically excluded Palestinians. There was no knowing how closely they identified with which of their cousins' ideologies, how reluctantly they carried those Israeli papers, how deeply they felt the disgrace of enduring Israeli sovereignty at the Haram al-Sharif, the Temple Mount, or what Israeli-initiated tragedy may have struck one of their relatives. At Rimon, a café at the foot of Ben-Yehuda Street downtown, married assistant chef Othman Kianiya had just negotiated a pay raise with his appreciative bosses when police arrested him in September 2002 for allegedly plotting with others to kill patrons by introducing a chemical substance into their drinks that slows the heart rate.

Then there was the case, in mid-December 2002 (reported on by the Hebrew newspapers), of the security guard at the Amit High School in Lod, outside Tel Aviv. A clean-cut young man in his early twenties, he had performed his duties with quiet professionalism for the two weeks he had been protecting the students. Halaf Kadah, who turned out to be a Ramallah native, had faked an Israeli ID card to get the job. But while the parents heaved huge sighs of relief that the scandalous incident had ended without their kids' being harmed, it's important to point out that Kadah hadn't abused the position to try to perpetrate violence, nor was it ever suggested that he had intended to do so; he was just desperate to find work.

Demonizing all Arabs—as indeed many Israelis, albeit a minority, were tempted into doing—and demanding their "transfer" to who knows where else demeaned us. It also could not square with the reality exemplified by the case of one particular Palestinian worker who every day sneaked illegally into Israel from his West Bank home in order to work. This man knowingly risked arrest for such lawbreaking by stepping forward and putting the country out of its misery in December 2002, when thousands of volunteers were scouring the Jerusalem area for Hodayah, the twenty-two-month-old daughter of estranged couple Roni Kedem and Eli Pimstein. Pimstein had been tearfully telling the cameras that his daughter had disappeared from his home when his back was turned for a moment. The Palestinian man saw Pimstein's picture and went to the police to inform them that days earlier, he now realized, he had seen the "grieving" father coldheartedly preparing the grave for the daughter he would later confess to having murdered. This was a premeditated act, carried out at the behest of whatever demons had entered Pimstein's soul.

Demonizing all Arabs left no accounting, either, for the death-defying courage of Rami Mahameed, a boy of just seventeen from the northern Israeli town of Umm al-Fahm. He was waiting at a bus stop there on September 18, 2002, when another young Arab came up and stood alongside him, carrying a backpack. Suspecting that the backpack contained a bomb, Mahameed calmly asked the man if he had a cell phone, then pretended to call a friend. In fact, he called the police and whispered that he was standing next to a man he thought was a suicide bomber. When the police screeched up minutes later, the bomber, realizing that the game was up, detonated the device he was indeed carrying, killing himself and one of the policemen, Sgt. Moshe Hezkiyah. But the lives of the passengers on the next bus, the one the bomber was presumably waiting to board, were spared. Mahameed was badly hurt in the blast—his hand was broken, and he was wounded in the neck, stomach and liver—but he was arrested and chained hand and foot by policemen, who figured he might have deliberately telephoned to get them killed. For a week, until he regained consciousness, he was handcuffed to his hospital bed, his parents evidently unable to persuade the police of his innocence. There were plaintive apologies, needless to say, when the true story emerged, but few wider lessons were learned, I suspect, about avoiding preconceptions and stereotypes and at least trying to remember the presumption of innocence.

The reliance on anything but buses, and the consequent use of taxis when no car was available, had its complications, too, extending beyond the financial. Until the conflict took hold, a cab in Jerusalem was one of the few places one might have an unremarkable and, therefore, telling conversation with an East Jerusalem Arab. But as the months went by, the Jerusalem taxi companies gradually reduced the ranks of their Arab drivers. The rise in Jewish unemployment meant that there was no shortage of Jewish drivers. And Jewish passengers were telling the mainly Jewish dispatchers not to send them Arab drivers, as they didn't trust them. Between 1967 and 2000, the taxi drivers blithely flitted back and forth from the Jewish west to the Arab east of the city. They took Arab passengers to West Jerusalem hospitals, and Jewish passengers to Arab restaurants and religious and tourist sites in the east. No longer. Now there was only mutual fear and a resurrected, albeit invisible, border.

We used to depend on Hatayelet, the nearest taxi firm. Most of Hatayelet's drivers were pleasant and reliable, and Arab. But in late spring 2002, our local newspaper reported that a certain twenty-four-year-old Hatayelet taxi driver, a Palestinian from East Jerusalem's Um Tuba neighborhood, had been indicted for membership in the Tanzim, the Arafat-affiliated group responsible for many of the year's suicide bombings. It was he who had checked out the "safest," roadblock-free routes into the city from the West Bank for the bombers who had orchestrated a series of attacks, including the March suicide bombing at the Kiryat Yovel supermarket. The driver had enjoyed free passage in and out of the city because of his job. The story spread incorrectly that a Hatayelet driver had ferried in the bombers. Demand for the firm's services plummeted, all the Jewish drivers left and Hatayelet temporarily closed down.

After that, we used any one of several firms, but not the Rehaviah taxi company, which was based in one of the city's more exclusive neighborhoods. That stemmed from one of the other unlovely realities about life here in the second Intifada: It appeared to be driving what may have been previously reasonably adjusted people to near-lunatic behavior.

Lisa needed to go to Hadassah Hospital at Ein Karem, on the northern edge of the city, for what proved to be a routine checkup. She was in her car, waiting in line to enter the parking lot—which was not a simple matter of pressing a button, taking a ticket and waiting for a barrier to rise, as it would be in much of the Western world. It was, instead, a protracted security process, as at Malkha, involving a minor interrogation by the uniformed guard at the entry gate, a cursory inspection of the vehicle's interior and a more stringent inspection of the contents of the trunk. Inevitably, all this checking took time, and though we all recognized why it was necessary, frustration, impatience and other emotions could take over. After fifteen minutes or so in line, Lisa was two cars away from the entrance barrier when a taxi driver for Rehaviah squeezed up alongside her in a lane most definitely intended for one and attempted to cut in front. Lowering the window, my wife gave the line jumper a quizzical look and raised both palms and one eyebrow, a gesture intended to convey mildly disputatious bafflement, which she reinforced merely by calling out something—entirely nonprofane, she insists—to the effect of "Excuse me, can't you see that I'm here?"

A large, red-faced and frankly intimidating individual, Avner (we were to discover his name only later) responded by turning off his engine and proceeding to scream at my wife. Not all the epithets are easily rendered in everyday English, but the following constitutes an expletive-deleted summary of his position, delivered at top volume and with menace: "You are an absolute piece of trash. A nothing. What do you know about this country? I built this country. You're lucky I've got passengers; otherwise, I'd . . . Go back to wherever you came from. We don't need you here. We don't want you here. To hell with you."

He did indeed have passengers—an elderly couple, who sank lower into the backseat as their driver's invective gathered force and pace. Lisa rolled the window back up and made no further effort to impede his passage into the parking lot, but she did have the presence of mind to make note of her verbal assailant's employer, Rehaviah Taxis, as advertised in his front windshield, and his driver number, which was displayed on the taxi's roof. She then parked the car and, crying, made her way to the hospital, where the concerned staff assumed she was nervous about the tests she was to undergo and tried to reassure her that she had nothing to worry about. Composure restored, she later called Rehaviah, which evinced no particular concern, and then called me. "For all he knew, I could have been going to the hospital for some terrible illness," she noted through her tears. "How can people behave like that?" I then called Rehaviah and demanded an apology on my wife's behalf.

"What was the driver's name?" I was asked.

"No idea," I said. "My wife wasn't about to interrupt him to inquire. But his driver number was thirty-one."

"Thirty-one? Oh, Avner," said the voice on the phone, as though that explained everything. Avner was a raging recidivist, apparently. "Yes, he should apologize," the voice allowed, then asked me for Lisa's cell-phone number so that Avner could effect his contrition. And I, displaying impeccable common sense, promptly supplied it.

"You gave him my phone number!" shrieked Lisa, not unreasonably, when I delivered the news of the imminent apology. "Are you insane? You've complained to his bosses that he's a menace and now you've given him my phone number?"

However, Avner never called. A horrified friend of ours, Eli, a longtime Rehaviah user, also telephoned the firm. "Every day until you make a proper apology to my sister Lisa," he threatened, employing a little genetic license, "I will call another friend and tell them not to use Rehaviah." There was still no apology. We let it pass, because, after all, if Avner lost it amid the strain, so did many of the rest of us, including me.

I gathered several more driving tickets than I would wish to confess to here—for speeding or failing to come to a complete halt at stop signs—all of which, naturally, I would ascribe to the tension. Such tension revealed itself in other ways, too. I was at Ben-Gurion Airport, returning home from a brief trip, when a kindly lady behind me in the long line at passport control overheard me speaking English and, assuming I was a tourist, tapped me on the shoulder. When I turned, she graciously attempted to explain in her halting English that I was waiting in the line marked, in Hebrew, ISRAELI PASSPORT HOLDERS ONLY. Unthinking, I snapped back at her, *"Mah echpat lach?"*—"What's it to you?" This was truly horrible behavior. Gracious to the end, she accepted my immediate apology for such rudeness.

I also had a major row with the owner of a café over the quality, or lack thereof, of his kitchen's grapefruit cutter, man or machine—yes, it was as absurd as that sounds. I had ordered half a grapefruit, which arrived in a semivirginal state, the fleshy segments inseparable from the skin. I calmly alerted a waitress to the problem. She returned with disinterred grapefruit flesh on a saucer, acknowledging as she delivered it that this wasn't quite what I was supposed to get, and removing it before I could demur. Then she came back with an entirely nondefiled grapefruit half. Still fairly calm, I walked over to the owner, who was at the cash register, and told him in the most reasonable terms that I couldn't, physically couldn't, eat the grapefruit. He erupted into a torrent of abuse, telling me that the kitchen staff weren't prepared to serve me anymore and he didn't want me eating in his café. At least that's the way I remember it. Seconds later, when I returned to the cash register to try to pay for the coffee I'd already drunk, he apologized profusely, said there'd been a misunderstanding and, holding a hand to his forehead, mentioned the security and financial pressures of maintaining such an establishment in this climate. He implored me to remain, then brought over a sublimely separated grapefruit half. Assuring me he didn't want me to pay for it, he then sent over a complimentary plate of assorted fresh fruit.

. . . • . . .

Bomb attacks and other acts of terrorism are nothing new, either in the Middle East or beyond it. And while they were never tolerable here—how can the premeditated murder of innocents be tolerable?—the frequency was such that most of us in Israel could afford to reassure ourselves that the odds against getting injured were pretty healthy. This was not true during the second Intifada, the armed Intifada. Now there was no one in Israel who hadn't been unnervingly close to such violence. The incidents were coming so fast that many times the victims of one attack had not yet been laid to rest before new bodies were brought into the morgues—and this in a predominantly Jewish country, where the norm is to bury the dead on the day they pass away. The attacks were so frequent that the badly injured were *always* still in the hospital when the maimed from the next attack were carried into the wards. Emergency rescue workers were being treated for cumulative trauma, the devastating impact of having seen so many scenes of horror.

How closely did we personally feel the chill winds of terror? A good friend who works in an office near the junction of Jaffa and King George streets honestly couldn't remember how many bomb blasts had rattled his windows. Our dentist returned from his economically crippled native land, Argentina, where a relative had just been robbed in his home, but as he was expressing his relief at being back somewhere financially stable at least, he heard that the son of his insurance agent had been shot dead by Palestinian gunmen in Hebron. The driver on the number 20 bus that got blown up in Jerusalem on November 21, 2002, looked familiar to us. As we watched him explain on TV how he had mistaken the bomber, who was wearing a satchel on his back, for a student, and as others were detailing the heroism with which he had helped rescue some of the injured and doused the flames in a soldier's hair, we realized he lived on the corner and that we had nearly bought his apartment before settling on the one down the block. We lost count of the number of people who were killed in "drive-by shootings" by gunmen on the roads outside the home of close relatives in a West Bank settlement. A friend's secretary was killed in a Jerusalem bus bombing, and his cousin died in the Hebrew University bombing.

One Friday afternoon at the start of February 2002, I went cycling with Josh to the Tayelet, a labyrinth of stone paths interspersed with beautifully maintained gardens at the edge of our Talpiot neighborhood. We enjoyed the spectacular view of the Old City, the glowing golden Dome of the Rock at center stage. We pedaled down the hill and into adjacent Abu Tor, a mixed Jewish-Arab neighborhood that crosses the old dividing line that until 1967 had separated Jordanian East Jerusalem from the Israeli west of the city. When we got home, and I told Lisa where we'd been, she was horrified. "Didn't you realize that's where a jogger was stabbed and nearly killed not long ago?" I hadn't realized, of course. A week later, at much the same time of day, Lisa, the kids and I were having coffees and milk shakes across the street from the Tayelet—at Shakespeare, a thoroughly non-Stratfordian café-cum-bar that has brought a slight injection of hipness into our comfortably dull residential neighborhood. A little white helicopter buzzed overhead. "Traffic helicopter, most likely. Pay no attention. It's nothing," I assured Lisa, albeit unconvincingly.

"David, it's Friday afternoon. There's no traffic. And it looks like a police helicopter," she retorted, sensible and worried.

Indeed it was. On the other side of the road, down the hill where Josh and I had been cycling a week earlier, in what is known as the "Peace Forest," a twenty-five-year-old Israeli girl named Moran Amit was being murdered, stabbed to death by a gang from Abu Tor, kids in their early and mid-teens. She was a second-year law student, born and raised at Kibbutz Kfar Hanasi in the Upper Galilee, and was profoundly in favor of peace with the Palestinians. She had been out walking with her boyfriend when the murderers approached. He ran one way, she the other, and they opted to chase after her—all this as my kids slurped their shakes across the street.

On June 18, 2002, I woke up just as Lisa was leaving the house around 7:40 to take our two boys and a friend's son and daughter to school. Her route ran from the south to the west of the city, skirting the Talpiot industrial zone, through the working-class Patt neighborhood, past Malkha, with its mall and industrial park, and into the Bayit Vegan district, where Josh and Adam were then in grades four and two, respectively. As she moved north, I was in the shower, so I barely registered a dullish thud in the middle distance. It didn't sound like an explosion, but that's what it was: A suicide bomber from a refugee camp outside Nablus had boarded a number 32A bus heading into the city from the Gilo neighborhood, also via the Patt route. The bomb, an unusually large device that ripped the bus to smithereens, was detonated at the bus stop just up the street from where Lisa was driving. Not far behind the bus, the children of our closest friends in Jerusalem, Vee Vee and Sid, were being driven to school in their car pool. Lisa didn't hear the explosion—she was only a couple of hundred yards away, but the sound was drowned out by the loud music that the kids played en route to school most days. However, long before the ambulances arrived, before the first policemen closed off the street, she passed nearby and saw the twisted metal skeleton. As her stomach lurched, she had the exceptional presence of mind to tell the kids to cover their eyes for a moment, which they did, while she executed the next right turn toward school and away from the scene. At least the children do not have that awful picture embedded in their memories. Only she does.

As serenely as she could, she ferried them to their classrooms, where all the parents and children were clustered in panicked conversation about the blast, its proximity to the school and the fact that numerous children were missing and feared dead (eleven-year-old Galila Bugala and fifteen-year-old Shani Avitzedek, from other schools, were among the nineteen Israelis killed in the bombing; many more children were among the dozens of injured). So she gave the kids a calm version of events, acknowledging that the bang hadn't been all that far away. Adam is still convinced he saw gunmen in black masks running away. He didn't want to go into school that day, consenting only when Lisa told him, accurately, that they would be saying prayers for the children who might have been hurt and, plausibly, that every little boy's prayer might make a difference. It was around this time that Adam felt moved to take some pink sidewalk chalk and inscribe SUPPORT THE ARMY FOR PROTECTING US in big bold letters on the stairs down to our front door.

So how close did we come to the terror? Not that close by second Intifada standards.

. . . • . . .

Why have I been prepared to take such risks with my children's lives? Because just two generations ago, Lisa's father, who grew up in Lodz, lost almost his entire family—his parents, and all but one of his seven siblings (Hirsch Machel had died of appendicitis before World War II)—murdered in Nazi concentration camps, and he survived the camps himself only through a combination of astonishing resilience and good fortune. Because my father, together with his siblings, had to be dragged out of Germany by his parents in the nick of time, severed from the place they had never conceived could be anything other than home to them. Because the Jews have been refugees for centuries, the appreciated, tolerated, despised or loathed minority, but always the minority, dependent for survival on the good graces of others. And now our nation of refugees has restored its ancient refuge. And if that refuge, this homeland, falls again, I see no reason to expect a flowering of Jewish culture, a stabilizing of Jewish demography, a sensitive integration of Jews around the world. Anything but. So I'd like to think I've been putting them through this for their own sakes, a shortish-term risk for a hoped-for long-term benefit, for them and for their children and for their children's children.

My personal commitment to Israel, in fact, has been anything but weakened by the new round of conflict. As I will elaborate later on, I have this powerful belief, founded on what I consider to be firm evidence, that we did genuinely try to make peace with the Palestinians, and essentially offered the right terms for coexistence. And so it would have been entirely dishonest to say, in the face of the agonies we were now facing, "To hell with it. This is something we, with our stupid, stubborn leaders, brought on ourselves." I'm not saying our governments prior to this conflict were perfect. And I think they could have grappled with it more effectively after it broke out. But I am convinced that with an Anwar Sadat or a King Hussein, rather than an Arafat, across the negotiating table, we would have been living side by side with Palestine, with a shared determination to marginalize and thwart the extremists.

But that is a grown-up analysis. And it is our children we are subjecting to its repercussions. Unlike their father, with his reduced period of initial military service and his ultrasafe reservist's duty as a lecturer, my sons will have to serve three years in an army that, much as we would wish it otherwise, we must assume will still be deeply embroiled in life-and-death combat when they turn eighteen. My daughter will have to do two years in green. I never wanted my children to so much as play with toy guns, but how can I tell them not to do so? How can I tell them that guns are evil when their beloved cousin wears a uniform and carries one? And they will do the same, and Israel could not survive without them. Unlike their father and mother, my kids didn't choose to live here. We have made that choice for them. Is that fair, responsible, sensible? "Are we as bad as the Palestinians?" Lisa asked me once, knowing I'd have no answer. "Do we also sacrifice our children for this land?"

One recent summer, the kids spent a few weeks with Lisa's parents in Dallas and attended a summer camp at the local Jewish community center. The camp had a special "Army Day," on which the kids were given green Israeli army–style T-shirts and dog tags. When Josh and Adam came home with theirs, Lisa started crying. Josh asked why. "Because for all the other kids it's just a costume," she told him, trying to smile through the tears. "But for you, it's real."

A few months earlier, in the midst of our suicide-bomber war and with 9/11 still fresh, Josh told us he'd had a dream: He'd been on board a plane, and there was a suicide bomber there. Josh had dressed up like the bomber, convinced him that they were in this together and asked him to come to the back of the plane. There, Josh tricked the bomber into blowing himself up, thereby, in the dream, saving everybody aboard. It was around the same time that Josh asked Lisa why American Jews weren't coming to save Israel, and reasoned, "If the bombers kill us, won't they kill the Jews in America next?"

Lisa says that it was only after hearing all this that she realized how important it is for the children to escape the sense of being defenseless victims, that they need to feel empowered. And despite her instinctual antipathy for the military, she recognized that it is only the army, the army in which they will have to serve, that can give them that strength. "I finally understood how crucial the army is to everything that we are in this country. Without it, we are just victims. After all these years here, I understood what Israeli parents mean when they say so proudly, 'My son is a soldier.' "

On one of our weekend outings, we visited "Kibbutz Hill" outside Rehovot, where the pre-state Haganah fighting force managed to construct (in just three weeks in 1945) and maintain an underground bullet-manufacturing plant almost under the noses of the British forces deployed nearby. We were shown how the two entrances to the factory had been hidden beneath a laundry and a bakery, which also served to explain the noise and smoke to any curious British passersby. We learned how the machinery had been smuggled in from Poland, and how the bullets—more than 2 million of them, for the Sten machine guns used in the 1948 war—had been smuggled out in fake compartments built into gas tankers. We saw the tanning room, in which factory operators had to sit periodically in order to reinforce the cover story that had them disappearing early each morning to work in distant fields. We were told that a single accident in the narrow, crowded subterranean workroom would have doomed the lot of them—and accidents are not unlikely when gunpowder is being sealed into bullet casings, one at a time, with primitive equipment that requires just the right amount of manual force. And at the end of our tour, when we stopped by the little souvenir desk and the kids asked if we could buy them the cheap necklaces with the (empty) bullet pendants that everyone else was taking home as keepsakes, we said yes.

. . . . • . . .

On the day after I wrote the above lines, Lisa and Kayla were heading home past the zoo in northern Jerusalem, close to a side road that feeds in traffic from the West Bank. Lisa was driving on a main road, two lanes in either direction, divided by a metal-fenced central reservation. As she rounded a bend, a Subaru, followed by a small truck, came directly toward her at high speed—against the traffic, on the wrong side of the road. She swerved instinctively to the right, almost colliding with the car alongside her, whose driver also managed to swerve to safety. She realized that both the vehicles that had come at her were driven by Palestinians. Ahead of her on the other side of the road, she now saw an army roadblock, temporarily erected to check all traffic from the West Bank amid warnings of possible suicide bombers. Evidently, the two vehicles that had almost hit her—and that might have been driven by would-be bombers or gunmen, or quite possibly by Palestinians who simply had no permits to be in Israel and so were desperate to skirt the surprise roadblock inspection and consequent arrest—had avoided the soldiers by pulling onto the wrong side of the road and speeding away.

Lisa stopped the car at the roadblock, where about a dozen Palestinian men were standing in the road and raising their shirts to demonstrate to the police that their belts were not bombs. She wanted to approach one of the policemen, so that the two rogue cars would be chased down. But she didn't want to get too close to the roadblock, in case there was a bomber about. So she waited until she was signaled forward by the police, then reported her near miss. "We know about those cars," the cop reassured her. Other units were already in pursuit. She then phoned me and drove home, shaking.

When she described all this to Josh at home a little later, he told her that he was sure the drivers had been suicide bombers and that had they killed her, "You'd have saved other people's lives, but I would have been mad forever." To show that he could contemplate his own demise with similar selflessness, he added, "I'd die if it meant I could save the whole world from suicide bombers."

When I got back from work, soon after that, Lisa, Josh, Adam, Kayla and I sat on the sofa, hugging one another.

"You're lucky to find Kayla and me here today. We could have been somewhere else," said Lisa, attempting to make the point without elucidating it.

"Yes, Daddy," said Kayla, smiling, pleased that she'd figured out the riddle. "We could have been dead."

3.

Scared and Saddened and Sobered and Scarred

In the land that was supposed to be the Jews' safe haven, the advent of the second Intifada meant that the privilege of determining our own destiny was now accompanied by the perpetual threat of detonation. That the Jews were still flowing into the Jewish state, thousands each month, was, unfortunately, less a testament to Israel's attractiveness as a destination than a reflection of just how grim it was becoming elsewhere. Argentina's Jews had shrugged off two colossal bombings in the early 1990s—at the Israeli embassy and the main community offices—and stayed put, even though their president and his government were manifestly making no effort to bring the bombers to justice. But the Jews couldn't ignore the fact that the economic collapse meant that doctors were living off food trawled from trash cans, and along with others from elsewhere on the continent, they flooded into Israel. France's 600,000 Jews, outnumbered ten to one by Muslims, and all too conscious of their diminishing importance to France's always-pleased-to-appease politicians, started to stream this way as well. About a million Russians had come in the previous decade or so, and they still came—tens of thousands a year, bombings notwithstanding.

But for those of us who had come here not to escape crisis in our native lands but because we really wanted to—because we felt a palpable bond—the armed Intifada put that affiliation to the test as never before. Uzi Arad, a former senior Mossad man and top Netanyahu aide turned prominent academic, reminded me that life in modern Israel had almost always been tough, and that Israel had survived against the odds only by repeatedly using initiative and knuckling down when things looked bleakest. We had allowed ourselves some exaggerated optimism in the early to mid-1990s, he thought, but now it was simply time to put our shoulders to the grindstone and cheerfully, philosophically, fatalistically battle for our survival again. That was the veteran Israeli's view, and I'm sure it was valid. But for those of us who hadn't been here in those earlier years, the new round of conflict constituted an extremely rude awakening.

In my little social circle, dominated by people my age, who had young children and who had most deliberately chosen to build their lives here over the past twenty years or so, it inflicted considerable attrition. Close friends from the United States and the United Kingdom, having been here for near on twenty years, are back there now. Others, who had moved here from various American cities, also returned there. Our children were no longer surprised when familiar faces disappeared, although that didn't make the parting any easier or the baffled hurt any less acute. I wouldn't dream of criticizing any of those who left, and least of all those for whom the move back was an economic necessity. The threat of a bomber, however potent, is intangible until the blast. Having to send your children to school by armored car, the last straw for one couple we know who headed back to America from the outskirts of Jerusalem, is miserable and immediate. The reality of having no work—because your overseas investors have chosen somewhere safer and more accessible for their high-tech firm, or because the tourists you used to guide for a living don't come anymore—creates an urgent imperative for action.

The various government ministries and immigration agencies claim not to keep figures for *yerida*—those who "go down" from the rarified heights of the Holy Land. (They're much happier providing the statistics for *aliya*—those "going up.") But anecdotal evidence would suggest maybe one in ten or fifteen of those in our non-Orthodox Western immigrant world abandoned the Zionist ship after September 2000. I'm sure the proportion was far lower among veteran Israelis. For one thing, they don't all have places to go. For another, while some did indeed up and leave and others would have loved to, for many, even most—people like our friends the Kapahs, of whom more later—leaving was unimaginable. They're Israelis. This is where they live, come what may. Even come the bombers.

I think the immigrants who dominate our little social circle are quite impressive for, overwhelmingly, having toughed it out—precisely because they have the easy overseas option: Make the quick visit to confirm the appropriate stateside neighborhood and check out the day school, put the house on the market, call in the shippers, book the flights, survive the short, sharp social shock and they could all have been gone. They toughed it out despite relentless pleas from brothers and mothers overseas to take the nieces and grandchildren somewhere safer: "It's enough already. Go back when it's quieted down." They toughed it out, too, in many cases, despite reservations about the means Israel was using to defend itself, and the deepest pessimism about things getting better in their lifetimes.

Back in the London suburbs where I was raised, where you can live next door to someone for decades and only ever see her as a shadowy figure watching from behind the net curtains, friends, even good friends, don't always speak heart-to-heart about how they're coping. In America generally, by contrast, and certainly in Dallas, where Lisa grew up, people seem to be considerably more open and forthcoming. And here? Here, we have few secrets from our friends, our social support group. My friend Vee Vee fessed up that she found herself making an extra check of the house before she left in the mornings—to ensure that it looked clean and neat—and realized she was doing so because, subconsciously, she was worrying that the next time the front door opened, it might be relatives and friends coming to pay a condolence call following her death or that of her husband or children in a bomb blast. Not much point keeping secrets in that kind of world, was there?

Still, at the height of the second Intifada, when you sat down to talk about the *matsav*—the situation—it was striking how quickly the different perspectives made themselves clear, between those of us who'd made the journey here ourselves and those whose parents, grandparents or great-grandparents had made the choice for them. Between, say, Nikki Hasson-Moss and Sid and Vee Vee Merlin-Knopp in the former category and Ruby Sharabi and Avshalom Kapah in the second. It was also striking how all of us, in one way or another, had felt the impact of this conflict and been changed by it. We were all scared and saddened and sobered and scarred.

. . . . • . . .

Nikki told me the following story:

"I was on the bus on Hebron Road, on the way to work, about a year into the second Intifada. I always go in by bus in the morning [she works at a school for developmentally disabled children across town in Ramat Eshkol], although I get a lift home. The bus was about half full; it was quite early, maybe seven-thirty, and there was a group of about ten schoolkids, young teens, sitting together at the back.

"This kid got on—dark-skinned, tallish, with a backpack slung over his shoulder and wearing a heavy coat on an already warmish day—at the stop near Abu Tor, a mixed Arab and Jewish neighborhood, and he walked straight past the driver, head down, toward the back of the bus, passing me, sitting halfway in. He had his hands in his pockets—holding the detonator, I assumed.

"Well, I just panicked. I kept it inside, but I panicked. This is it, I was saying to myself. This is the end. He's going to blow himself up any second. I was asking myself, Why did I insist on taking the bus? I knew I shouldn't take the bus. And now I'm going to die on the bus. Now this is going to happen to me. And who is going to pick up my children from school?

"Then the bus driver called out to this kid, told him to come back to the front. And I was a complete nervous wreck. But I remember thinking, Why is nobody else panicking? Because they weren't. The other passengers were just calmly sitting there, watching. At least they looked calm. Maybe I looked calm, too, but I doubt it.

"So the kid walked slowly back through the bus, still with his head down, still with his hands in his pockets. And I shuddered as he walked past me. And then, when he reached the driver, I heard him speak this perfect Hebrew, talking about whether he'd paid or not paid or something. And so straight away, I breathed this huge sigh of relief, and, of course, I felt like such an idiot.

"Now he was walking past me again and the kids at the back, obviously his schoolmates, were in hysterics. 'What, he thought you were an Arab?' said one of them, cracking up at the idiocy of the idea. 'A terrorist?' "

Nikki is one of the finest people you could wish to meet, a woman who simply won't think badly of others and is trying to raise her eleven-year-old twins, Saul and Ariella, with a "do unto others as you would wish to be done by" mind-set. She and her husband, Moose (real name Hilton Moss), a TV lighting whiz and former heavy smoker turned cycling enthusiast, grew up in Johannesburg, met on a train to a Jewish youth camp in Cape Town when they were eighteen and, evidently discovering they had much more than manes of black hair in common, got married and immigrated to Israel in the mid-1980s. Both consider themselves to be left-wingers, fervently supportive of territorial compromise, strongly opposed to the settlement enterprise. Moose thought he was too old and creaky to be summoned up for any more reserve duty, but when a call-up notice seemed imminent in 2002, with the army under strain as it redeployed throughout the West Bank, he sat down with Nikki and the twins and told them he'd go to jail if necessary rather than serve in the West Bank. He wasn't prepared to enforce any more weeks of occupation, not in a conflict he regarded as being far short of a war for Israel's existence. (He has dutifully presented himself for various training stints since then, but he hasn't been dispatched to the territories.)

Still, Nikki and Moose were also disillusioned with the Palestinian leadership after the Camp David summit, and largely bereft of hope. It was at their house that I watched Palestinian television, which isn't generally available in Israel—their building is set on an incline and it has a high antenna, so they pick up the signals my building, just a few hundred yards away, can't receive. We all got to see the gruesome hospital scenes and the martyrdom-extolling music-video clips and the long hours of footage of Israeli soldiers shooting Palestinians, maliciously edited to show Israelis shooting Palestinians even in places where they hadn't. Moose gave me occasional updates about how many hours of specifically anti-Israeli programming was running. (Israeli satellite and cable packages offer TV stations from around the world, including those from Egypt, Jordan, Lebanon and other Arab countries. The PA rejected approaches for Palestinian TV to be similarly available, knowing that its manipulative programming could only heighten Israelis' antipathy to the cynical Arafat regime.)

Moose fantasizes about moving his family to New Zealand and spending his leisure time fishing in the middle of nowhere. He could do precisely that if he wanted it enough, and if he were prepared to pressure Nikki, who would have to be torn away from here.

Nikki told me her bus panic story on a Friday afternoon, when I'd popped into their house, as I often do on the Sabbath eve, for a break in the midst of an afternoon cycle ride with Josh and Adam. "The truth is," she said, running her fingers through that mass of hair, "that I'm terrified on lots of mornings. I can't tell you how many times I've sat there worrying that this or that passenger was a bomber and wondering whether I should get off at the next stop, just in case. And I don't know if I've communicated that fear to my children. . . .

"For me, I think the murder of Yael Ohana had a really heavy impact." Yael was gunned down in her home, along with her mother, at Moshav Hamra, an agricultural settlement in the Jordan Valley, on February 6, 2002. The gunman disguised himself in an army uniform, killed an army reservist he encountered, then made his way to the Ohana house. Yael's father was out shopping, and the gunman fatally shot Yael and her mother, Miri, before rescue troops broke into the house and killed him. Born with physical and mental disabilities, Yael, who was eleven when she was killed, had been a student at Nikki's school years earlier, and Nikki said she remembered the devotion with which her mother, a former teacher, had looked after her. "Miri sent Yael in by taxi, with an escort, every day. And she always used to send in roses, grown at the moshav, to brighten the school. When they were killed, it wasn't just names for me. It was people I knew. People I knew to be wonderful and innocent and no threat to anyone. They killed a helpless little child, who had difficulty even walking easily by herself. We've killed children, too, I know. But not deliberately. This was deliberate.

"My biggest fear is of something happening to one of us. I do ask myself, all the time, what we are doing here. I vacillate. My parents, who live in South Africa, are constantly asking me, 'How can you bring up your children in a country like this?' But I also feel that this is where they belong. That here their life has meaning. That this is the place of the Jews. When I wake up in the morning, I never know which feeling will be dominant—the 'What on earth are we doing here?' feeling or the 'This is the only place for us' one. I'm totally schizophrenic. And I fear that I'm passing it on to my children. I think it is important for children to feel good and comfortable about where they live. And I think they lack that and miss that. Sometimes, because of that, I'm jealous of, say, the settlers—because of their certainty, their resilience. I wish I could be totally consumed with faith and could say, 'This is it. This is where we are. Nothing to discuss.'

"And then there's the knowledge that my son will have to serve in the army. He's anything but that gung ho paratrooper mentality. It'll be hard for him. Not long ago, in a shop, he saw a card with the message *'Giyus kal'*—'Have an easy call-up.' And he said, 'Mum, we have to buy that for Shimon,' a friend his own age who *is* the gung ho combat soldier type.

That tore me apart. His friends are already talking about what they want to be in the army, and who wants to be a fighter. And he knows he doesn't and that this friend does.

"Moose and I are the biggest antiviolence people. And we're bringing up our kids in a militaristic country. It's against all my principles. Israeli schools are the most violent in the world. The surveys confirm it. Well, of course they are. Every day when you turn on the TV, it's all violence. What message are we giving our children? We left South Africa—Moose left specifically—to get away from the army there and from apartheid. He did his service here, and years in the reserves, as a medic, because until recently it didn't feel so much like the occupying, oppressing army. But on the other hand, if we just roll over, they'll destroy us and we'll have no country. What should we do? Run away to New Zealand? But our parents have been running away for generations. This is the only place we can call home."

. . . • . . .

Vee Vee and Sid Knopp are two of our very closest friends, soul mates in the ongoing struggle to stay sane and do right by our children. Sid and I both grew up in Britain, come from Orthodox backgrounds, play guitar (he considerably more effectively than I) and like soccer (he infinitely more obsessively than I). We met at university twenty years ago, shared an apartment in our final year and never let the connection slide. Our similarities, though, pale by comparison to the frankly eerie Vee Vee–Lisa parallels: Our wives are both American-raised, married to Brits, mothers of three, hold Columbia master's degrees in social work, are fourth of four daughters, and redheaded to boot. They empathize a lot.

With his soft northern accent, amiable grin, extrovert personality and niche-market products, Sid makes a living as a marketing and sales manager of a firm selling and integrating industrial computers to Israel's once thriving, now struggling high-tech industry. This he supplements with his true love, music—writing songs and singing them for an Israeli firm that produces English-language teaching book-cassette packages. Vee Vee works three-quarters of the time for a nonprofit organization on neighborhood programs for the elderly, and part-time running pet-assisted therapy groups at the zoo for children with emotional and mental difficulties, in between shuttling Talia, Eitan and Shira—eleven, nine and five, respectively, when we talked—to school, kindergarten and after-school classes, and looking after their dog and cat.

They live in a bright, airy, fish- and music-filled three-bedroom apartment in Gilo, a southern Jerusalem neighborhood. It is part of the Jerusalem-area territory captured by Israel in the 1967 war and subsequently annexed, although regarded by the Palestinians as an integral, and Israeli-occupied, area of the West Bank. In the first months of this Intifada, Gilo was almost continuously on the front line. Gunmen from the Arafat-affiliated Palestinian Tanzim commandeered homes in Beit Jala, a Christian village across the valley that divides Gilo from the West Bank, and opened fire most every night on buildings in the Israeli neighborhood, drawing escalating return fire. The Sharon government eventually sent the army into Beit Jala in the summer of 2001 and arrested or forced out the Palestinian gunmen. While Arafat publicly complained to the international community about the invading aggressors, purporting to have been helpless to prevent the original shooting, he simultaneously cut a quiet deal with Israel and promised to rein in the gunmen in the future. The army pulled back out and the zone fell relatively quiet.

In retrospect, admitted Vee Vee with a sigh, perhaps choosing to buy an apartment in Gilo wasn't their smartest move. A masterly understatement. And yet, she added in the same breath, she had no regrets. Their building never came under fire—it was a massive (by frontline standards) seven hundred yards from the heart of the shooting gallery, and largely protected by a hill. "And I wouldn't feel any safer living anywhere else in Jerusalem," she noted. "Still, if I had been living on one of the streets that was shot at, I probably would have moved out of the neighborhood long ago. My thinking was that the bullets hadn't reached here, so we were safe. That was pretty silly when you think rationally, but that's how you think when you live here."

Sid said he was aware when he bought the apartment that Gilo was over the Green Line—the pre-1967 Israel-Jordan border. But he said he'd made some inquiries and "ascertained that Gilo was not remotely considered disputed territory," which he asserted it wasn't until the conflict erupted again. "It wasn't a settlement—where I wouldn't have lived. And I wouldn't have bought if we'd actually been directly across from Beit Jala or any other Arab homes. And it wasn't like Pisgat Ze'ev"—another edge-of-Jerusalem neighborhood of similar status to Gilo—"where I'd also looked for an apartment, but where the houses for the Jews were being built literally next door to the homes of the Arab villagers."

With the dry self-deprecation that is something of a trademark, Sid recalled that after searching in vain for appropriate, affordable three-bedroom apartments throughout Tel Aviv, where he works, Jerusalem, where friends and family live, and most places in between, he had been won over to Gilo by an advertiser's copy line. "How did I buy a million-dollar home for $450,000?" ran the seductive text, actually promoting new homes in a different neighborhood, Givat Mesua, not far away. The smaller print beneath asserted that the farseeing, if quite possibly fictional, homemaker concerned had backed his foresight and purchased early in a luxury housing project in this up-and-coming area, and been rewarded for his prescience with the rapid appreciation in value of his, needless to say, impeccably constructed residence. Sid wasn't—still isn't—a millionaire, and he quite fancied the prospect of becoming one. He didn't have the $450,000, but he did have enough for the early purchase in a new Gilo development of a slightly less spacious home than the one advertised. In Sid's case, given Gilo's subsequent notoriety, the advertising copy might have been more accurate if reversed: "How did I buy a $450,000 apartment for a million dollars?" But the Knopps rightly love their home. "Our view is not of more and more houses, like most Jerusalem neighborhoods, but of trees and the Cremisan Monastery on the facing hillside—the unpopulated hills of southern Jerusalem," said Sid. It's just that its location in a neighborhood unexpectedly drawn to the center of conflict helped heighten what Sid calls his "long-standing pessimism as the son of Holocaust survivors," and it wearied even the instinctual optimism of his wife.

"I never thought there'd be peace," said Sid, exuding gloom from the depths of my living-room sofa. "As a child of Holocaust survivors, I'm always cynical, expecting the worst. I was skeptical, to put it mildly, about the Oslo process from the start. I didn't trust the Palestinian leadership, and I was right, wasn't I?"

In May 1994, under what is known as the "Oslo A" or "Gaza and Jericho first" accord, when the initial group of PLO fighters made their way from their longtime base in Iraq, through Jordan, then across the Allenby Bridge to take up their duties as the policemen of Jericho, Sid was part of the welcoming committee. "These men were being charged with maintaining law and order in West Bank and Gaza areas being handed over by Israel to Palestinian Authority control, and with preventing attacks on Israeli targets. Israel had agreed to arm them. And I"—as a reservist who happened to be on duty at the Allenby Bridge—"was handing over the guns." Speaking like a man who couldn't quite believe the story he was telling, he repeated himself: "They'd line up and we'd give them guns, one at a time, and bullets, and stamp their papers."

Most of the people serving with him, said Sid, were of the emphatic opinion that the Israeli government of the day, the Rabin government, had lost its collective marbles. "We did the job we were told to do. But the private grumbling was all 'What on earth are we doing? This is madness. It is just not going to work. These people are dreadful—Saddam doubles who must be laughing their heads off at us for voluntarily supplying them with the weapons that, sure as anything, they'll be firing at us before long.' My thoughts were pretty similar, although I also felt that, having come this far in the negotiations, just maybe we ought to give it a try. I certainly didn't share that government's view that 'No, it's going to work. It's got to work. We have to give up control of the territories, and these men, like it or not, are our partners.' "

For Sid, the incessant suicide bombings and intermittent gun battles of the 1990s, and what he regarded as the orchestrated eruption of Intifada violence following the Camp David summit, constituted confirmation of that fundamental misjudgment, the impossible attempt at forging a partnership with Arafat. "The Palestinian leaders have proved that they didn't want peace," he said, shrugging. "They look back on this Intifada, in which they have dragged their people backwards—there are no jobs, no chance to travel, curfews, closures, violence, month after month of murders and bombings of Israelis—as more successful than building a state and establishing infrastructure and going forward. Because their ultimate aim is that Israel not exist. And they don't care how much their own people suffer, so long as they are weakening us."

Vee Vee was less categorical, but not much. "I used to think there'd be peace in five years," she said, shaking her head at her naïveté. "Now I think it's going to take a generation or two, at least. In fact, I can't see how it's going to be resolved." But she opted for foolishness over malicious strategy as Arafat's flaw: "The Palestinian leaders are idiots," she asserted. "They messed it up for themselves. They had people like me, who wanted to give them more and more, so that we could live side by side. They've lost me now. Now I say, 'You had your chance, and you obviously didn't want to take it.' "

Sid and Vee Vee watch the news most nights, and read a newspaper each weekend. But they don't obsess about the minutiae. They don't discuss clauses and subsections of the 1998 Wye River Agreement with their guests at the Friday-night dinner table (unless it's our table, and then there's no escape). But to a considerable extent, they were speaking for the new Israeli consensus: the grimly vindicated skeptic and the disenchanted optimist, coalescing in that hitherto nonexistent concept of an Israeli mainstream—a solid two-thirds, and sometimes even more of the electorate—that, with a variety of interpretations, blamed Arafat for the collapsed attempt at peacemaking and concluded that Israeli-Palestinian coexistence was oxymoronic for "a generation or two, at least."

Typically, too, Sid and Vee Vee drew a careful distinction between the Palestinian leadership and the "ordinary people." "The ordinary people don't want to live in squalor," said Sid. "Their leaders have condemned them to it."

Vee Vee: "Ordinary Palestinians have been brainwashed by the leaders to hate Israelis, and Americans, for that matter. They've been taught to blame us for their real trials and tribulations—most of which are simply not our fault. I wonder whether we are partly to blame. Maybe we could have offered them a solution earlier. But I'm not sure that's true. We're certainly not killing them now for the hell of it. I may not agree with some of our tactics, but overall, we go into their territory because there are warehouses of ammunition where they are building bombs. And, sure, Arabs get killed on the way—it's tragic. And we've killed relatives of Intifada leaders when we've tried to get the leaders. But that's war. I wouldn't say we shouldn't go after these people, who are trying to blow us up, because of a fear that someone else, someone innocent, could get hurt. Like I say, that's tragic. But these people have to be stopped before they kill us."

Sid and Vee Vee have learned to live with the nightly gunfire. It was Patt Junction that had them really scared, and the blown-up bus my wife had driven by.

"The first night of firing at Gilo from Beit Jala," said Sid, "I didn't really know what was going on, or how far away it was, or how afraid to feel. The shooting went on for months. We grew accustomed to helicopters roaring overhead, bright surveillance lights blazing as they reconnoitered over Beit Jala. And planes flying over, with no lights at all. About two weeks into the conflict, there was an almighty crash one night, the loudest noise we've ever heard; we think it was the army knocking out a weapons factory in Beit Jala. Bullets landed as far away as Malkha, a few miles away. And the thought that we might get shot did cross my mind. But the truth is that we realized pretty quickly that there was not much likelihood of our apartment, with that hill blocking the line of fire from Beit Jala, being hit. And we got used to living alongside the front line. The living room has double glazing. The bedrooms face away from Beit Jala, on the other side of the building, so you hear less anyway. The kids sleep in the *mamad*"—the reinforced sealable room that every new Israeli building has to have by law (a post–Gulf War ruling) as a potential refuge from nonconventional weapons attack—"so that's even more soundproofed. It's tragic what you can get used to. We'd watch TV some nights, and they'd report shooting at Gilo, and that would be the first we'd know about it. We'd tuned it out. Friends and relatives would call in a panic, and we'd ask them what they were talking about.

"Still, after a while, the kids were affected. They'd hear about stuff in school. And then, of course, there was the day when Talia and Eitan, in their car pool, were two hundred yards behind the bus as it blew up on the road down from Gilo to Patt Junction, their route to school. I was already at work—had been since seven—when Vee Vee called at five to eight to say there had been an attack, that she couldn't get hold of the kids on the cell phones because all the lines had gone down"—the lines are always overloaded after suicide bombs, as panicked relatives try to reach their loved ones—"and that they must have been right there, or very near, when the explosion happened.

"How did I spend the next twenty minutes? I was pacing my office, trying to get through to the car pool's driver, Amos. I was calling friends to hear if anybody had seen them. No one knew anything. They knew there had been an explosion; they didn't know anything about Talia and Eitan.

"I was numb. I had always known it was inevitable that somebody close to me, or I myself, would be near to an attack. I had been in Mahane Yehuda"—the much-bombed outdoor fruit and vegetable market in Jerusalem—"earlier on the day that it was blown up by two suicide bombers in May 1997. I'd seen a SCUD missile fly overhead when I was on duty in the army reserves in 1991. But now I was just numb. I kept on trying to dial to anyone who might have heard anything, and at the same time I was listening to the radio, hearing the first reports of the explosion, and that the area was closed, and that there was a fear of fatalities—that it was a serious attack. Yes, I thought my children might have been killed. But I told myself I'd just keep on trying till I got through and heard that they were okay. Dialing and hoping. I certainly didn't start rethinking, in those twenty minutes, whether I had done the right thing to bring them up in Israel, whether I had taken indefensible risks with their lives."

Vee Vee took up the story: "Lisa called me and said, 'Where are the kids?'

"I said, 'Why?' I know that tone of voice. And I realized right away that something was wrong. 'What's happened?' I asked.

"Lisa said that there was a bomb at Patt Junction. That she'd seen the blown-up bus. I said, 'Oh my God, the kids are right there, or just ahead or just behind, right now.' I hung up and tried to call Amos. But I couldn't get through. Shira was at home with me, and saw me flipping out. I started crying, saying, 'Oh my God' over and over. Shira was asking, 'Mummy, Mummy, what's wrong?' I was trying to calm her down, saying, 'It's nothing,' but I couldn't stop myself from flipping out.

"I don't how long it took to get through to Amos. It felt like hours, but it was probably about twenty minutes. I was watching the coverage on TV all the time, and thinking my son and daughter were in the middle of it. All I could think of was to find out if they were okay. The phone kept ringing—friends and family, sisters, asking me if we were all okay. I kept having to say, 'I don't know, and I need to keep the line clear so that Talia can get through.' Finally, the phone rang—and it was Talia calling, telling me, 'Don't worry, Mummy. We're all right.' They were safely at school. I started crying more—with relief, I suppose. I was trying to calm her down, but really she was calming me down. She was crying; I was crying. I called Sid to tell him they were okay.

"My first instinct was to go and find them and hug them and take them home and just sit with them. On the other hand, I thought the sight of me rushing into the school, struggling to be calm, might freak them out even more. Lisa, who was also at the school, said they looked okay. So I didn't go, although that was very hard for me.

"Once I knew they were safe, I started asking myself whether this was the right thing to be doing, bringing them up in Israel. And I've wondered since then, Are they going to turn around to me one day and ask us why we put them through all this? Because I don't have to. We don't have to live here. We have American passports. So why don't I use them and move the family? If we get into out-and-out war, with bombs exploding everywhere, biological attack, then I don't know if I would stay. Actually, it is the economic situation that might push us out, although the political reality wouldn't make it harder. The fact is, though, that I can clearly get over the fact of my children being two hundred yards away from an exploding bus—because I want to stay here. I wouldn't want to live in America, where it's hard to feel Jewish without becoming religious.

"How can I take these kinds of chances with my children's lives? Because this is my country; this is my life. Maybe if it happened five days in a row, it would push me out. Maybe I'm living in denial: It's not going to happen to me. Even though I know how close we've actually come. Still, I don't feel like I'm being irresponsible to my children, because there's a reason why I'm doing this. I am thinking about their welfare. I can't see them in America, with their friends and their Christmas trees. They have such a great life here, bomb threats apart. As crazy as it is, it is safe enough for the kids to ride around on their bikes in our neighborhood late at night. There is a lot more freedom here for them than there would be in America. They're not part of a minority. And being part of a minority is not fun, I can tell you. As a child, in Buffalo, I hated being the only Jew in my class at school. And being asked to tell the rest of my class, on Hanukkah, what it meant. And them singing a token Hanukkah song, while I had to sing all the Christmas songs and draw trees at Christmas, bunnies at Easter.

"When the kids got home that day, I talked to them about it. They didn't see any body parts, thank God. They heard the boom. They saw the smoke. But they didn't see the flying limbs. They had to drive past the twisted shell of the bus. Eitan told me about that. He described how the roof had been blown off, and he told me about the remnants of a car alongside it that had been wrecked.

"I've felt the repercussions of the bombing ever since from the kids. Talia started insisting on sleeping with the light on. She'd never done that before. She'd never been afraid of the dark, afraid to go to bed. She's told me she wants to live in America because it will be safer. She wants to move there with my two sisters and their families, who are also here. If we're out in the car and draw up alongside a bus, Eitan asks us to try to get away from it, because maybe it's going to blow up. If we go to the mall, he asks how long we're going to be in it—maybe there'll be an explosion. Downtown, he'll ask, 'Isn't it dangerous to be here?' So, obviously I only go to town when I have to with him—like for allergy shots every three weeks.

"Nowadays, we drive up and down that road every day. By the end of that same day there was hardly a sign that anything had happened there, that nineteen Israelis had been killed. There was no blood on the road, just flowers.

"I was actually supposed to be going for a meeting about a new job that morning. And I wound up going, as scheduled. My hands were shaking, but everything was fine and normal. That's how it is. You go on with life."

Sid again:

"I've never had real doubts about Israel being the right place to live and raise my family—because of my 'child of survivors' background, and always having felt that I didn't belong in Britain. Living in Israel is almost impossible—financially, emotionally, even culturally, and now from the point of view of safety. But most of my ancestors were murdered because they were Jews. Today, deep into this conflict, I'm probably more of a Zionist than I've ever been. We have to have our own country.

"I'm pessimistic about what will unfold here now, but my main day-to-day concern is economic. I don't think the Arabs will ever make peace. They'll never be offered so good a deal as they were by Barak. And we'll never be able to trust them. Terrorism is so much more global, so much more of a threat, so we can take fewer risks, I think. Twenty years ago, when I came here, there were isolated stabbings in the street, a very occasional bus hijacking or bombing. We'd had the plane hijackings. Now you have September eleventh. Incidentally, I was in the army that day—just about to go on guard duty at Megiddo jail. A guard shouted down to us, 'A plane has just hit one of the Twin Towers.' Soon after, I'm up on the roof, looking down on two hundred Palestinian security prisoners, and there's this joyous hubbub as the tragedy unfolds. They are gathered around the radio, rejoicing. You have day after day of suicide bombings. Dozens of intercepted blasts. Fears of megaterror—downing skyscrapers or hitting nuclear plants or gas-distribution centers, as they have tried to do here twice. It's reached the stage now where you can get blown up anyplace, anytime. But I won't be driven out.

"As for the Palestinians, I do feel sorry for some of them. The people of

Beit Jala, most of them Christians, had lived in peace with Israel for decades. They were forced into harboring terrorists."

Vee Vee: "The residents of Beit Jala were definitely taken advantage of. Beit Jala lived in harmony with Gilo for years. The heads of Beit Jala and Gilo used to get together, to eat together. The Palestinian Authority gave them no choice. It took over their houses. They feared for their lives. Every day that we were firing at Beit Jala, I'd feel terrible. But when the shooting at Gilo stopped in Beit Jala, we stopped firing back. Of course. We didn't initiate the shooting—we fired back at the gunmen. We could have bombed the hell out them, but we didn't do that."

Sid: "But part of me also feels, as regards the rest of the Palestinians in the West Bank and Gaza, that they made their own bed. They allowed this leadership to champion them, never revolted against the corruption. They allowed themselves to be the pawns of the Arab world. When Israel was founded, and Arab leaders decided that the Palestinians would not live side by side with the new Jewish state, they allowed themselves to be forced to live in squalid refugee camps down the decades, when Israel, in equally, if not more, unpromising conditions, set about absorbing its hundreds of thousands of Jewish refugees from Arab lands. The entire crisis—their entire misfortune and now, of course, ours—stems from their initial and continued refusal to accept Israel. And the bottom line: I'm much too caught up in the Jewish tragedy right now to worry too much about their tragedy."

. . . • . . .

Ruby Sharabi has never given the slightest consideration to the notion of living anywhere but Israel. He is native-born, his family working-class Sephardim. And he is still recovering from the Palestinian bullet that nearly killed him a few weeks into this conflict—two weeks before the scheduled end of his three-year military service. Would he ever think of living in America? I asked him as we waited to board a flight back to Israel from the States. He looked up at me quizzically, eyes scrunched and nose wrinkled, pretty sure I was kidding, perplexed to see that I wasn't. "Come on," he scoffed. "What would I do here? I'm Israeli."

I first met Ruby on a summer's night outside Entrance 3 to Ben-Gurion Airport. I was flying out to speak at a conference of young American

Jewish leaders in Arizona, and so was he. I was the professional veteran, invited to give an overview of Israeli current affairs—the mood, the media coverage, the political prospects. He was the rookie, an Israeli caught up in the Israeli-Diaspora relationship because of what had happened to him on October 11, 2000. That was the day he was shot by a Palestinian sniper outside Hebron. In the speech he'd prepared for the conference, with a lot of assistance from a friend of his in Tel Aviv—a Jews for Jesus freak, who, he cheerfully acknowledged, had been trying to convert him—he referred to his injury in the briefest and vaguest of terms. "I was hit in the groin," he said. In fact, a bullet had gone right through him, front to back, ripping through his flesh. He wasn't quite as good as new, but he was close. And he knew how lucky he was not to be paralyzed, or dead.

The people who had invited me to the conference had asked me to meet up with Ruby on the way, to help him negotiate the paperwork and travel complexities en route to Phoenix. His English wasn't dreadful, but they wanted to be sure he didn't mistakenly head off to Bermuda or Mexico City on the connection. I recognized him easily enough at the airport—he is bespectacled, wiry and tall. An ex–army paratrooper with the height and build of someone well able to take care of himself, he nevertheless struck me as vulnerable, hesitant, anything but pushy. We sat separately on the plane, so it wasn't until we got to Toronto and had an hour to kill before the connection that he told me in detail how he had gotten hurt.

Then twenty-one, Ruby was deployed with his unit, escorting convoys of army vehicles around the Hebron area. Returning to base at the end of one such session, they came upon a tire placed upright in the middle of the main road. Stuck to it were pictures of various Israeli prime ministers—Golda Meir, Rabin, Netanyahu—overlaid with a large black swastika. Trailing off from the side of the tire was some wiring. "It was obviously meant to look like a bomb," he recalled. "But we still had to assume that it might genuinely be a bomb. So we radioed for the bomb squad and kept the traffic safely back in both directions until the sappers arrived. A crowd of Palestinians built up as we waited, and it got dark, and then shots rang out from the Palestinian town, Halhoul, alongside us. We turned on some projector lights and tried to spot the source of the fire. I saw two flashes, and fired back at them, and there was a heavy gun battle for a few minutes. Then one of the Palestinian gunmen fired tear gas at us. I had been stepping out to fire and then taking cover behind the armor-plated door of our jeep, but the tear gas was overpowering, and by the time I could see straight again, one of their gunmen must have moved to a new position, where I wasn't covered by the door. When the bullet hit, it felt like I'd been struck by a hand grenade. A massive explosion of pain. I tried to walk forward, backward, but I couldn't. I just collapsed on the floor."

Initially, the unit's field medic told Ruby he'd sustained only a minor injury. "He found the exit wound, teaspoon-size, in my butt and thought I'd just been scratched. I didn't argue, but I knew it was much worse. I was telling them jokes as they evacuated me"—by ambulance and, later, by helicopter to a Jerusalem hospital—"and telling myself just to stay awake. I didn't know what would happen if I allowed myself to drift into unconsciousness."

At the hospital, the doctors told him they'd have to remove part of his stomach, and asked him to sign a consent form. "I'm not signing anything without my parents," he retorted. No time for that, they told him. He signed.

Recovery involved months of agonizing operations and physiotherapy. But after about six months, Ruby was back roaring around on his motorbike and paddling his kayak. And the long-term damage, he knows, is relatively mild. His various organs are in pretty good shape; his sex life is unhampered, as is the prospect of fatherhood. "Was I lucky?" he mused. "Well, I've been to the funeral of a friend whose outpost was hit by a TOW missile in Lebanon. So, yes, I was lucky. But I was the only soldier injured in my battle, and I was hit because the projector light we'd set up was right over my head. I was an easy target. And we were *freierim* [saps] to have been caught up in it in the first place. We walked straight into their trap. They placed the tire, waited for us to stop, then opened fire on us."

I asked him whom he blamed, steering him out of his immediate battle zone toward the bigger picture. He began with a helpless shrug and words of sympathy for the Palestinians. "Look, they've got nothing, these people. We go into their houses to make arrests in the middle of the night, and so on, and you see there's nothing there. There's nothing in their homes."

"So are you saying we shouldn't be there, the army shouldn't be there?" I asked. "I mean, you were deployed in the Hebron area, outside the borders of sovereign Israel."

"No, we need to be there," he said firmly. "Those few hundred Jewish families who live in Hebron"—the number was closer to five hundred Jews in all: sixty families and two hundred or so yeshiva students—"are protecting us! If we give away that area, we'll lose the whole country."

. . . • . . .

Avshalom Kapah, father of Dekel, one of Josh's best friends, shares Ruby's Sephardic background—his family immigrated from Yemen—and, thus, an instinctive familiarity with the Arab world that Ashkenazim like myself can never match. Upbeat and prone to think well of people unless the evidence proves otherwise, he also had a wake-up call in the course of the second Intifada, less direct than Ruby's, but no less dramatic.

The Kapahs live in a fairly new area of the Bayit Vegan neighborhood. For years, while the building contractor was finishing the complex, a Palestinian man in his twenties, Shahdi, was employed as a kind of security guard–cum–janitor. The Kapah family got to know and like him well enough to entrust him with the key to their home. "He became both a friend and something of a symbol for us," said Avshalom, an archaeologist, "living proof of the Palestinians as friends, as good neighbors, people we can trust."

Early in 2002, Shahdi disappeared for a while, and he came back looking battered, literally. Avshalom asked him where he'd been, what had happened. Shahdi said he'd had an argument with someone from his village, a "collaborator" who had provided intelligence information to the Israeli authorities, and that this man had made trouble for him with the Shin Bet, who had arrested him and beaten him up. "I didn't know what to make of it," said Avshalom. "I'd have thought that if anyone was collaborating with Israel, it would have been Shahdi."

That March 26, at a roadblock on the southern outskirts of Jerusalem, two Palestinians died when their car exploded. The circumstances were unclear. Initial reports suggested that soldiers manning the roadblock had opened fire on the vehicle when it failed to stop, and it had then burst into flames. Subsequent reports made no mention of Israeli fire. What was not disputed was that the passenger was nineteen-year-old Khaled Mohammed, a member of the Fatah-affiliated Al-Aqsa Brigades, and that when his dead body was removed from the wreckage of the vehicle, he was wearing a suicide bomber's belt. TV stations later screened parts of his "farewell video," in which he declared that he was heading off to "sacrifice myself to defend the land of Palestine," a statement made explicit by the visible assault rifle and bomb. What was also not disputed was that his dead driver was Shahdi Hamamreh, from the village of Al-Khader, south of Jerusalem. That Shahdi.

Avshalom told the story with an apologetic smile, still not sure what to make of it. Police sources later said the intention had been to carry out a bombing at the Malkha mall, and that they'd had a tip-off and were looking out for a suspicious vehicle. Part of Avshalom wanted to believe that Shahdi gave the tip-off, that their family friend was the "good guy" who warned the police and would have delivered the bomber to them, and that his death was an accident, explosives in the car detonating unexpectedly. But he couldn't be sure. He'd never told Dekel what became of Shahdi, just shrugged off the question.

Avshalom is warier of all Palestinians now, he acknowledged. "When the first Intifada erupted, in 1987, I was responsible for archaeological work in the whole area north of Jerusalem out toward Ramallah," he said, "and it took me a full year, during which I got stoned a few times in my car, to realize that some of these people wouldn't mind killing me. Before then, I'd been aware, of course, that there were daily protests and lots of deaths, but I was so familiar with the villages, I knew the area like the back of my hand, knew the people I was working with, so I just didn't take the threat seriously. Shahdi's death has forced me to take the level of danger more seriously still. I've maintained work-related friendships with some Palestinians, but I'll meet them somewhere public and neutral nowadays, not in my house or theirs anymore—not because I mistrust them, but because you never know."

For all that reluctant wariness, Avshalom remains one of the most optimistic Israelis I know, instinctually disposed to viewing the glass as half full. "Look back a century, and see how far we've come," he said. "Look back to the founding of the state, in 1948, when there were only six hundred thousand Jews here, and no guarantee we'd survive as a nation. We've made peace with Egypt, with Jordan. We're First World—comparing ourselves not to Middle America but to Manhattan. Look at Israeli youngsters—sure, there are some unpleasant characters on the margins, but most of them are smart, talented, full of initiative, able to hold their own with anyone.

"We'll survive here," he insisted, "as long as we really show that we want to. The more we prove to the Palestinians that we can match them for *sumud* [unshifting, dedicated commitment to the land], the easier it will be to make peace with them. They have to know that we cannot be budged. And I think we have taught them a great deal about our resilience since this conflict started. Still, lots of my friends have two passports, Israeli and, say, American, just in case—in case we Jews have to run for our lives again. The less there is of that kind of thinking, the less it becomes self-fulfilling prophecy. The more we remind ourselves that this is our home, and that we're not going to be forced to abandon it, the less likelihood there'll be of us needing to abandon it."

It's a potent assertion, one that appeals to my purist Zionist sensibilities, my conviction that Israel is the only place where Jews can take charge of their own destiny. "I want to come here every week for a dose of your passion," I told Avshalom the night he set out his thinking.

"With pleasure," he said. "For Israel pep talks, I'm your man."

4.

How Did We Get into This Mess?

In the summer of 2002, *Harakiri,* a book claiming to detail the paranoia that had characterized Ehud Barak's record-breakingly brief and unhappy prime ministership, topped the local best-seller lists. It was written by Raviv Drucker, who had covered the highs and (mainly) lows of the Barak era as the diplomatic correspondent for Army Radio. The book, whose English title was the more prosaic *Ehud Barak: The Failure,* presented Barak as an almost comically flawed human being: a man incapable of trust who eventually alienated even his most loyal associates; an egotist whose exaggerated faith in his own abilities masked a devastating tendency to indecision and prevarication; a leader seemingly pathologically disinclined to follow a straightforward path to his goals when more circuitous routes were available; a prime minister who would habitually assign the same task—including a specific element of policy planning or the drafting of a particular speech—to two, three or more purported intimates simultaneously, assuring each of them that only he or she could do the job, with predictably catastrophic consequences.

Earlier that year, for a project I was then working on, I spent many hours in Barak's company. I found him to be a no-nonsense, methodical individual with a strong memory for detail. He also exuded a truly extraordinary self-confidence and self-belief, the cumulative result, no doubt, of his decades of almost uninterrupted success in the military. I had the sense of a man who knew, absolutely knew, that he could achieve whatever he turned his hand to and set his heart on. And I think it was essential to that self-image that, in the aftermath of the Camp David debacle, he was able to convince himself—and then set about the vastly more problematic task of persuading the rest of us—that he had succeeded there, too, in "removing the mask," as he likes to put it, that had hidden the true face of the duplicitous Arafat.

My time with Barak confirmed one of the damning charges in *Harakiri*—that concerning his tendency to invite more than one person to carry out the same task. And while there was no doubting Barak's ability to advocate a position effectively, I came away from the experience less persuaded of his facilities as a listener, a not unimportant quality in a would-be peacemaker. I also had conversations with him on subjects that he asserted we had discussed earlier, although we had not.

I write this because, among those who would defend Arafat's decision to walk away from the Camp David peace summit in July 2000, there are many who place principal and very personal responsibility for its failure on Barak, who is said to have humiliated Arafat by not spending enough time face-to-face with him, and by not treating him with sufficient respect. But I firmly believe, on the basis of interviews with Camp David participants and hangers-on, and an examination of much that has been published about what unfolded there, that Arafat ensured the collapse of the summit, and much of the deterioration since—not by accident, either, and much less through weakness than by design. I know from personal experience that Barak can be frustrating to work with, and I can imagine how much more frustrating he could be to work opposite. I am anything but a Barak acolyte. But Camp David did not fail because Barak wasn't nice enough to Arafat, or didn't listen closely enough. When the president of the United States is on hand, those kinds of problems are simply not allowed to destroy fleeting opportunities for historic regional breakthroughs. Arafat and Barak actually got along just fine. They were still engaging in amiable conversation months later—days before Ariel Sharon visited the Temple Mount and the second Intifada began—when Arafat and his advisers were invited to Barak's home in Kochav Yair and the pair stepped out onto the balcony for a tête-à-tête. Barak may have been a far from ideal negotiating partner, but he had come to Camp David to make peace. The failure was one of substance, not of niceties. Solomon, I suspect, would have fared no better.

. . . • . . .

I believed, and I wasn't a complete fool. I never had Yasser Arafat down as the Palestinian Mother Teresa, or even the Palestinian Nelson Mandela. Not even close. But along with 60 percent of Israelis, I wholeheartedly supported Yitzhak Rabin when he strode out onto the White House lawn, flanking President Clinton on one side while Arafat walked on the other. I understood Rabin's self-described "butterflies in the stomach" about embarking on a partnership with an ex-terrorist—or rather, a purportedly ex-terrorist. But I absolutely shared his assessment that it was a partnership Israel owed itself to attempt.

There were 9 million Israelis and Palestinians between the Jordan River and the Mediterranean Sea. And if we Jews couldn't agree with most of the Arabs on terms for a separation, we faced the demographic overwhelming of our renewed Jewish homeland. Rabin had tried to reach an accommodation with what was described in those days as "the PLO inside"—Palestinian leaders living in East Jerusalem, the West Bank and the Gaza Strip with whom the previous Yitzhak Shamir–led government had entered into public negotiations in Washington in the wake of the 1991 Madrid Peace Conference. But those talks had led nowhere. Every Israeli proposal put to Faisal Husseini, Hanan Ashrawi, Haider Abdul-Shafi and the other Palestinian delegates was transmitted to Arafat, still exiled in his Tunis seaside villa, and his unchanging riposte was that if Israel wanted to make headway in the peace effort, it would need to talk directly to the PLO and give him a direct role. So long as it did not, he would not allow his loyalists to sanction the most negligible move forward. And the Palestinian delegates deferred to Arafat: They never defied him, never sought to exercise independent authority.

Rabin was not convinced of the PLO chief's professions of a desire for peaceful coexistence in an independent Palestine alongside Israel—rather than in place of Israel, as had been the PLO's long-standing declared ambition. Hence the butterflies. He worried that Arafat was merely maneuvering to save himself and his organization from extinction: Having put the PLO where his gut was in the Gulf War, and having pledged unfailing loyalty to Saddam Hussein, Arafat hadn't merely alienated Western supporters; he had lost the support, and financial backing, of much of the Arab world and was in danger of passing away into loathed irrelevance, a terrorist footnote to Middle East history. But Arafat, it had gradually become plain to Rabin, was the only leader with the authority to negotiate for those Palestinian millions. If there was to be an accord, it could be achieved only via Arafat. And we were six years into an Intifada, a genuine widespread uprising against the Israeli occupation. More than eleven hundred Palestinians had been killed. So had 160 Israelis. We needed to find a way out. If Arafat was committed to coexistence, and would keep his promises to both abstain from and prevent terrorism, we might find it. *If.*

Almost all Israelis are familiar with most aspects of the peace process, its successes, its setbacks. How could we not be? This is life and death for us. Put one hundred Americans or Britons in a room and ask how many of them are passionately interested in their domestic politics, and a few hands might be raised. Put one hundred Israelis in the room and ask them the same question, and they won't really understand it. Of course they're profoundly interested. When an apparently minor clause in a peace agreement—such as the one, say, in the 1994 "Gaza and Jericho first" accord that provided for continued Israeli control over the crossing points between Egypt and Gaza, and Jordan and Jericho—can have such profound implications for us, a national obsession with the minutiae is plain common sense. (Had Israel relinquished control of those crossings, as the Palestinians demanded during a two-month negotiating deadlock, Arafat would have had the legal, Israeli-sanctioned authority to invite unilaterally hundreds of thousands of Palestinians from Jordan, Lebanon, Syria and elsewhere, and their descendants, to make temporary homes in Gaza and Jericho, with the possibility of a subsequent relocation, by force if necessary, to sovereign Israel. Equally, absurd though it may sound, he could have asked Saddam Hussein to loan him a few elite Republican Guard units, say, or the Syrians to send over their best fighters, and have them deployed in Jericho and Gaza, ready to lead the next military confrontation with Israel.)

But I think that even the Middle Easterner least obsessed with the peace process, and much of the rest of the world, watched that potentially era-changing ceremony on the White House lawn that day, September 13, 1993, and saw a tableau that said everything about Arafat's mind-set, Clinton's mind-set and, most especially, Rabin's mind-set as they signed the Oslo peace accords. For me, the moment when Rabin and Arafat shook hands, with Clinton standing paternalistically behind them, redounds through the years as an image that emblematizes not merely

Rabin's "butterflies in the stomach" but also the uncertainties of the Israeli nation—an image, moreover, that remained emblematic for a full seven years.

It's all there in the body language. Arafat thrusts out his hand with tremendous enthusiasm. He's delighted to shake hands, to cement the perception, before the watching notables and countless millions around the world, that he—a man who wouldn't have been allowed to so much as set foot on American soil just a few months earlier—is making the transition from terrorist to statesman. As for Clinton, standing behind the two Middle Eastern protagonists, he's encouraging them to touch flesh. He wants the moment immortalized: the president of the United States making peace in the Middle East, even though, of course, the talks had taken place in Oslo and he hadn't known the first thing about them. But Rabin visibly hesitates. It looks like he doesn't really want to go through with the handshake. It is only Clinton's helping nudge that ensures consummation. And this is all the more remarkable because, we later learned, Rabin knew full well in advance that he was going to be asked to shake hands. There'd been some dispute about who was going to attend the ceremony. Would it be the number twos—Shimon Peres and Mahmoud Abbas (Abu Mazen), or Rabin and Arafat? When it was decided that the top men would attend, the White House sent word to the prime minister's office in Jerusalem that a festive handshake would be the appropriate way to culminate the ceremony, and Rabin replied that this was acceptable. But through his bureau chief, Eitan Haber, he stressed that he would not tolerate Arafat hugging or kissing him. The story goes that they even held rehearsals at the White House and assigned certain unnamed officials the unenviable task of trying to intervene were the PLO chief to attempt to plant one on the prime ministerial cheek. And yet, despite the foreknowledge, Rabin hesitated, wordlessly confirming his misgivings over rehabilitating a man who had sent terrorists to murder Jewish men, women and children, over whether or not this Oslo process would prove to serve Israel's long-term interests.

As a nation, for the next seven years, we were similarly uncertain, and sometimes violently divided, as to the efficacy of the partnership. Consider our elections, when the stakes couldn't be higher. We're not only determining priorities in areas like education and health and social services; we're making a decision that can affect the size of our country: whether tens of thousands of people may have to leave their homes in the

West Bank, Gaza Strip and Golan Heights or whether more Israelis are going to be given financial incentives to move to precisely those disputed territories. To a large extent, we're determining how safe we're going to feel when we get on a bus in the morning over the next few years, depending on the stewardship of our prime minister in the relentless battle against terrorism. And yet, if you look at how we've behaved as a nation on election days over the last decade or so, a superficial glance at our voting record might suggest that we don't take our elections seriously. We've seemed to flip capriciously back and forth across the political spectrum. As the 1990s began, we had the uncompromising right-wing Shamir as our prime minister, a man who had seen his own family murdered in the 1930s by the villagers with whom he had grown up in Poland, and whose overriding concern as prime minister was to do nothing that might weaken Israel and again make Jews vulnerable to Gentile enemy forces—which, for him, meant an ideological refusal to relinquish territory in any attempt at peacemaking with the Palestinians. In 1992, we swung leftward, electing Rabin on a promise to accelerate the peace process. After he was assassinated in November 1995, he was briefly succeeded by the like-minded Shimon Peres. But Peres was voted out in May 1996, in favor of the hawkish Benjamin "Bibi" Netanyahu, a relentless critic of the Oslo accords, who mockingly derided the notion of Arafat safeguarding Israelis' security. Next, after three years of Bibi, we lurched to the left again, and voted in Barak, who promised to finalize a permanent accord with Arafat. And finally, after that effort had failed, we shifted starkly back to the right again, with the election of Ariel Sharon in February 2001 and then his reelection in January 2003. Right, left, right, left, right—five flips in barely a decade.

But the truth is that we're anything but capricious. People fly back from overseas to cast their ballots. Voting turnouts are sky-high, nearly 100 percent in some areas. Dinner-table conversation revolves endlessly around the "process," the "situation," how we can best find a path to tranquillity and who might most effectively blaze that path. Candidates' qualities and failings are scrutinized. Party platforms are pored over. Newspapers are devoured. In many households, the nightly news is watched at 7:00 p.m. on one channel, 8:00 p.m. on another and 9:00 p.m. on a third.

So why, then, if we are neither capricious nor pointlessly fickle, did we switch so restlessly between such radically differing political leaderships—the right-wingers with their desire to boost Jewish settlement, their reluctance to relinquish captured territory in the Golan Heights, the Gaza Strip, the West Bank and, most especially, East Jerusalem, and their scorn for Arab claims to want peace; and the left-wingers with their readiness to dismantle settlements, withdraw from captured territory and put those Arab claims to the test? We vacillated precisely because, as a nation, just like Rabin on that fall day in 1993, we were unable to make up our minds about where our long-term interests lay—whether we would achieve security by bringing Arafat and his coterie from Tunis to the West Bank and Gaza, and embracing him as a peace partner, or whether we would be inviting in a viper. For parts of those seven years, in periods when few of our buses were blowing up and we seemed to be building a people-to-people relationship with our Palestinian neighbors, most of us believed that Rabin had been right to go through with the handshake. At low points, when terrorism was at its rampant height, and the right-wing assertions were most credible that Arafat, far from fighting the extremists, as had been his pledge, was subtly and not so subtly encouraging them, the consensus was that the entire Oslo experiment had been a grievous mistake.

I was one of those—sometimes part of the narrow majority, sometimes part of the narrow minority—who, during most of that period, was prepared to believe that Arafat was forswearing terrorism, even if he patently wasn't doing everything in his power to prevent others from planning and executing attacks. I was infuriated at his refusal to smash Hamas, but I was prepared, albeit tentatively, to ascribe this more to weakness than to malevolence, a weakness of power and character. The question I asked was not whether he was an ideal partner. The answer to that was always no. The question, rather, was whether the partnership with him, however problematic, was better than all the alternatives. And it seemed to me then that the answer was yes. The Islamic extremists were a threat to Arafat himself, Rabin and Peres would typically opine. If he moved too harshly against them, he might himself be swept away in the ensuing violence. It made a certain amount of sense. Arafat had to work within the consensus in order to create goodwill gradually.

Even in hindsight, with Arafat having regressed to orchestration of terrorism in the second Intifada, I don't blame Rabin for signing the Oslo accords. I think that we, as a nation, had to know that we had tried to reach an accommodation. Otherwise, we could never have mustered the unity and resilience required to hold firm in the subsequent conflict. As it is, there are those Israelis who contend that we could have done more to satisfy the Palestinians, and that this round of bloodshed would thus have been averted. But they are a minority. Those voices would have been far, far louder if we had not—first under Rabin and then under Barak—so plainly attempted to finalize an accord. When Rabin took the plunge, six years into the first Intifada, the occupation had plainly become untenable. The Palestinians were not prepared to suffer under our rule any longer, even if they had to die trying to force out the army. And it was brutalizing our society as well, with our soldiers ordered to use an "iron fist" to suppress the opposition. We had sought to negotiate with a nonterrorist Palestinian leadership, but no such creature existed. What was left was to try to make peace with our enemies, led by Arafat, who were insisting they had their hearts set on coexistence.

I do most definitely blame Rabin's negotiating deputies—and he, of course, bore overall responsibility for their failures—for some of the Oslo architecture, the process by which Arafat was able to gain control over slices of territory without having to concede on any of his demands. They failed to secure explicit recognition from Arafat for Israel as a mainly Jewish state, a nation he would not seek to defeat by weight of numbers. Presenting the central equation as one of "land for peace"—concrete concessions from Israel in exchange for something all too vague—they failed to pin him down on what should have been the central, genuinely peace-yielding equation, "land for refugees," providing for a new state of Palestine alongside Israel, a new state within which all Palestinian refugees would build new lives.

We'll never know, of course, whether the process would have unfolded differently had Rabin lived longer. Eitan Haber, ever the loyalist, insisted in an interview with me and my colleague Ina Friedman, in February 2001, that Israel would absolutely have reached a permanent accord with Arafat if his boss had survived the assassin's bullets on November 4, 1995. "The main drawback of Oslo was that it was designed to fit Yitzhak Rabin, according to his will, his intentions, his ideas, his plans," Haber asserted. "He assumed that he'd be the man to see it all through." According to Haber, Rabin "didn't have a shadow of a doubt" that all the problems could be solved, including the refugee issue and the vexed matter of Jerusalem, which, Haber believed, "Rabin would not have divided." Asked about fallback plans, Haber claimed that "there was a plan at every stage" were things to have gone wrong, but he again insisted that the process would not have collapsed overall had his old boss lived.

Pressed on the question of Arafat's true commitment to the process, Haber began to waver. "Perhaps Arafat just wasn't a partner?" I asked. "Perhaps the whole thing was a mistake?"

"I don't know," he conceded.

"We were expecting to hear you say, 'I'm sure that's not so.' "

"Look, you're asking me hypothetical questions all the time. . . . I so envy those who have certain answers. With me, it's all question marks. But am I allowed to try to make peace? We always said, 'Let's at least try.' "

"Because we're strong enough if it all collapses?"

". . . The army is stronger than you can imagine. The spirit of the people of Israel is sagging by the day."

To my own sorrow, I have doubts about whether it would all have worked out had Rabin lived. That 60 percent of the Israeli public who had endorsed the Rabin-Arafat handshake in 1993—confident, or at least hopeful, that our world was about to change for the better—had slipped down toward 50 percent by the late summer of 1995 as erstwhile supporters reluctantly became opponents of the partnership because the violence was all too plainly continuing, with intermittent suicide bombings all over Israel. In that climate, Rabin would quite likely have lost the next election to Netanyahu anyway. Terrorism would have brought him down, whether directly encouraged by Arafat, as the Israeli right claims it was, tolerated by Arafat, or deeply opposed by Arafat, as Haber believes it was. "Arafat was really panicked by the bombings," Haber insisted in our interview. "He made very serious efforts to prevent them. He turned things upside down."

To some extent, I feel Rabin was himself a victim of that terrorism. The timing of his assassination was not happenstance. It came just a few weeks after Rabin and Arafat had signed the most significant accord in the Oslo series—the "Oslo B" deal, under which Israel relinquished control of the major Palestinian population centers in the West Bank, pulling the army out of all the big cities, from Jenin in the north, via Tulkarm, Nablus, Kalkilya and Ramallah, down to Bethlehem and, later, Hebron. Heaven knows what psychological makeup is required to gun down any fellow human being in cold blood at point-blank range. I'm sure that Rabin's killer, a right-wing Orthodox psychopath named Yigal Amir, drew personal encouragement from the awareness that all around him were Israelis who hated Rabin for bringing what they saw as the Oslo disaster down upon them. He must have drawn nourishment, too, from the knowledge that prominent rabbis were engaging in earnest theological debates as to whether, were modern Israel not a democracy but a theocracy governed by a biblical-style Sanhedrin of learned sages, the prime minister might merit the death penalty for the crime of abandoning divinely bestowed territory to Israel's enemies. But without minimizing Amir's crime, Arafat and his regime are also culpable. Every suicide bombing that Arafat had failed, or chosen not, to avert in the previous two years had chipped away at Rabin's credibility and heightened the loathing for the Oslo process in some sectors of Israeli society, as well as boosting the prospects of a murderous individual feeling public sentiment would be with him if he killed the prime minister.

After the Rabin assassination, many Israelis put aside their misgivings over Oslo and reembraced the peace process, partly because they loathed the notion of being identified with Amir and his extremism. Surveys showed a wild rise in support for the partnership with the Palestinians and, personally, for Peres over the Likud candidate for prime minister, Netanyahu. But another flurry of bombings changed that. Over just eight days in late February and early March 1996, in the run-up to Election Day two months later, Islamic extremist bombers carried out four attacks, killing sixty Israelis. In Jerusalem, on the main Jaffa Road, they blew up a number 18 bus on a Sunday morning and staged another attack that day in Ashkelon. A week later, rubbing our nose in our own inability to stop them, they blew up another number 18 bus on the Jaffa Road. And the next day, a bomber exploded his device at a Dizengoff Street shopping mall in Tel Aviv; seeing the security guards at the door, he simply waited until a small crowd encircled him at the adjacent pedestrian crossing.

Implored by Israeli officials to crack down on the bombers, at the very least by arresting the bomb makers and orchestrators whose names and addresses were supplied to him by military intelligence, Arafat did nothing. It was later claimed by some of his defenders that he'd had little choice but to "allow" the first two strikes, as fitting Hamas revenge for Israel's assassination weeks earlier of the chief Hamas bomb maker, Yihya Ayash, known as "the Engineer," who was blown up by a device planted in a cell phone he was tricked into using. The defenders also claimed that Arafat had then been "misled" by the Islamic extremists, who had carried out the third and fourth bombings without his sanction. Such assertions, of course, merely highlight what might most kindly be described as Arafat's ambivalent attitude to terrorism at the time. Credible Israeli intelligence assessments indicate that rather than use what must have been one of the highest proportions of armed men of any regime anywhere in the world to confront the killers, he sometimes reined them in but also eased the pressure on occasion, effectively letting them loose when he deemed appropriate, as one more element in a strategic armory.

After the Oslo process collapsed in a shambles at Camp David, and more so a year later, after Sharon first came to power, Palestinian journalists and academics would moan about how Israel had destroyed Palestinians' hope by slowing the process in the Netanyahu years, expanding settlements, never learning to treat the Palestinians as equals but, rather, always regarding them as enemies. There is truth in those charges. But it was the terrorist extremists, and, above all, Arafat, who bore fundamental blame. It was terrorism that destroyed the chances for peace. It was, unarguably, for instance, Arafat's refusal to prevent terrorism that got Netanyahu elected. "With all due respect to Rabin's memory," I remember a friend of mine telling me in May 1996, as he prepared to vote for Bibi, "we're being blown to pieces here. I can't support a partnership with a man who is letting bombers murder us at will in the streets." The four February–March 1996 bombings redrew the political map in Israel, transforming Netanyahu from the ranting, egotistical opposition leader, whose own party had been contemplating dumping him, into the sensible skeptic. Before those attacks, with the newly dead Rabin well on the way to iconic status, much of Israel thought of Netanyahu, loathingly, as the upstart who had whipped up right-wing mobs into frenzied hostility against the prime minister and who had publicly accused Rabin of having "fallen on his head" in trusting Arafat; after the attacks, much of Israel was sorrowfully inclined to acknowledge Netanyahu's point. And on May 29, 1996, by what we then imagined to be the narrowest of margins—less than 1 percent of votes cast, a majority of 29,457—it elected Netanyahu prime minister.

The Bibi years were a period of settlement expansion, which certainly fueled popular Palestinian disillusion with the Oslo process. They were also the years in which the forebodings of my friend Sid and his fellow reservists on the Allenby Bridge became fact: The Palestinians turned their Israeli-issued guns on their Israeli issuers in September 1996, after Netanyahu approved the largely inconsequential opening of the second entrance at the ancient underground water tunnel that ran alongside, but crucially not under, the Temple Mount. A far more significant unilateral alteration of sensitive soil was taking place on the Mount itself, where the Waqf Muslim Council, which administers the holy sites, was bulldozing a massive enlargement of a subterranean area in the southeastern corner, known as Solomon's Stables, and reconstituting it as the vast Marwani Mosque. But while Israel chose to swallow in silence that gross violation of the status quo, the Palestinian Authority capitalized on Netanyahu's secretive opening of the tunnel exit to provoke furious opposition, disseminating absurd but widely accepted assertions that the new digging—which merely saw a pathway less than one hundred feet long cleared to allow visitors to the tunnel to exit via the Old City's Christian Quarter rather than retracing their steps along the narrow passageway back to the opening at the Western Wall Plaza—was designed to destabilize the foundations of the Al-Aqsa Mosque and the Dome of the Rock. In the consequent rioting and street fighting across the West Bank, Gaza and East Jerusalem, seventy Palestinians and fifteen Israeli soldiers lost their lives. It was a foretaste of what was to recur in 2000.

They were years in which Netanyahu—having reluctantly sanctioned a military pullout from the last of the West Bank cities, Hebron—demanded "reciprocity" from Arafat and the Palestinian Authority, at first with American sympathy but later with mounting American frustration. He sought a concerted crackdown by Arafat on the bombers, as well as the confiscation of illegal weaponry, a reduction in the ranks of a Palestinian police force bloated far above the limits set in the accords and a formal convening of the Palestine National Council to do what Rabin and Peres had accepted had been done already—revoke from the PLO's guiding Palestine National Covenant those clauses (almost the entire document) that urged the armed struggle to eliminate Israel. And he had mixed results. The demand for the covenant's annulment led to an assembly of the council, in Gaza in December 1998, and the offending clauses were revoked by a show of hands. But while right-wingers dispute to this day whether the necessary quorum was in attendance and wonder whether this was not merely another piece of Palestinian leadership trickery, there can be no debating the one concrete consequence of Netanyahu's demand: It brought President Bill Clinton, unprecedentedly, to Gaza to oversee the ceremonies and speak movingly of the Palestinian right to independence, and thus, effectively, to signal what would later become more formal American endorsement for full Palestinian statehood. Typically, Netanyahu never so much as dreamed of attending the meeting along with the American president (though whether Arafat would have hosted him is a moot point), a gesture that might have indicated partnership and cooperation on the path to moderation.

Netanyahu's greatest success, unarguably, was in the reduction of the incidence of suicide bombings. There were several attacks in the Bibi years—on the Ben-Yehudah pedestrian mall and at the Mahane Yehuda fruit market in Jerusalem, among others, and at Tel Aviv's Apropo café—but nothing on the scale of the bombings that had preceded his election, and nothing, of course, on the scale of the attacks that would follow. For Netanyahu, this was vindication, proof of the potency of his message to Arafat that there would be no more territorial handovers until the terrorism stopped. For Yitzhak Mordechai, Netanyahu's defense minister, it was the direct result of the army's improved ability to thwart such attacks. And for Netanyahu's critics to the left, it was a mixed blessing: Fewer Israelis were being killed in the short term, they asserted, because Netanyahu's simultaneous settlement building and reluctance to relinquish further territory was turning all Palestinians into disheartened extremists, and the international political leadership into impassioned advocates for accelerated Palestinian statehood, leaving Hamas with no immediate need to risk alienating other potential supporters by targeting Israeli civilians.

A few days before Netanyahu's unsuccessful bid to wrest the Likud party leadership away from Prime Minister Sharon in November 2002, I met with Uzi Arad, the former top aide to Netanyahu, and we discussed the dramatic decline in terrorism during the 1996–1999 Bibi years. I told him what a Palestinian acquaintance, Yussuf, a plumber who lives in the Al-Arub refugee camp outside Hebron (of whom more later), had once proffered by way of an explanation: Arafat had come back from Tunis only in July 1994, Yussuf recalled, and it had naturally taken him some time to establish his authority. Hence the terrorism of the Rabin years. But when, after the February–March 1996 attacks, interim prime minister Peres appealed to him to thwart the bombers, Arafat took the necessary action, and relative tranquillity prevailed, with Bibi the coincidental beneficiary. Arad chose not to dignify this theory with any kind of response, but he offered two different explanations, the one most favored by Netanyahu, he said, and his own. Netanyahu believes, most of all, that Arafat was scared of him, Arad said, and that when Netanyahu threatened to deport him if there was more violence after the Temple Mount tunnel riots, Arafat was truly afraid and cracked down on Hamas for his own self-preservation. Arad himself believes that it was the Netanyahu administration's emphasis on "linkage" that forced Arafat to intervene against the bombers. "We kept the process alive, and made clear that we were prepared to move substantively ahead, but Arafat also knew there would be no significant progress unless the terrorism was halted."

Personally, I think that among the most significant aspects of the Netanyahu years was the decisiveness of his ouster. Here was a man who, for whatever reason, had presided over three of the most bomb-free years in recent Israeli history. They were years when, by our bloody relative standards, the country felt safe. American Jewish mothers did not bite their fingernails down to the quick at the thought of their carefree offspring spending a summer or a semester in an Israeli study program. We sent our kids off to school fairly confident that they would come home intact. And yet, at the end of those years, when Netanyahu's impossible coalition of bickering leftists and rightists collapsed as, under the 1998 Wye River Agreement, he handed over one small chunk of West Bank territory in the Jenin area, we voters of divided Israel dumped him in what was, for us, a landslide, the colossal margin of 12 percent. There were myriad factors behind that ouster, including widespread reservations about Netanyahu's character—his arrogance, his financial propriety or lack thereof, his predilection for inciting sectors of society against one another—but perhaps the decisive factor was the sense that while the world was gearing up to recognize the independent state of Palestine, our prime minister was refusing to engage in meaningful negotiations with the Palestinians. A state next door was about to be foisted upon us, essential security issues needed to be resolved and there was no dialogue.

In the international climate of the second Intifada, with parts of the United States, much of Europe and the entire Arab world convincing themselves that the Israelis were the brutal aggressors, and that Israel had sowed the seeds of the new conflict by refusing to grant the Palestinians their fundamental rights and by its hawkish insistence on maintaining its rule over territory to which it has no international claim, the defeat of Netanyahu stood as incontrovertible evidence to the contrary: evidence that Israelis, far from eschewing compromise and reconciliation, thirst for nothing else. I think it's entirely fair to say that the crushing electoral defeat of Netanyahu—and his replacement by Barak—constitutes proof positive of the Israeli electorate's desire, indeed desperation, for peace. Complacently and erroneously assuming that the relative calm we had begun to take for granted would be maintained, we threw out a leader under whom we had felt safe, risked that precious sense of security and elected a political novice, whose sole claim to our vote was his pledge to finalize a permanent peace deal with Arafat. Barak is the innovative genius who transformed the Sayeret Matkal commando unit into a peerless counterterror team capable of assassinating PLO terror chiefs in their apartments in Beirut in 1973, a "Nothing is impossible" thinker who at least partially devised the awe-inspiring Entebbe airport hostage rescue in 1976. And he is the most decorated soldier in Israeli history and a former army chief of staff. But as a politician, he was an unproven rookie, a minor player in the final months of Rabin's coalition and the brief tenure of Peres's. Yet he promised us peace, and so we elected him.

. . . • . . .

As I've said, to my mind nothing compares to the hesitant Rabin handshake on the White House lawn for sheer, undisguisable political drama, the public expression of the currents swirling out of sight. But there was a telling moment of truth on public display, too, at Camp David, when Clinton hosted Barak and Arafat for the first serious bid to forge the terms for a permanent accord.

The Camp David summit was Barak's idea, coordinated with Clinton, imposed on a deeply reluctant Arafat. There'd been all sorts of preparatory meetings between Israeli and Palestinian leaders, from which the Israelis came away with the overwhelming impression that a deal was there to be done. They believed they would be able to strike an agreement that would leave at least a small proportion of the West Bank in Israeli hands, enough to encompass the majority of the settlers, although the vast majority of the settlements would have to be dismantled; that an arrangement could be found to satisfy both Jewish and Muslim claims in the Old City of Jerusalem and, especially, on the Temple Mount; and that the Palestinians would agree to realize the "right of return" solely in the new Palestine, rather than in Israel, with a face-saving provision for a small proportion of refugees to be allowed into Israel under a "family reunification" criterion, without radically altering Israel's Jewish-Muslim demographic balance. I've heard from some Labor leaders that, on the basis of those preparatory meetings, they were convinced they'd be able to retain as much as 12 percent of the West Bank in a permanent accord; others spoke of 7 or 8 percent. But there was a great deal of confidence that a viable accord could be made. The only problem with such optimism was that Peres, Barak's foreign minister Shlomo Ben-Ami and the various other Labor interlocutors had been dealing only with Arafat's advisers—top advisers, to be sure, such as Ahmed Qurei, one of the prime Oslo negotiators and the speaker of the Palestinian Legislative Council (and, later, the PA prime minister)—and not with Arafat himself.

Clinton, the savviest of all media manipulators, was in prime form on day one of Camp David, July 11, 2000, inviting the camera crews to film him, Barak and Arafat as they walked amid the foliage. But then he made a most uncharacteristic error: He stepped through the narrow doorway into the first cabin, where the talks were to start, ahead of Barak and Arafat, leaving the pair of them, unsupervised for only the briefest of moments, to negotiate an aperture insufficiently wide to accommodate them both simultaneously. Each motioned politely to the other: After you, Mr. Prime Minister. No, after you, Mr. Chairman. But neither would give way. And there ensued what was widely described as a friendly little wrestling match. Except it wasn't actually all that friendly. And given that Barak is considerably younger than Arafat, who is not in the best of health, and that Barak is an ex-commando and a former chief of staff, fairly well developed in the upper torso, it wasn't hard to guess who'd win the impromptu bout. So if you replay the footage, you'll see that Barak basically shoves Arafat into Camp David. Arafat may be smiling, but he's plainly being heavily manhandled.

I once mentioned this to Barak. "It didn't look too good," I said. "I mean, you pushed him through the door."

"Oh, David," Barak said, smiling indulgently. "You with your Western sensibilities." (Apparently, in the Middle East, it is perfectly acceptable to shove people through doorways.) Arafat, he said, never subsequently mentioned the undignified entrance. It wasn't important. I was making too much of it.

Well, maybe. But to me, it reflects the deeper truth of an Israeli prime minister elected by his public to make peace, and impatient to do so, and a

Palestinian leader who didn't even want to start the talking. And if we're speaking metaphorically, you might say that, two weeks later, Arafat shoved Barak back out of the door of Camp David, rejecting what most Israelis consider to be inadequately perceived as the best terms any Israeli leader had ever offered for peace. What Barak showed readiness to concede at that summit and during the subsequent abortive contacts was as much as Israel can *ever* offer for peace, for beyond those concessions lies only national suicide.

Camp David is the cracked foundation stone on which everything crumbled so completely in the subsequent years, which is why understanding what happened there is critical to the perception of cause and blame and to any solution. But the great difficulty with Camp David is that there is no independent, unarguable account of what went on, who said what, how it fell apart. There was no silent American factotum sitting in a corner writing a protocol; that was at Barak's insistence. If they reached a deal, it would be drafted and signed, and the festivities would begin. But if they did not, ran his thinking, however unrealistic, he did not want to leave Arafat in a position to cite chapter and verse on what Israel had been prepared to relinquish, and use the protocol as the starting point for the next round of negotiations. And that's what has led to what you might call "the battle of the narratives": the Israeli versions, the Palestinian versions and the American versions. I use the plural form here because there aren't just three accounts of what went on at the Maryland retreat, but dissensions and contradictions from within each delegation as well—most starkly among the Americans, from whose Camp David team Clinton's leading Middle East envoy, Dennis Ross, emerged with a depiction of the negotiations that accords overwhelmingly with the Israeli narrative, while Rob Malley, a special assistant to Clinton for Arab-Israel affairs, somehow managed to witness a radically different summit, and he formed a conception of what unfolded that accords much more closely with the official Palestinian version.

Having spent a considerable amount of time with Barak, and spoken at length with other Israeli delegates to the talks, I have no doubt of one thing: Barak went to Camp David certain that he would be able to reach a permanent peace accord with Arafat. That's not what he said publicly when the second Intifada was in full swing, mind you. He said that he had hoped to achieve a deal but that he could not lose either way: He would finally be putting Arafat to the test. If Arafat proved willing to make the necessary compromises—on land, security arrangements, sharing Jerusalem, refugee rights and so on—the deal would be done, to everybody's benefit. If not, the charade would be ended, mercifully, before it was too late. The worst fears of Israel's uncertain electorate would be unequivocally confirmed. The world would recognize Israel's thirst for peace and Arafat's refusal to reciprocate. Israel would rise in the international estimation. Arafat would fall. Israel's most hardened leftists would shrug sadly and unify with its rightists in giving up on Arafat. The misled Palestinians would eventually oust their failed president and choose a leadership that could steer them to statehood and coexistence. And Israel would still be left with some of the territorial bargaining chips for that future effort at peacemaking.

Personally, I incline to the assessment of Barak's state of mind offered during our interview with Eitan Haber, self-described close friend of Barak, seven months after the summit's collapse. Haber said Barak was sure he would strike a deal at the summit because he had drawn up the pragmatic, correct terms for a viable compromise, and pragmatism had triumphed every time for Barak, from his years building up the Sayeret Matkal commandos in his revolutionary, freethinking, courageous image, his time as chief of staff, the process by which he then took the Labor party by storm, and finally when he defied the pundits who mocked his leaden TV style to beat the supposedly unbeatable Netanyahu for the prime ministership. At Camp David, said Haber, Barak "thought that in a week or two they could put everything on the table and go home. Because that's Ehud's logic. As of this moment, as of yesterday at five p.m. at least, Ehud still doesn't understand what happened to him. How is it that for thirty years he managed to persuade heads of state and army commanders and enemies of the logic of his theses? And suddenly it didn't work, because there are other interests at play."

Britain's ambassador to Israel at the height of the second Intifada, Sherard Cowper-Coles, unlike some of his predecessors, empathized deeply with the challenges faced by the country where he served. He was a clear-sighted friend of Israel and spoke quite radically about the need for a kind of international godfather, some sort of protectorate authority, to steer the intemperate Palestinians toward maturity and the genuine peacemaking that would end the conflict and resolve the septic tragedy of the refugee camps. And yet Cowper-Coles, when I hosted him one evening at the Yakar educational center in Jerusalem, took what I thought was a shockingly forgiving view of Arafat's conduct at Camp David. Speaking before an audience of about a hundred people, who, to their credit (and that of the ambassador), had gathered on the very night of the Patt Junction bombing, in a hall, moreover, where no security guard was on duty, Cowper-Coles averred that the terms on offer to the Palestinians had indeed been reasonable, but he said he felt that the Palestinian leader had merely overplayed his hand, erring tactically, in rejecting them. "Arafat made the mistake of his life at Camp David," he asserted.

I do not believe Arafat made the mistake of his life at Camp David. I think he knew exactly what he was doing. In retrospect, indeed, as I've already said, it seems unarguable that he had no intention of striking a deal. When the elderly (now late) President Hafez Assad anticipated that a dramatic treaty with Barak might be near, he had the streets of Damascus festooned with banners proclaiming that his people had fought valiantly through many wars and now were battling for peace. Did Arafat, in the year after the election of Barak, an unmistakably pro-peace prime minister, seize the moment and do anything similar? Hardly. Did he stop poisoning the minds of his schoolchildren? Anything but: Palestinian schoolbooks still rarely referred to Israel, and when they did, the reference was usually negative—as a foreign entity, artificially and forcefully imposed on Palestine in 1948. According to an October 2002 report issued by the Center for Monitoring the Impact of Peace, Israel did not appear on maps in the textbooks, nor did Israeli-established cities such as Tel Aviv. The New York–based center, which had been analyzing PA textbooks for the previous five years, found that Jerusalem was described almost exclusively as Palestinian, and the Jewish role in its history never acknowledged. In short, the report stated, "Palestinian education does not foster peaceful relations with Israel." Israel was presented as "a source of aggression, death and destruction to the Palestinians. . . . Hence no peace is sought after, but rather a war against Israel as the usurper and aggressor and occupier is to be waged." Did Arafat deliver stirring orations underlining the need to set aside the dream of a return for refugees to their ancestors' homes in Israel, in order to grasp the reality of true independence? Far from it. Instead, he continued to spout the same message he had been delivering throughout the Oslo years.

While Rabin, Peres and now Barak had been making abundantly plain to their people that there could be no final accord without massive territorial compromise and the widespread dismantling of settlements, Arafat chose not to speak of compromise. He kept on signaling, in those Arabic declamations that the Oslo supporters had wanted to believe could be explained away as a short-term consequence of narrow political expediency, that he had been taking what territory he could get via "peace" accords but that the dream of a Palestine from the river to the sea lived on, that he was following the glorious tradition of the Prophet Muhammad in acknowledging his weakness and accepting temporary cease-fires with the enemy, but only in order to become stronger and eventually prevail. Much of this was recognized, not in retrospect, after Camp David, but many years earlier, by Israeli right-wingers. But all too often, because their predictions of doom were inextricably tied to their pronouncements on the need to boost the Jewish population of the West Bank and Gaza, their justified vilification of Arafat was discredited by the unreality of their impossible Greater Israel vision. Some of this was recognized, too, by Israeli left-wingers, outside government and within. But either they—we—didn't want to believe that what we were hearing and reading was the genuine voice of the Palestinian leadership or we knew that it was real but wanted to believe that progress on the ground—economic improvements, the gradual attainment of control over territory—would start to change that mind-set, to inculcate the virtues of compromise.

I've heard from more than one participant that at Camp David, Palestinian Authority "moderates" like Mohammad Dahlan, then Arafat's Gaza security chief, urged the chairman to sign the deal or at least show readiness to sign a slightly improved version, telling him it was the best the Palestinians would ever get. If so, maybe that shows them to have been more duplicitous than Arafat, ready to endorse an accord and gain control of prized territory while happily contemplating the emergence of a pretext that, later, would enable them to resume the bloodletting. Or maybe it shows them to have been decent realists, honorable men who had the best interests of their people, and mine, at heart.

I've also heard from more than one participant that in a confrontation that saw Clinton pounding on the table and insisting that Arafat take the plunge, with the threat that if he did not, the United States government would turn its back on him for good, Arafat retorted that to sign such an accord would be to sign his own death warrant. If he put pen to paper, he apparently told the president, the next time Clinton would see him would be at his funeral. (I wonder if Clinton had become too personally involved for his threats to move Arafat, who would have long since recognized the president's fundamental good nature. I wonder, had it been former secretary of state James Baker coldly informing Arafat he'd never set foot in the United States again . . .) Arafat was telling Clinton the truth: Had he signed the deal, he would likely have been gunned down by his own extremists. But that was a situation of his own creation. He had chosen, strategically, to foster a climate of such hostility to Israel that to accept viable terms for a two-state solution would have cost him his life. (It could be argued that Barak, too, was knowingly putting his own life at risk in offering to share Jerusalem with Arafat's state-in-the-making, having seen Rabin murdered five years earlier against a background of concessions incalculably less religiously and historically significant.)

In the Palestinian narrative, Arafat's sympathizers would have us believe that he wasn't offered what Barak says was offered at Camp David, that no Palestinian leader could ever have agreed to what they say the Israeli terms envisaged, or to the improved terms presented as the subsequent, last-ditch Taba talks of January 2001, or even to Clinton's final desperate "bridging proposals." Barak wasn't ready to partner the Palestinians toward anything remotely resembling independent statehood, they insist. Israel was bent on maintaining control over borders and airspace and water resources, and the territory it was grudgingly contemplating conceding would have been crisscrossed by Israeli-controlled highways, its contiguity compromised by security zones, leaving "Palestine" as a patchwork quilt of disconnected minicantons, South African Bantustans reincarnated in the Middle East. "Our historic compromise was to accept 22 percent of pre-1948 Palestine—and still they want to divide it up," Mohammad Dahlan would tell Britain's *Guardian* in July 2002. It was terrific propaganda with which to convince great swathes of gullible world opinion that your subsequent "resistance" to the ongoing Israeli occupation—the campaign of shootings and suicide bombings—was nothing but the justified response of a stateless people denied all other avenues to freedom. But it was also quite untrue.

Clinton subsequently made this plain. So, too, did State Department senior envoy Ross. "The Palestinians would have in the West Bank an area that was contiguous. Those who say there were cantons—completely untrue," Ross would insist in a Fox TV interview the following spring. "His [Arafat's] negotiators understood this was the best they were ever going to get. They wanted him to accept it. He was not prepared to." (Israel did indeed seek ongoing control at the borders—not surprisingly, given the constant efforts to smuggle in arms from Egypt and Jordan, the cross-border tunnels, the intercepted weapons shipments, the rumors that, before Israel blew them up, Arafat had even used his own private, unsearched helicopters to import materiel. Still, Israel made clear that if it became evident over time that the new Palestine really was intent on living in peace, it would have gradually sanctioned international supervision, and ultimately Palestinian supervision, of the border crossings and over airspace.) And a handful of more honest Palestinian leaders, two years into the second Intifada, also began acknowledging as much, publicly confirming that the Clinton proposals, if not the earlier Barak offers, constituted viable terms for peace, ones that Arafat had been criminal in rejecting.

From my understanding of Camp David, it is clear that Barak would have paid almost any territorial price for peace. Indeed, the talks didn't break down over territory. The map that the negotiators worked on, from the very first day, already showed almost all of the West Bank—88 percent—in Palestinian hands, and that was just the starting point. As the talks progressed, the area increased to more than 90 percent—territory, remember, that Israel had captured in warfare, from which it had been relentlessly attacked, which had previously been under Jordanian, never Palestinian, sovereignty, and over which Jordan had relinquished all demands. That 100 percent of the Gaza Strip would become fully sovereign Palestine went almost without saying. The Palestinians assented to an Israeli expansion of sovereignty into a handful of small "blocs" of West Bank territory, within which Israel would have encompassed as many settlers as possible, conditioning such assent on territorial compensation—in the shape of sovereign Israeli land, most probably alongside the Gaza Strip, that would have been annexed to the new Palestine. By the time the talks had moved on to Taba, Israel was telling the Palestinians it would effectively relinquish 100 percent of the West Bank territory—retaining only more minor settlement blocs, and fully compensating the Palestinians with land alongside Gaza and the "safe passage" route across Israel—this according to Shlomo Ben-Ami. What all that means, of course, is that the summit didn't fail over what Palestinian spin doctors have since presented as the key obstacle: the occupation. Barak went to Camp David determined to end the occupation. Arafat wouldn't let him.

Rather than territory, occupation or settlements, then, the talks broke down over two other areas—control of the Temple Mount and the issue of Palestinian refugees. Israel had captured the Temple Mount—the holiest site in Judaism and the third holiest in Islam—in the 1967 war, then annexed it with the rest of the Old City and East Jerusalem, but made immediately clear that it had no intention of practically realizing its claim to sovereignty: The army's chief rabbi, Shlomo Goren, wanted the mosques blown up to clear the path for the construction of a third Jewish temple. The senior army commander in the area, Maj. Gen. Uzi Narkiss, told Goren he'd be thrown in jail if he didn't pipe down. And the defense minister of the day, Moshe Dayan, assured the Waqf—the Muslim Council that administered the holy sites atop the Mount, on behalf of the hitherto sovereign Kingdom of Jordan—that it would continue its work unaffected. (The pragmatic Dayan invoked the Orthodox Jewish tradition that considers the Mount so holy that no Jew should dare set foot upon it, for fear of inadvertently treading on the former site of the Temple's Holy of Holies. This was the chamber where the Lord's spirit was so powerful that only the high priest could enter, and only on the year's holiest day, Yom Kippur, and from which he would not emerge alive if his soul were anything but pure.)

For all the dissenting Camp David narratives, there is no argument over the position Arafat took with regard to the status of the Temple Mount: He demanded full Palestinian sovereignty, and was deaf to all suggestions that fell short of that. The deceptively elegant notion of "divine sovereignty" was raised at one point—let no man claim to rule over an area of such extraordinary holiness—a seemingly Solomonic resolution, so long as none of the rival protagonists got to debating the precise nature of the divine being. But Arafat was having none of it. Clinton later conceived the construct of Palestinian sovereignty at ground level and above, and Israeli sovereignty beneath the surface, where Jewish tradition would have the remains of the temples. Again, Arafat would not be moved. He insisted that the Islamic world would rise up against him if he formally signed away so much as partial control. Whether or not this was the case, he also derided the very notion of a Jewish link to the Temple Mount, his delegates asserting on his behalf that the Israelites' Jerusalem Temple was a myth and that the Jews knew this as well as he did. The Jews had controlled the site for more than thirty years, one member of the Palestinian delegation noted contemptuously to Clinton, and yet they hadn't tried to build so much as a synagogue there. Israel's profound respect for the holiness of the site, and its deference to Muslim sensibilities, was now being cited as evidence of Jewish indifference. I write this on the basis of my own interviews, but if anyone doubts Arafat's mocking dismissal of the Jewish connection to the Jews' most sacred place, they need not take my word for it. In an interview with the London Arabic daily *Al-Hayat* in October 2002, the Palestinian chairman openly asserted that "for thirty-four years they [the Israelis] have dug tunnels [a lie]. . . . They found not a single stone proving that the Temple of Solomon was there, because historically the Temple was not in Palestine."

Again, despite all the contradictory accounts of the Camp David talks, there is also no dispute surrounding the positions taken by the two sides on the issue of the Palestinian refugees, those who fled or were forced out of sovereign Israel during the War of Independence in 1948, and their descendants. By a unique feat of accounting, achieved by employing quite different criteria from those used to resolve refugee disputes in every other conflict area around the world, the United Nations has managed to compile a register of some 4 million such refugees, a figure that includes those who have long since taken Jordanian citizenship and those who, as residents of the West Bank and Gaza Strip, would automatically become citizens of Palestine the moment such an independent state was internationally recognized. And at Camp David, Arafat insisted in principle that those 4 million people be afforded a "right of return"—not to the new state of Palestine that Barak was so earnestly attempting to partner him toward establishing, but to the state of Israel, with a population of some 6.5 million people, of whom 5 million or so are Jews and 1.2 million are Arabs. You do the math. By holding out for such a "right," Arafat was demanding nothing less than the legitimacy to bring down the Jewish state, not through regional conflict (which he had vainly encouraged in the past), not through terrorism (the tool to which he would shortly return), but through the sheer weight of Palestinian numbers. His former deputy, the late Abu Jihad (assassinated in Tunis in 1988, ironically, by a team led by the very man with whom Arafat was negotiating in such bad faith, Barak), was wont to remark that the Palestinians' greatest weapon against the Jews is the womb. Arafat was now seeking to use it.

Arafat's defenders would have us believe that a formula on the refugee issue was close to hand at Camp David, and closer still at Taba—a formula that would not have drastically altered the Israeli demographic balance because, among other clauses, it would have offered refugees so generous a financial incentive to rebuild their lives anywhere but Israel as to render a "return" thoroughly unpopular. It would have meant an influx of no more than 40,000 refugees into Israel, according to some accounts; 25,000 over three years and an undecided number over the next twelve years, according to others.

Personally, I find this hard to credit. In the middle of the Camp David summit, Clinton broke away from the talks to attend the Okinawa, Japan, summit of the G8, where he raised the issue of the refugees in behind-the-scenes contacts with the other world leaders. When he got back to Camp David, he was able to tell Arafat that the leading countries would offer citizenship to hundreds of thousands of Palestinians, and contribute to a colossal international compensation fund. Arafat was not to be budged. As he opined in that same October 2002 interview with *Al-Hayat,* as far as he was concerned, "no one can abolish the right of return." There are those who claim that at Taba, where Barak's ultradovish justice minister Yossi Beilin played a leading role, the delegations did near agreement on some kind of formula, under which huge numbers of refugees, perhaps even all of them, would have been formally granted the "right of return," with the Palestinian negotiators having persuaded the Israelis that this right would not be widely exercised. If so, I'm only glad that no such deal was ever signed. Because in most surveys I've seen of Palestinian refugees in the West Bank and Gaza Strip, close to 100 percent insist that there can be no peace without the "right of return." More than 95 percent say that if such a "right" is promised, they would exercise it, no matter how inviting the financial benefits of not doing so. And few can seriously doubt that the hundreds of thousands of refugees in Lebanon, who were fuming with Arafat from the very start of the Oslo process for not immediately securing their return rights, would begin their journey en masse the moment such a deal was signed, and that Syria would make sure its Palestinian refugees were soon heading in the same direction. (One 2003 survey, its questions curiously worded, did find very different figures—suggesting a much-reduced insistence on "return.")

I often give talks and briefings to fairly worldly groups visiting Israel, groups that can include senior legislators and other prominent players on Capitol Hill who are not Middle East experts. And sometimes when I detail the positions Arafat took on the refugee issue, I can see they are having trouble believing me. It makes no sense to them. Arafat cannot seriously have been demanding that the majority of his people be given the right not to live in the new state of Palestine, taking its place for the first time among the family of nations, but in the country next door, the enemy state they were so delighted to be separating from? But it is all too true. And for many Israelis, I think, it was the very root of their sense of betrayal by Arafat. The voting split in the 1999 elections, when Barak defeated Netanyahu 56 percent to 44 percent, would indicate that 44 percent of Israelis had never placed much faith in the partnership with Arafat. In the light of Camp David, and most especially of Arafat's stance on the refugees, another 20 or 30 percent of the electorate lost their faith, too—people like me, who had considered it a partnership worth pursuing, and who could only conclude that they had been wrong, that Arafat had been dissembling from the start, that when he purported to recognize the state of Israel and its right to a secure future, as the basis of the Oslo process, he didn't have an Israel with a Jewish majority in mind at all.

The Israel of summer 2000, as Camp David was taking place, was a country markedly free of hysteria. We were not tearing ourselves apart in an orgy of demonstration and counterdemonstration, even though it was becoming clear that Barak was contemplating territorial compromise on a scale far exceeding that overseen by Rabin. Rather, I had the sense of a nation engaged in a kind of collective soul-searching. There was a degree of shock at the dovish positions Barak was taking—more generous than many of his own voters, never mind the opposition, had wanted him to adopt or imagined he would adopt. In essence, people were saying, This is the price we are being asked to pay for peace? Wow. Should we do it? Isn't it too risky? Can we be sure?

Barak, whose coalition had collapsed in the run-up to the summit and who no longer commanded anything like a parliamentary majority, had promised the public that he would seek their approval by referendum if a deal were reached. There is no way of knowing how Israel would have voted. When he came home from the talks, and the full dimensions and implications of Arafat's positions had yet to become clear, there were two groups of demonstrators outside the prime minister's residence in Jerusalem. And the pro-Barak rally hugely outnumbered the opposition protest. But I wouldn't read too much into that. Ironically, I think much would have depended on the precise status agreed for the Temple Mount. Ironically because, never having utilized its claimed sovereignty between 1967 and 2000, Israel closed off the Mount altogether to Jews after the riots there following Sharon's visit. Such realities, however, are not quite the point.

Psychologically, I think most Israelis would have shrunk from a deal that formally conferred jurisdiction over the most sacred place in Judaism to another people, a people, moreover, demonstrably indifferent, or worse, to Jewish sensibilities there and at other Jewish holy places. Speaking personally, I know I would have been troubled if Israel had relinquished it, partly because I think it would have weakened us as a people to be severed from the site at the center of our identity, and maybe partly for all the emotional and religious reasons that I so decisively and derisively reject when it comes to places like Joseph's Tomb or Rachel's Tomb or even Hebron. Lisa, by contrast, is withering: "You look at the Old City walls and your heart moves," she said to me when we discussed this. "I look and I see buildings, land. I look at the Temple Mount and I see buildings, land. They're not worth dying for. They're not more important than life."

Had Barak conceded full sovereignty at the Temple Mount to the Palestinians, then, I think, Israelis would have rejected the accord. But Barak was manifestly not prepared to do that. And, for what it's worth, I believe a Clinton-style bridging proposal, in which Israel continued to have a significant stake and say in the area, would have won over much, and quite possibly most, of the public. In this context, it may be worth noting that when Benjamin Ben-Eliezer, defense minister in the Sharon government in 2001–2002 and leader of the Labor party for most of that period, stated publicly that an outside "special regime" would have to be established to administer Jerusalem's holy places, he provoked little public antagonism. That position then became official Labor party policy. Barak's referendum prospects would have been boosted further if he had been able to garner evidence, as he expected he would, to suggest that this deal was more than just an Israeli-Palestinian permanent accord—namely, that, with his and Arafat's signatures, Israel was well on the road to fully normalized relations with its immediate Arab neighbors and much of the rest of the region as well, including Tunisia, Morocco, Saudi Arabia and the other Gulf principalities—the kind of turning point most Israelis had hoped and believed, inaccurately as it proved, they had reached on signing the peace treaty with Egypt twenty-one years before.

But nothing—no graceful solution to the Temple Mount dispute, no generous expansion of West Bank sovereignty to minimize the number of settlements being dismantled, no ironclad guarantees of successive peace treaties with Arab regimes, not even Syria and Lebanon—would have persuaded Israelis to vote in favor of an accord that offered Palestinian refugees the right, no matter the conditions, to make their homes en masse inside the state of Israel. Barak refused to contemplate the notion, and no Israeli prime minister would have acted, or will act, any differently. And any Palestinian leader who demands this "right" is bent not on making peace but on destroying Israel.

The second Intifada began a little more than two months after Camp David broke down on July 24, with Sharon providing the pretext. Blamed by Clinton for destroying the talks, Arafat began a global tour aimed at regaining international sympathies—to some effect in parts of the Arab world, but little, tellingly, in European capitals, where Barak was simultaneously working the telephones, both disseminating his narrative and pleading with every statesman he could collar to use his or her influence to bring Arafat back to the negotiating table and a deal. But Arafat was not listening. (Has a U.S. secretary of state ever suffered such humiliation as did Madeleine Albright at the residence of the U.S. ambassador in Paris that October, reduced as she was to running after Arafat to try to prevent him from bolting from one more doomed effort at reconciliation? She ordered the gates to the residence shut just before Arafat could make his escape, but he trumped her by boycotting that night's planned ceremony for the signing of a tentative Intifada cease-fire.) Rather than honoring his pledge to resolve disputes through negotiation, he incontrovertibly began stirring his people up into an anti-Israeli frenzy by the simple expedient of lying to them: The account he and his colleagues disseminated of what had happened at Camp David was of an uncompromising Israel that stubbornly refused to cede significant areas of occupied territory (false), insisted on retaining full sovereignty throughout Jerusalem (false) and would not countenance a right of return (true). Barak was conning the Palestinians, Arafat said, and Clinton was his hopelessly biased accomplice. Arafat returned to Gaza a hero—for purportedly rejecting much poorer terms than he had, in fact, been offered—and some Palestinian leaders, ministers included, began discussing openly an imminent all-out confrontation with Israel, a so-called Battle for Jerusalem.

I do not know whether, as has been reported by *Jerusalem Post* journalist Khaled Abu Toameh, rumors now began circulating in the West Bank and Gaza Strip that Israel was promoting cancer among Palestinians via innovative "radioactive belts" or sexual promiscuity via doped chewing gum. And I have no personal proof that Fatah began giving Intifada training to teenagers at dozens of camps—again, as Abu Toameh has reported. But those who monitor Palestinian TV note that even before the collapse of Camp David, it carried lengthy inciteful broadcasts featuring footage of Israeli troops shooting at Palestinian and other Arab targets down through the decades, and of bloodied victims in the grisliest condition—footage that I personally did see broadcast, for hour after hour after hour, once the conflict was in full swing. And then we have the acknowledgments of some of the key players themselves: Marwan Barghouti, Arafat's West Bank Fatah-Tanzim chief and confidant, bragging to London's *Al-Hayat* that Sharon's visit had been identified as the ideal pretext to launch the preplanned Intifada—"the most appropriate moment"; and Imad Falouji, Arafat's minister for communications, positively ridiculing the notion that the conflict was some kind of spontaneous response to the Sharon visit, an outpouring of popular anger against the reviled Israeli opposition leader so profound as to be unquellable by the would-be peacemaking PA. "Whoever thinks that the Intifada broke out because of the despised Sharon's visit to Al-Aqsa Mosque is wrong, even if this visit was the straw that broke the back of the Palestinian people," Falouji told Palestinians in the Ein al-Hilwe refugee camp in Lebanon in March 2001. "This Intifada was planned in advance . . . ever since President Arafat's return from the Camp David negotiations." It was a strategic resort to violence and terrorism, acknowledged by its own protagonists, to regain international sympathy, weaken Israel, unite the Palestinian people and its factions behind their leader and quash the growing criticism of his corrupt regime by refocusing all anger on Israel. It had the added attraction of bringing the Arab masses behind Arafat, too, rivaling or eclipsing the unbending Saddam, as the man who held firm against Israel, the United States and the might of the West for the sake of Islamic Jerusalem.

As opposition leader, incidentally, Sharon needed Barak's permission to make his visit to the Temple Mount, which the prime minister granted, ironically, after being given assurances by Arafat's security chiefs that it would not be used as a pretext for violence. Sharon, worried by Netanyahu's plans for a comeback that would oust him, and bent on demonstrating to his party members that he shared their determination to maintain Israeli control of the Mount, knew that a tour there by him might not pass entirely without response, which is why he was accompanied by several hundred security personnel, itself something of a provocation. But he could not possibly have imagined how widespread the repercussions would be. Sharon did not set foot inside the mosques, and

spring of 2001, he freed a dozen more, among the most dangerous terrorists, including men who had been in his jails since 1996 for orchestrating the February and March bombings that year.) He sat back as mobs torched the Joseph's Tomb compound in Nablus on October 7, 2000, and started a fire at the ancient Shalom Al Yisrael synagogue in Jericho five days later—a synagogue for which the PA had formally assumed responsibility under the 1994 accord. He began what would become his daily appeals for a million martyrs to march on Jerusalem. With time, his regime would try to smuggle in a fifty-ton consignment of weaponry aboard the *Karine A* cargo vessel, as part of a secret alliance with Iran that could hardly have been hatched without Arafat's guidance: His most senior financial adviser, Fuad Shobaki, supplied the cash to buy the ship; Omar Akawi, the captain, was an officer in the PA naval police, and acknowledged in a TV interview that he had been given orders by a PA official and had been bound for Gaza when he was intercepted in the Red Sea. Three earlier, smaller arms shipments from Lebanon aboard a vessel called the *Santorini* are said to have reached their Gaza destination. In November 2002, the Israeli army released documentation captured in Gaza that it said detailed plans to manufacture chemical weaponry there, a project overseen by Rashid Abu Shabak, then acting head of the PA's Preventive Security apparatus, and Samir Mashrawi, the Preventive Security general director. Israel would eventually garner incontrovertible evidence that Arafat was personally signing off on funding for such self-acknowledged murderers as Tulkarm Al-Aqsa Brigades chief Raed Karmi, months after Karmi had bragged on TV about killing two Israelis who had made the fatal mistake of visiting a Tulkarm café. Following his arrest by Israel in April 2002, Barghouti explained the dynamic to his Shin Bet interrogators as follows: "When Yasser Arafat wanted a cease-fire, he would say so, and when he remained silent, it was understood as a green light to continue terror attacks." (The transcripts of Barghouti's interrogation were made public by Tel Aviv District Court in April 2003.)

Arafat would repeatedly resort to despicable distortions to try to mask the fact of his refusal to counter terrorism and his incitement of it, with no little success. His aides would claim, first, that Barak had planned the Intifada as some kind of Machiavellian "exit strategy" to free him from the concessions he had offered at Camp David. Then, after Barak was defeated, they would portray the Israeli antiterror incursions into the West Bank as part of Sharon's "grand plan" for reconstituting Greater

Israel. Arafat branded the battling in Jenin in April 2002 "Jeningrad" and knowingly propagated false massacre charges there—and much of the world's media faithfully reported the allegations. He falsely claimed, as Israel lifted one of its sieges on his Muqata headquarters on May 1, 2002, that the army was in the process of storming the Church of the Nativity in Bethlehem "using all kinds of fire and rockets," and accused Israel of behaving like the Nazis. Watching flames flickering in a tower in the church compound on the live coverage that night from CNN, the BBC and the Arab Al-Jazeera network, I thought of the millions of Christians around the world, looking in, horrified, wondering if there were no depths to which those Israelis would not sink. Only hours later, after who knows how many viewers had been deliberately misinformed by the chairman, did most of the networks confirm that his claims had been falsehoods. The fire had been small and apparently arson, and nobody had been storming the church.

If Arafat had wanted an accord but was unhappy over the precise terms, the way forward would have been to keep negotiating. If an Israeli opposition leader's visit to a holy site had then inflamed his people and taken him by surprise, the way forward would have been to urge restraint, to plead for calm, to tell them to hold firm because a solution was imminent. His sympathizers claim that Arafat was hamstrung at Camp David by insufficient preparation, or by insufficient support from moderate Arab leaders, or by a thousand and one other factors, and would ask us to suspend our disbelief still further and accept that Arafat neither initiated nor enabled the Intifada and was desperately seeking a return to the peace table. None of this withstands even cursory scrutiny.

There was just one compelling reason for him to have taken the plunge in Maryland, or to have indicated a desire to do so in subsequent rounds of talks: He would have led his people to the promised land—brought them statehood on almost all the territory they sought, economic partnership with Israel and the Arab world, with international acclaim and international financial support, and vast sums of compensation for refugees with which to build the thriving Palestine they had forfeited half a century earlier. Like Israel's first prime minister, David Ben-Gurion, fifty-two years before, he would have been settling for only slightly less than he could expect for his people, and history would have acclaimed his wisdom. He might indeed have paid with his life—as Anwar Sadat did so shortly after he had engineered the economic salvation of his country, regained prized territory and averted endless rounds of further bloodshed by making his peace with Israel. That was a price Arafat evidently was not prepared to pay. Why do so when, in the absence of a deal and at the price of a tiny percentage of dead Palestinians, time would surely ensure so much more advantageous a resolution? Why do so when failing to lead, failing to challenge and reorient his public, was just so much easier? "The Camp David agreement," as Joe Klein wrote in his book on the Clinton presidency, *The Natural,* "would have required Yasser Arafat to stop being Yasser Arafat, an extremely unlikely capitulation." Dennis Ross was even more succinct: "For him to end the conflict is to end himself."

5.

The Other Side

Army helicopters often circled late at night near our home in Talpiot. The copters were generally engaged in reconnaissance work above adjacent Bethlehem, sometimes shining bright beams down on areas in that city where soldiers were in action, enforcing curfews and tracking down "wanted" Palestinians. Some nights, at the height of the Beit Jala–Gilo clashes, there were great pounding booms as rockets were fired. After the louder noises, one or another of my kids would moan in his or her sleep and shift position. During the most intense of these periods, when the rumble of warfare sounded anything but distant, Josh didn't fall asleep for hours and was clearly troubled; it really did feel as though the war was in our backyard, or one yard over at the most. Even during relative lulls, there was no escaping this conflict, and no keeping it completely from the children. Fortunately, Kayla didn't register what was going on down the road, and Adam only barely—although he started to get concerned in the winter of 2002, before the war with Iraq, about whether we had the right size gas mask for him. But Josh got it, and he was worried by it.

I would not be so arrogant as to try to write from the perspective of ordinary Palestinians. I know there are Palestinian writers and journalists, and parents, too, who are doing that with, hopefully, the same effort at honesty that I'm trying to exercise in describing Israeli life in this round of conflict. But from my vantage point next door, and intermittent venturing across to the Palestinian side of this venomous divide, I am acutely conscious of how awful we looked to them, and how the guilt and worry I felt about having my kids sleep uneasily as helicopters rumbled and boomed overhead was playing out just down the road. There, the war truly was in their backyards, and sometimes in their very homes. Our tanks came storming through their streets, crushing everything in their paths. Our helicopter missile attacks and commando-unit gunfire on militants and suspected bomb factories were seen there as the brutal Israeli army imposing its might on a defenseless, stateless people. Our imposition of curfews as the elite units used hard-won intelligence to try to locate the bombing orchestrators' hideouts was perceived there as the heartless deprivation by Israel of basic human liberties—the freedom to walk around one's own town, to shop and play and sit at a sidewalk café. There, our insistence on stringent travel restrictions, including roadblocks where trucks were unloaded and checked, was detested, as was our searching even of ambulances, which could be turned back; the same bitterness applied to our barring of pedestrians from leaving their home city and sometimes asking them to strip to their underwear to prove that they were not concealing explosives. All this was regarded as deliberate collective humiliation, reflecting Israel's desire to oppress and suppress, to prevent Palestinians from leading anything that might resemble a normal life.

I am acutely conscious, too, that the context in which all this awfulness was unfolding was entirely different from the context I understand to be accurate. Before Camp David, most Palestinians were telling their pollsters that they believed in coexistence and reconciliation, albeit in vague terms that gave no indication of what compromises they'd be prepared to make for it. Suicide bombers were supported only by a minority. The fundamentalist Hamas group, despite its educational and social networks, was easily outpolled by Arafat's Fatah faction of the PLO, which had endorsed the Oslo peace process. And, as I said earlier, the people of Bethlehem, Hebron and Ramallah were not all poised with knives behind their backs to stab us when the signal came. Deep into the second Intifada, all of that was reversed. Many, sometimes most, Palestinians in polls now said they regarded the aim of the conflict to be not merely the liberation of territory captured by Israel in the 1967 war but the liberation of all of Palestine—the destruction, that is, of our sovereign state. The majority of Palestinians expressed support for the "martyrdom operations" of the suicide bombers. Hamas was neck and neck with Fatah in the polls, and Fatah, in any case, had become a prime practitioner of suicide bombings.

In one of his many inopportune but presumably honest utterances, then Labor leader Ehud Barak remarked in March 1998, "If I were a young Palestinian, it is possible that I would join a terrorist organization." It was not the smartest comment to make to the Israeli electorate, but it reflected his realistic appreciation of the overpowering Palestinian desire for independence and the extent to which the perception had spread among Palestinians that such statehood could be achieved only through violence. And he was speaking more than two years before this conflict erupted. That sense among ordinary Palestinians of Israelis as heartless brutes who could be tamed only through bloodshed deepened immeasurably once the Intifada was raging. Hundreds of Palestinian innocents were killed and thousands were injured; hundreds of thousands of families lost their incomes, and endured days and weeks confined to their homes, months confined to their cities. Joblessness was above 50 percent in many areas; half the population was living below what the UN defines as the poverty line. If many of them hadn't liked us much before, many more truly came to loathe and despise us. If most Israelis became despondent and untrusting and less willing to contemplate compromise, most Palestinians traveled the same road, only farther.

And whatever ordinary Palestinians thought about how they and we had gotten into this cycle, that was history. The awful present was one in which an Israeli missile could streak from the heavens at any moment and, though intended for this or that Tanzim leader or Hamas bomb maker, could kill them or their parents or their children in the blink of an eye, death from out of the clear blue sky. I wrote about our daily lottery. This was theirs. There were no safe havens for them, either. With no warning, their home might be commandeered by the Israeli army for whatever purpose an unseen commander had determined, and their family ordered to manage, somehow, in one remaining room, or to go live with friends or relatives. And there was no telling what condition they'd find the place in when they were allowed to regain it—perhaps it would be smashed and looted, or tidier than when they had left it. As Israel constantly sought information about possible bomb plots, they might be obliged at any moment, if they had the misfortune to be male and between the ages of about fifteen and seventy, to present themselves to Israeli troops for questioning. They faced arrest without charge, handcuffs, blindfolds, interrogation.

Hundreds of young men, sometimes thousands, were kept in jail under "administrative detention" orders, imprisoned for months without trial. From the Israeli point of view, this was all in the cause of the battle against terror, and who could wish the army to do anything but its utmost to keep us Israelis safe? From the Palestinian point of view, it was intolerable; it was among the factors that created the next waves of vengeful bombers, fodder for the indoctrinators.

What was the long-term impact for the young children in the orphanage alongside Holy Family Hospital in Bethlehem, twenty of whom reportedly vomited in terror one night when Israeli tanks passed by outside, amid heavy exchanges of gunfire? Not so long ago, we had all marveled, amid the horror, that young suicide bombers would be so devoid of the will to live, or so brainwashed, or whatever analyses we invoked to try to make sense of the incomprehensible, as to willingly throw away their lives in this way. Now it became routine. Hamas crowed that it was overrun with volunteers. It had to step up bomb production to meet the demand. The wife of Hamas leader Abdel Aziz Rantisi might have been embarrassingly recorded on her home phone firmly withdrawing her teenage son Muhammad from a "martyrdom operation"—"Bless you, but my son is busy with his studies," she curtly told the recruiter who'd telephoned with the "good news" of his selection, and promptly hung up—but Hamas had long since gravitated far beyond the disgruntled, impressionable young male stereotype, and now managed to draw in young women, and even older women, and older men, and married men. And a feverish, semifriendly rivalry persisted as to who could send out the most—Hamas, Islamic Jihad or the Fatah Al-Aqsa Brigades.

For Israel's governments, meanwhile, there was a wafer-thin line between, on the one hand, ordering the kinds of measures necessary to enable troops to thwart Palestinian attacks and, on the other, ordering measures that might boost the Palestinian motivation to carry out attacks. Or maybe there was no thin line anymore. Maybe you simply could not do one without the other; maybe that was the very deadlock at the heart of this mutation of our conflict.

In an interview that he gave to Britain's *Guardian* newspaper in August 2002, Britain's chief rabbi, Jonathan Sacks, declared that the Intifada was forcing Israel "into postures that are incompatible in the long run with our deepest ideals." He said things were happening on a daily basis "which make me feel very uncomfortable as a Jew," and that "this kind of prolonged conflict, together with the absence of hope, generates hatreds and insensitivities that in the long run are corrupting to a culture." One of Israel's most passionate spokespeople to the sometimes overwhelmingly hostile British media, Sacks was savaged in the Anglo-Jewish community, both for the forum in which he chose to express his comments—the *Guardian,* which notoriously described the Israeli military action in Jenin in April 2002 as having been "every bit as repellent" as the September 11 terrorism, is widely regarded as the British newspaper least sympathetic to Israel—and, especially, for the content. There were even, ridiculously, calls from some extreme Jewish corners for him to resign.

Rather than brazen it out, reminding his critics of his staunch identification with and support for Israel and declaring that he stood by what he had said, however, Sacks wriggled. He claimed he had been quoted out of context. The headline—ISRAEL SET ON TRAGIC PATH, SAYS CHIEF RABBI—had been unfair, he contended, and the newspaper had been guilty of sensationalism. One of Sacks's aides actually read out to me long chunks of the wider interview to try to prove how sentences that had been left out of the printed text rendered his criticisms less stinging, while actually achieving the opposite: The headline may have been sensationalist, but the newspaper appeared to have recorded the rabbi's views relatively faithfully. Sacks, of course, had no need to wriggle: This conflict *was* forcing Israel into "postures . . . incompatible with . . . our deepest ideals."

What else could anyone with moral backbone say about a reality that necessitated soldiers and policemen to order Palestinian men to stand in line for inspection and lift their shirts at roadblocks? "Of course there's no comparison, and of course the context couldn't be more different," an Israeli woman whose family had been decimated in the Holocaust said to me shortly after she was caught up in a traffic jam at a Jerusalem-area roadblock. "We're not marking people for death. It's the opposite: We're trying to preserve life. But when I saw those half-dozen Palestinians standing there by the side of the road, for all the world to see, heads down, bedraggled and humiliated, well, the echoes were obvious."

What was worse was that, too often, it seemed as though Israel was becoming engaged in acts of violence that went beyond the scope of the defense against terrorism in which, regrettably, innocents are caught up as collateral damage. In a period of barely two weeks near the end of 2002, for instance, Israel did the following:

November 30: The army blew up a three-story building in Beit Lehiya, in the north of the Gaza Strip, the top floors of which, it alleged, were being used as a terrorist hideout. But presumably the army searched the building for the alleged terrorists before it razed it. And stored on the ground floor of the building were vast quantities of food to be distributed by the UN-affiliated World Food Program, enough food, indeed, to feed 38,000 people for a month—$200,000 worth of wheat flour (over four hundred tons), rice (over one hundred tons) and vegetable oil (over one hundred tons). Formal complaints all the way up the UN hierarchy yielded an army response that the UN had failed to follow the usual practice of cocoordinating with it over the use of the site. The next day, two Palestinians were killed in the same town, only one of whom was said by the army to have been a gunman who was firing on troops. The next day, a Palestinian boy was killed in the West Bank when he climbed onto an armored personnel carrier.

December 3: A ninety-five-year-old Palestinian woman was shot dead by troops while traveling in a taxi north of Ramallah, on a road that the army had ordered closed to Palestinian vehicles. She was returning home from shopping. The soldier involved allegedly fired seventeen bullets at the vehicle, aiming for the tires, military sources said. The victim, Fatima Hassan, was hit in the back by one of them.

December 6: Of ten Palestinians killed in an army raid on Gaza's Bureij refugee camp, during which Israel was attempting to locate a leading Islamic terrorist, most were believed to be Hamas members, but at least one, Ahlam Riziq Kandil, thirty-one, was an employee of the UN Relief and Works Agency (UNRWA), a female elementary-school teacher. (Two weeks earlier, the UNRWA chief in Jenin, Briton Iain Hook, was shot dead by troops in the course of another clash; they apparently mistook the cell phone in his hand for a grenade.)

December 8: Nahla Ajel, a thirty-six-year-old resident of Rafah, at the foot of the Gaza Strip, was shot dead when walking to her home near the settlement of Rafiah Yam. The army said troops thought they had spotted a group of six armed men trying to infiltrate the settlement. Ajel's three young children, walking alongside her, were injured.

December 9: Troops fatally shot a twenty-five-year-old Palestinian woman who was driving with her husband and mother on an unlighted road outside Nablus, breaching a dusk-to-dawn curfew; the same day, a mentally handicapped man was killed near Tulkarm after he ignored soldiers' orders to halt and started running.

December 12: Troops shot dead five Palestinians who were crawling toward the fence separating Gaza from Israel; they were equipped with ladders but unarmed. The army said the soldiers had feared a terrorist infiltration; the men were believed to have been trying to cross into Israel to find work.

As ever, this was also a period of attempted infiltrations into Israel and into settlements by armed Palestinians, and of sustained Palestinian attacks, and foiled attacks, on Israeli civilians and military personnel: two soldiers gunned down in Hebron; innumerable bombs defused close to settlements and on army patrol roads; daily clashes with Hamas and Islamic Jihad gunmen across the West Bank; several suicide bombers thwarted, including one in Rafah who walked toward soldiers, ignored their shouted orders to halt, was shot and was found to be wearing a belt packed with explosives. Late November had also seen a Hamas suicide bombing in Jerusalem's Kiryat Menachem neighborhood, in which eleven Israelis were killed, and an assault by Fatah gunmen in Beit She'an, in which six Israelis were killed, not to mention the Al-Qaeda attacks on Israelis in Mombasa. What's more, the Rafah mother may indeed have been hit by machine-gun fire directed at stopping a genuine infiltration attempt. The schoolteacher who was killed in Bureij was clearly an unfortunate victim of a fierce gunfight with acknowledged Hamas gunmen. The soldiers involved in the other incidents were deployed in areas where a bomber or gunman could appear at any moment. Life-and-death decisions had to be made in an instant. Holding fire could condemn Israeli innocents to death. And yet . . . And yet, the killing of the ninety-five-year-old woman outside Ramallah was the result of a clear breach of the army's open-fire regulations, which bar such shooting unless soldiers feel their lives to be in danger, and prompted an internal army investigation. The deaths of the five unarmed Gazans prompted another such internal probe. The army was forced to investigate time after time, week after week, and still the killings continued. More than twenty Palestinians, most of them fifteen and under, were shot dead by troops when breaching curfew orders in the second half of 2002 alone—almost all of them in incidents that required army investigations. Incidentally, several Israelis who failed to heed, or didn't hear, shouted orders to halt at roadblocks were killed, too.

In late 2001, I tried, via the army spokesman's office, to get to the bottom of several of the dozen-plus cases of Palestinian civilians reported to have been killed in Bethlehem in late October, during the army's two-week incursion into the city following the October 17 assassination of Israeli tourism minister Rehavam Ze'evi. Several of the fatalities were reported in the daily press to have occurred during gun battles with the army; others died under murkier circumstances. I asked about four specific cases when I wrote to the spokesman's office: Musa George Abu Aid, who was shot in his living room on October 19 by an Israeli sniper, according to an eyewitness account; Maryam Sabih, who died with her unborn child after being barred from getting to a hospital in Jerusalem by soldiers at the checkpoint near Rachel's Tomb, according to a Christian source in Bethlehem in an e-mail forwarded to me; Johnny Thaljiah, seventeen, who was shot dead on October 20 by an Israeli sniper as he played with his baby nephew a few feet from the entrance to the Church of the Nativity in Manger Square, according to his family and local clergymen; and Rania Kharofah, twenty-two, who was shot dead in adjoining Beit Jala "while buying diapers," according to the B'Tselem Israeli human rights watchdog group.

Three of these cases were not widely reported; the death of Thaljiah was covered in numerous newspapers, and cited as the cause of a papal lament about violence in the Holy Land and the need for a return to "peace and fraternity." Thaljiah's family told me by telephone that he had been hit by a single bullet "that went from the left-hand side of his back into his heart" and that the source of fire had been a clearly visible Israeli position on a nearby hillside.

The spokesman's office declined to have someone meet with me to discuss the incidents and took almost a week to provide a written response, part of which read as follows:

> The Israel Defense Forces deployed in the village of Beit Jala and parts of the city of Bethlehem between the 18th and 29th of October, 2001, following continuous fire from these areas on the Jerusalem neighborhood of Gilo, in order to protect the security of the citizens of Israel's capital. While the IDF deployed its forces they were under continuous fire, forcing them to return fire. IDF forces throughout the area of Bethlehem do not fire at civilians. . . . The IDF does everything it can to prevent harming civilians or shooting towards populated areas. The Palestinians, however, tend to shoot at IDF

soldiers and Israeli civilians from within the hearts of civilian populations and close to religious places, endangering the lives of Palestinian civilians.

The only specific case addressed in the statement was one that I had not raised, concerning one Yusuf Abayat, "who attacked a soldier inside an IDF post and was therefore shot," according to the statement. It said the army had "no information regarding any of the other incidents mentioned . . . and these incidents cannot be linked to any incidents in which shots have been fired."

I went back to the spokesman for a more detailed response to the specific cases but made no further headway. Subsequent inquiries, via other officials, were equally unproductive, although a government spokesman out of nowhere assured me in a later phone conversation, off the record, that Thaljiah could not possibly have been killed by Israeli fire, since Israeli forces had had no direct line of sight to the spot where he died.

While it is demonstrable that Palestinian officials routinely lied about death tolls and the circumstances of death—Arafat brazenly more than doubled the Palestinian death toll in his November 2001 address to the United Nations General Assembly—the Israeli track record was anything but reassuring. How could one discount week after week of reports of innocent Palestinians being killed, when a little research turned up cases such as that of Shadeen abu-Hijla, sixty, shot dead in broad daylight on October 11, 2002, as she sat on the porch of her home in Rafidiyah, one of the tonier neighborhoods in Nablus, "with a needle and thread in her hand," according to her family? Her husband, a doctor, was also injured in what the family insisted was an unprovoked attack. An initial army investigation reportedly produced the finding that she had been hit by "a stray bullet." The family said it had collected fifteen bullet casings.

Or take the case of an eleven-year-old Gaza boy, Khalil Mugrabi, who died in initially unclear circumstances in July 2001. Following a request for information from B'Tselem, the army's military prosecutor's office mistakenly sent the organization internal army documents, in which the prosecutor details how Mugrabi, who was resting on a sand dune after a game of soccer, was hit in the head by a bullet fired from a tank-mounted machine gun at a time when neither he nor anyone else in the vicinity posed any threat to the troops. Clearly, the prosecutor wrote, the fatal shot had been fired in breach of all regulations. However, in a formal letter to B'Tselem—the only piece of paper that was supposed to have been put in the envelope—that same military prosecutor ruled out any criminal investigation of the case, asserting that there was no evidence to justify such a probe.

We rightly screamed to the world about the orchestrated terror campaign that we were enduring. And there can be no comparison between those deliberate killings and what were, even in the least justifiable cases, the genuinely regretted Israeli killings of Palestinians. There can be no moral equivalency between deaths achieved through the premeditated targeting of civilians, where success is measured by the size of the death toll, and deaths that unhappily stem from efforts to protect those civilians. But plainly, to be brutally pragmatic about this, overeager Israeli fingers on the triggers could only rebound against us. Every innocent Palestinian father, mother or child who was killed left behind a circle of relatives and friends who would have had to be superhuman not to want some form of revenge. And then, pragmatism aside, there was the little question of our own moralities, our desire to protect an Israeli state that is democratic, ethical, worth protecting.

By the end of 2002, when the Central Committee activists of the governing Likud party rapturously selected the former Shin Bet operative Ehud Yatom for a high place on its roster of Knesset members for the next parliament, our own respect for those moralities seemed in danger of disappearing into the clouds. Yatom is the self-acknowledged killer of two Palestinians who were captured alive after hijacking an Egged bus in 1984 and threatening to kill all its passengers. (The two other terrorists were killed when the bus was stormed at a roadblock by Israeli commandos, as was a female Israeli soldier.) He bludgeoned them to death on the orders of his superiors, then, during a series of inquiries, lied about what he had done. When the truth belatedly came out, he was consequently barred by the Supreme Court from holding a string of public positions, including one as Sharon's antiterror adviser, then later received a presidential pardon. Now he sits in parliament, in the party of government. This debilitating trend—the escalating public support for figures like Yatom and the rising hard-line politician Avigdor Lieberman, who have a questionable commitment to the moral values of a democratic state—was one of the gravest consequences of what Sacks called the "corrupting" of our society. And what a victory for Yasser Arafat.

In a coruscating piece in the liberal daily *Ha'aretz,* reporter Gideon Levy, one of Israel's most fiery self-critics, compared our "certainly grave" troubles with those of the Palestinians: "Are Israelis afraid to sit in cafés?" he wrote. "It's been a long time since Palestinians could even dream of that. Is it scary to travel on a bus in Israel? There is no longer any such travel in the territories. Afraid to fly? Most Palestinians have never flown. Unemployment is rising? That is nothing compared to the malnutrition and near hunger in the territories, where the great majority of the residents are not terrorists." He went on: "No terrorist threat, however murderous, is grounds for a wholesale annulment of values; no suicide bombing can justify the daily killing of innocent people or the large-scale incarceration of others without trial; and nothing, but nothing, can justify the absence of a public discussion and the total disregard of what's going on in our backyard."

I would agree with some of that. I was troubled and discomfited by too much of what was being done in my name to protect me and mine, even as I profoundly appreciated the life-threatening situations that soldiers placed themselves in to protect me. But in trying to shake the Israeli public out of its indifference to the plight of the Palestinians, I also believe that Levy unduly escalated the self-flagellation. I do not think there was "a wholesale annulment of values" in Israel. And neither do I think that the suicide bombings were being used to "justify the daily killing of innocent people." That kind of prose suggests, falsely in my opinion, that filtering through the army was an attitude that said "Screw them" and produced casual killings of Palestinian civilians. I wonder why there was so ready a resort to live ammunition in so many troubling circumstances, especially when there are so many other methods that one would think could have been applied. In late spring 2001, an acquaintance fresh from a stint of reserve duty near Jenin detailed for me the circumstances in which one of his colleagues, having "run out" of rubber bullets, fired live rounds at Palestinian youths who were stoning his position from a nearby hill and killed one of them. How is it that Jordan, with a military that stands no comparison to ours in funding and expertise, manages to disperse large crowds of angry demonstrators without the automatic resort to live fire? But I was not on the front lines, and I don't know how many of the deaths could have been prevented.

I feel, too, after reading so passionately argued an article as Levy's, that there was much that this kind of writing unrealistically ignored: How deeply could the Israeli public, engrossed in its own struggle to stay alive, realistically be expected to empathize with a neighboring population that was telling its pollsters it considered itself to be an existential enemy of Israel's, proudly supporting a deliberate strategy of murder to rid the Middle East of the Jewish state? Why would Israelis have protested the fact that Palestinians could not sit amiably in cafés or travel freely between West Bank cities when they had so often felt the repercussions of such freedoms—given how often the lifting of a curfew or the easing of a blockade was exploited by suicide bombers to slip into Israel and wreak mayhem, and how those bombers were often cheered by hordes of celebrating Palestinians? Israelis didn't need to have long memories to know that the closures and curfews were a post–September 2000 reality, initiated not in peacetime by a whimsically vindictive Israel, but in a defensive war. And for all the humane sympathy Israelis might nevertheless have felt for ordinary people suffering from poverty and food shortages, those concerns were also affected by a knowledge that the prime source of much of that suffering was the Palestinians' own corrupt leadership, which consistently siphoned off substantial proportions of the colossal international aid packages provided precisely to alleviate Palestinian impoverishment, and at times allocated those funds to the terrorists. Most every business deal, Palestinian entrepreneurs would tell you privately, included a hefty under-the-table cut for the Palestinian Authority bureaucracy. Aides to Arafat and others in the PA establishment, the entrepreneurs alleged, demanded 50 percent of all profits in the cement and petrol industries, payoffs on every kind of business export and import, cuts even from the salaries they paid to their own employees.

All these factors were part of the context. They affected the way Israelis viewed and responded to what was happening on the other side of those roadblocks. And I believe that, similarly, if ordinary Palestinians had been more aware of these contextual factors, the course of the conflict would have changed. It must have been hard to consider anyone but the Israelis to blame when there was no food in your cupboards, you had not worked in months, and your son or your nephew or your son's best friend was in the cemetery, hit by a stray tank shell during a soccer game or gunned down when making the fatal mistake of crossing the road during a curfew. But a fair ascription of blame and an acknowledgment of its implications were crucial to breaking the bloody deadlock. Israel's conduct in this conflict was not beyond reproach. But it was plain that Israeli troops were not deliberately setting out to kill innocents; quite the reverse: The guiding policy was to minimize the risk of civilian casualties in every circumstance. It was equally plain that were the bombers to have stopped coming, the army would have had no need to go seek them out, and the roadblocks and curfews and humiliations and hardships would have come to an end. It is not remote coincidence that saw Jericho largely untouched when parts of many West Bank cities were pulverized in Israeli military onslaughts in the course of 2002: The bombers weren't coming from Jericho. If they hadn't been dispatched from Jenin, Nablus and Ramallah, those cities would not have been reentered, then reoccupied, either. What the Hebrew University philosophy professor Avishai Margalit observed in an article in *The New York Review of Books* in May 2001 still held true: "If the Palestinians were to stop the violence tomorrow, there is no question that Israel would stop its violence at once. But if Israel stops the violence tomorrow, there is no chance the Palestinians will stop theirs."

For the first two years of this conflict, almost nobody with any credibility on the Palestinian side would acknowledge the truth of Arafat's culpability in orchestrating the descent from Barak-era peace talks to armed Intifada. But that begun to change around the time of the second unhappy anniversary. It was then that Sari Nusseibeh, Arafat's Jerusalem representative, began trying to galvanize support for an end to suicide bombings and other attacks, at least on civilians inside Israel. It was then that Nabil Amr, who had only recently resigned as Arafat's minister of parliamentary affairs, wrote a landmark article in the official PA newspaper, *Al-Hayat Al-Jadida,* headlined AN OPEN LETTER TO PRESIDENT ARAFAT, in which he implicitly castigated his former boss for having rejected Clinton's bridging proposals for a permanent accord—thus essentially confirming much of what the Israeli delegates have always asserted about the viability of the peace terms on offer at the Camp David peace summit. "We failed in the management of the historical process we faced," Amr stated flatly. "Didn't we dance for joy when we heard about the failure of Camp David? Didn't we hurl mud at the pictures of President Clinton, who courageously put on the table proposals for a Palestinian state with minor border modifications? We are not being fair, because today, after two years of bloodshed, we are asking for exactly what we rejected then—except that now we can be sure it is no longer possible to achieve it."

And it was then as well that Abu Mazen (Mahmoud Abbas), the man whom Arafat had long ago designated as his successor, finally rediscovered his voice after two years of public near silence and began announcing, to the media and to public gatherings at home and abroad, that the decisive mistake of this Intifada had been to start killing Israeli civilians. In comments in September 2002, Abu Mazen told journalists invited to his home in Ramallah that "we made many mistakes from the beginning of the Intifada. . . . It's possible we went too far. . . . It's time to abandon all forms of violence." By late that November, he was using far harsher language. In a speech made all the more extraordinary by the fact that he was delivering it in Gaza, to the heads of "popular councils" representing Gaza refugees, Abu Mazen accurately but unprecedentedly described the Intifada as "a military battle, not a popular uprising expressing popular rage to which none can be opposed." It had been a dreadful mistake, he went on, to use "mortars, grenades and other things, and to shoot from homes and neighborhoods" against the Israelis. And he blamed himself and others like him for having "held our tongues in light of the terror." Even then, though, Abu Mazen refrained from pointing an accusatory finger directly at Arafat—despite the fact that his boss was, at that very moment, again frustrating Abu Mazen's efforts to broker a full Intifada cease-fire in talks with Hamas, Islamic Jihad and other Palestinian factions under Egyptian auspices in Cairo. Arafat was insistent that the agenda relate solely to a possible cessation of attacks inside Israel; he would not hear of an end to killing settlers, much less soldiers.

Of the three, it was Abu Mazen who was the most prominent and important figure, but it was his statement of the obvious that I found the least moving. This was the supposed voice of Palestinian decency, the angel on Arafat's right shoulder, constantly battling the terrorist devils on the left. But while I know he had been privately lamenting the return to "armed struggle" from the very earliest days of the second Intifada, he had made no effort to prevent the historic debacle at Camp David, and it took him two years to begin publicly assailing the resort to arms. And he didn't stress that the strategy was a mistake because it was wrong, because deliberately killing people is an intolerable thing to be doing. No, he emerged from hibernation to critique the armed Intifada primarily because it wasn't working, because Israel, in defiance of the Palestinian leadership's conventional wisdom, wasn't collapsing under terrorist pressure, wasn't making dramatic territorial concessions. Rather, he noted, the Intifada had had the reverse effect: The Palestinians, instead of gaining more territory, had seen Israel retake control of the territory it had previously relinquished.

Nusseibeh, Amr and Abu Mazen were rewarded for their outspokenness with intimidation of varying degrees of seriousness. Amr had shots fired at his house, and promptly retreated into his shell, shelving any further criticisms. Abu Mazen took to traveling a lot. Nusseibeh endured a series of death threats.

There could be little doubt that any and all of Arafat's critics were dicing with death. You crossed Arafat at your very real peril. Nobody can say for sure who it was that ordered the killing, in January 2001, of the Gaza head of Palestinian TV, Hisham Maki. But Maki, a close friend of Arafat, had clearly become an embarrassing inconvenience to the chairman, it being widely reported that he had siphoned off between $15 million and $17 million of PA funding into his private bank account. Jibril Rajoub, Arafat's former West Bank security chief, was still around, but he had lost that job after clashing with his chief over Arafat's refusal to let him take on Hamas—the chairman drew his pistol on Rajoub in the heat of one of their contretemps—and after refusing to sacrifice dozens of lives needlessly when Israel surrounded his security headquarters on the edge of Ramallah in April 2002, choosing instead to broker a surrender of the Hamas and other militants who were hiding out inside. Rajoub, a stocky Brandoesque figure, who speaks perfect, Godfather-style guttural Hebrew learned over many years in Israeli jails, was once the high hope of Israeli governments for the post-Arafat era. (Israel had identified Rajoub as a figure of moderation, and hoped to see his power rise in the Palestinian hierarchy. The best way to boost someone's standing in the implacable Palestinian reality was for him to be perceived as a staunch enemy of Israel. And so, in a nicely choreographed routine that nobody will acknowledge was prearranged, Rajoub left home one morning, returned to find heavy artillery damage to the premises and could then have himself filmed by Palestinian TV mournfully inspecting the shattered tiles in his bathroom.) But for a while after his dismissal, Rajoub seemed a spent force, broken by Arafat for having demanded a crackdown on terrorism.

There were other apparently reasonable prominent Palestinians out there—whether speaking out or still holding their tongues. Mohammad Dahlan, formerly Rajoub's equivalent in the Gaza Strip, was a public critic of the killings of Israeli civilians and of the missteps since Camp David—nevertheless, he managed to remain close to Arafat—and was one of the savviest and most credible younger Palestinian leaders, well liked by the Americans, at least in part because of the tailored elegance of his suits and his English proficiency. (In mid-October 2002, Dahlan was reported in the Israeli media to have told a gathering in Gaza, "After nine eleven, I implored Arafat to put the armed Intifada behind us—it's getting us nowhere—smash Hamas, and turn it into a popular [presumably non-armed] uprising. But our leadership didn't have the guts.") Dr. Eyyad al-Sarraj, a Gaza psychiatrist and human rights activist, was jailed on several occasions for protesting abuses and systematic corruption in the Arafat regime, but he was not cowed. I once accompanied *The Jerusalem Report*'s Palestinian affairs editor, Isabel Kershner, to the West Bank for an interview with a prominent Palestinian figure who consistently spoke out against the suicide bombers. He told us as we sat in his tranquil living room of the late-night visit he'd had from a very senior Arafat security official after making another such appeal against the attacks. The official delivered a pointed warning that, "at a time of war," it was his "national duty" not to talk like that. And that if he didn't change his tone . . . The threat was left unspecified.

But Arafat, improbable survivor of expulsion from one Arab country after another, openly reviled by most every Arab leader, given up for dead after a plane crash in the Libyan desert, then debilitated by consequent blood clots on the brain, suffering from Parkinson's and who knows what other physical or mental ailments, rejected by George W. Bush and repudiated by much of the Israeli peace camp, still reigned. And until that changed, the more humane voices would be shouting in the wilderness.

. . . • . . .

It was only a ten-minute drive from the well-ordered Jewish French Hill neighborhood in north Jerusalem to the sprawling anarchy of Ramallah. But that was more than enough time to appreciate some of the reasons why Palestinians regarded Israelis with such hostility. The crossing point just south of Kalandiya refugee camp, where more than ten thousand people live in an area of about one-tenth of a square mile, constituted an immovable barrier to any honest Palestinian who would seek to enter Israel for work, social reasons or health purposes. That dishonest Palestinians, and most especially those carrying explosives, could quite easily sidestep the main road and find their way to their targets via any number of smaller paths and open fields only confirmed the pointlessness of the crossing point for many Palestinians. In their eyes, the Israeli claim that this and the innumerable other roadblocks spread across the West Bank were positioned to try to improve Israeli security was ridiculous and insulting: Only the decent folk got checked and delayed and often harassed and sometimes abused at the official crossing points—and arbitrarily refused permission to cross on occasion, even when they had the appropriate papers, or a pregnant woman or dying child in the back of their car or ambulance.

On a good day, the line of cars and trucks waiting to be checked and eventually waved across stretched for hundreds of yards, and the process could take hours. Days were wasted. Products rotted in the sunshine. And all those in the line had the right papers. This long into the Intifada, everybody knew better than even to bother attempting to cross without them. As the hours passed, the only Palestinian beneficiaries were the young boys selling water.

On the hill overlooking the crossing point to the east sat the settlement of Psagot, sometime base camp of the Council of Jewish Communities in Judea, Samaria and Gaza, the settlers' umbrella organization. A neatly planned patch of red-roofed splendor in the grass, it contrasted starkly with the parched, dusty, gray streets below.

Through the checkpoint, towering from a strategically placed advertising placard above the potholed main road, loomed a vast rendering of Yasser Arafat in all his finger-waving glory. ALWAYS WITH YOU ran the Arabic inscription—comforting or intimidating, depending on your perspective. And, deep into this conflict, he was indeed still with us—albeit an Arafat much reduced from his globe-trotting early presidential incarnation. This was an Arafat who had been confined to quarters, his humiliation keenly and personally felt even by many of those Palestinians who opposed and loathed him.

Again, the distances, or lack of them, were startling: From the seat of Israeli power, the Knesset in Jerusalem, to Arafat's Muqata headquarters in Ramallah, traffic and roadblocks permitting, was perhaps a journey of twenty minutes. After months of increasingly close attention by Israel's assault helicopters, by late 2002 the once proud Muqata complex was simply a bomb site, ringed with wreaths of barbed wire. The military intelligence building, or what was left of it, had collapsed into narrow layers of rubble. The same applied to the general intelligence building. Across the street were the repaired offices of the Popular Front for the Liberation of Palestine, where Secretary-General Abu Ali Mustafa had been blown up in his third-floor quarters on August 27, 2001, by missiles fired with such accuracy from Israeli helicopters that, even as they plotted their revenge, his deputies could not suppress their admiration at the clinical precision. The PA prison compound had been obliterated. Rows of smashed Palestinian police cars and jeeps were abandoned in a parking lot. (There was no shortage of such lots: This city's police station, a few minutes away, where Israeli reservists Avrahami and Norzich had been battered to death on October 12, 2000, was now a parking lot, too, surrounded by a low breeze-block wall on which the ubiquitous graffiti sloganeers had spray-painted paeans of praise for the continuing Intifada.)

Under Israeli siege, the president held court in the last office of a three-story barracks with incongruous pink-and-yellow shutters, an office with a circle of concrete patching up a hole in the outer wall. A solitary Palestinian flag fluttered from the roof, alongside a torn wind sock—no need for that anymore; Israel had blown up his helicopters long ago. In interview mode, he remained defiant, reminding his international media interlocutors that they were "talking with General Arafat," strategist of repute, survivor nonpareil.

Home to maybe 100,000 Palestinians, Ramallah–Al-Bira looked like a town that had been striding forward, then ground to a sudden halt and was now in steep decline. It was the thriving capital of the West Bank in the mid- to late 1990s, abounding with new construction, new businesses, restaurants and nightclubs. Now, the elite Al-Masion neighborhood, with its incongruous fantasyland architecture, all crenellated towers and sweeping paired outdoor staircases, stood out like an ever-sorer thumb amid the general dilapidation, the dust, the garbage, the shut-down stores and beauty parlors and the abandoned cars.

Radwan Abu Ayyash, director of the Palestinian Broadcasting Corporation (PBC), had produced a lavish pamphlet detailing the reprehensible January 2002 bombing by Israel of the radio and TV building, which he later began tentatively rebuilding. On its fifty-six full-color pages, the pamphlet castigates Israel for its "brutal . . . state terrorism," and stirringly extols the PBC as "the lighthouse that shined in the sky of Palestine . . . the voice and image of martyrs and wounded. Yet they shelled the air that carried those dreams." On the outside column of every left-hand page is a picture of the pristine five-story PBC building "before the destruction." On the outside of each right-hand page is the same building, shown in flames on January 19. Abu Ayyash, a cordial, sharp-witted functionary who claimed, in conversation across an empty desk in his temporary offices around the corner, that he sought nothing more than a path out of the conflict and back to the peace table, would have had the world see in those twin images—that architecture of Palestinian achievement and Israeli destruction—the essence of what had gone wrong: the Israeli insistence on obliterating Palestinian freedom. In a valley not far from the Muqata, though, I saw a piece of architecture that provided a more honest metaphor. It was a building interrupted at a most peculiar stage of construction—its floors and countless staircases completed, but its walls unbuilt. So plentiful were the interior staircases, open to the elements because nobody had ever put up the exterior, that the building resembled one of those baffling M. C. Escher paintings, the stairs turning in on themselves, leading nowhere.

Khaled Abu Toameh, a journalist and friend for many years, lives in East Jerusalem. He has covered Palestinian affairs for twenty years, and his uncle Jamal Abu Toameh is Arafat's lawyer. Khaled described Arafat's regime as "functioning like a Mafia." It was "an open secret," he declared, "that Arafat ordered the killing of Hisham Maki." He recalled the day in August 2002 when he happened to be reporting from the Muqata and saw two plainclothes Palestinian security personnel emerging from out of the rubble with a prisoner; he decided to follow them and saw the man blindfolded and executed against a wall. "When I asked one of the policemen what was going on, he said, 'A criminal has been executed. What's the big deal?' They honestly didn't know why we would care." Speaking to me with the air of an extraordinarily patient nursery-school teacher explaining the same lesson over and over again to a phenomenally obtuse child, Khaled, who himself had shrugged off dark personal threats from senior aides to Arafat, insisted that Israel should have known better than to help rehabilitate the chairman, and that by doing so it had consciously imported a militaristic dictatorship, which, in turn, had changed a fundamentally moderate people and imposed a culture of uniforms, corruption, intimidation and execution. "Arafat always described the Oslo process as the rape of the PLO," Khaled claimed, "and said that accepting the process was the only way in which he could survive" from his post–Gulf War low. "He always presented the agreements in that light to his people, as, at best, a short-term truce. When I asked the first PLO cops what they were here for in Jericho, they said they had been brought to liberate Palestine. Making peace? Living side by side with Israel? That was never mentioned."

All through the 1990s, Khaled continued, still in his "This is so obvious" tone, the Palestinian Authority did anything but prepare its people for compromise. "On the contrary, they reassured the people, 'If we don't get what we want, we'll have other options'—that is, a return to armed struggle. They stockpiled weapons for the moment the day would come, the moment they'd launch plan B. And Israel helped out by, incredibly, giving them automatic rifles."

But wasn't Arafat also maneuvering within the confines of Palestinian public opinion? I asked, attempting a little devil's advocacy. Maybe he couldn't appear too conciliatory to Israel, too fast, for fear of being branded a traitor by his own public and brought down. Khaled was not convinced. "Arafat was plenty strong enough to arrest [the leading Hamas spokesman in Gaza] Mahmoud Zahar, and have his beard shaved off," he recalled. "Strong enough to jail [Gaza Hamas leader] Abdel Aziz Rantisi for years, from 1995 to 1999, without protest."

In short, Khaled asserted, "Arafat was waiting and hoping Israeli society would break down and that he would become the 'king of Palestine'—replacing Israel—with Jews a minority among the Muslims. As he said, he wanted to lead the hordes to liberate Jerusalem. By the summer of 2000, having seen what the loss of twenty Israeli soldiers a year in Lebanon could do to Israeli society"—that relentless annual death toll through the 1990s, as Hezbollah pounded away at Israeli army positions in the so-called security zone in south Lebanon, led ultimately to a unilateral, somewhat chaotic military pullout in May 2000—"he thought to himself, I can do better than that. Hence the new Intifada, and the expectation, at the very least, that the mounting civilian casualties on both sides would bring international intervention, to impose a solution more beneficial than the one he was offered by Barak."

When it came to a path out of this nightmare, Khaled, who stressed that he was speaking as a Palestinian concerned for the moral well-being of his society, suggested that Israel needed "to turn Area A into Area B," by which he meant to "clean the Palestinian areas of all heavy weapons" and leave the Palestinian Authority and/or its successors with only a rudimentally armed police force rather than a quasi army. (This was, incidentally, part of the recipe suggested by many Jewish settlers in the

West Bank, who regarded a permanent Israel reassertion of security responsibility over the major West Bank population centers, where it relinquished such control in late 1995, as the only viable means of co-existence, reducing the PA to an institution controlling civil affairs only.) "Perhaps," Khaled postulated, "in the course of a few generations under that arrangement, the Tunis Mafia mind-set might get swept away, and you might produce a generation that genuinely seeks compromise. Perhaps."

Khaled unburdened himself of this bleak prognosis as, along with Isabel Kershner and Danish TV journalist Steffen Jensen, we waited in another of those plentiful parking lots alongside the site of the former PBC building for our meeting with Radwan Abu Ayyash. Not surprisingly, Radwan, whom I had met occasionally down the years since he ran the Palestinian Journalists' Association in East Jerusalem well over a decade ago, offered a radically different assessment of the Intifada, its causes, Arafat's strategy and possible routes out of the deadlock. Like a man in thrall to the oversized portrait of a youngish Arafat that stared at us, bubble-eyed, from a dominant vantage point, propped up on the side cupboard behind Abu Ayyash's left shoulder, the PBC boss trotted out a flawless depiction of "Arafat as victim, Arafat as man of peace," buffeted impossibly by the heartless Sharon on one side and the impertinent Hamas on the other. "There is no master plan," he insisted. "We want peace. We just want Israel to leave us alone. Arafat is a peaceful person. You ask me, 'Why didn't Arafat compromise [at Camp David]?' But you gave him no evidence, no concessions on Jerusalem, on settlements."

As he warmed to his theme, Abu Ayyash pulled small pieces of square paper, little orange notelets, from the box on his desk and, apparently quite unconsciously, doodled light and heavy straight lines, little boxes and arrows in blue ink, to reinforce his points: "We didn't start this [Intifada]. Sharon went to the Temple Mount." Arrow into a box. "The Israeli army, the Israeli side, is the powerful one." Three heavy lines, drawn underneath one another. "Israel has to start. Don't ask the weak to give the concessions. Arafat can't even leave his front yard"—light arrow out of a box—"and you expect him to take control!"

Arafat, he went on, indignant, "uses all the bad words when he hears about the latest Hamas attack. He knows it will drive us back. He would love to say all the right things, but he is the leader of a people under occupation. Half the Palestinians believe that Arafat is a traitor. His own people look at Arafat as humiliated. They ask, 'Why do you limit us?' "—a presumed reference to the periodic calls for a halt to attacks inside Israel. "They say, 'We need to take revenge.' "

Abu Ayyash had an Arafat-exonerating answer for everything. Asked about Arafat's funding of the Fatah groups that had carried out so many suicide bombings and shooting attacks, he insisted, amid frantic underlining, that the president "didn't knowingly fund terror. He gave money to people for food, but he didn't know what it was used for. He gave money for social work."

But what of the documents seized by Israel that show Arafat specifying the sums to be paid to individuals known to be engaged in attacks? Abu Ayyash put down the pen. "The documents," he said solemnly, leaning back in his chair, "might not be true."

And what about the horrific battlefield and hospital footage Arafat ordered screened on Abu Ayyash's TV stations, the anti-Zionist and anti-Semitic diatribes from the mosques, the music videos in praise of the "martyrs"? "We don't produce those videos," Abu Ayyash countered. "We just screen it. And we use English subtitles, so it can't be mischaracterized by our critics!"

Only a few days before this meeting, I had watched a few of the musical clips. Among the most often played was a plaintive tune, sung by an olive-skinned beauty, in praise of an unnamed "young girl" who "like a flower is gone"—gone in circumstances that are not precisely detailed. All we learn from the lyrics is that she "offered her soul and sacrificed for her country," for a "people whose aim is to liberate ancient Jerusalem." Clearly no expense had been spared in the preparation of the clip, since the singer changes clothes, hairdo and backdrop several times while venerating the fallen heroine, one of the "dignified virtuous martyrs" who have "sacrificed for Palestine to live . . . bringing tomorrow a new dawn." Also frequently screened was the heartrending short film of a young boy comforting his mother in the destroyed ruins of the family home, intercut with black-and-white footage of Jews arriving in prestate Israel on boats, hammering home the message that the Jews are brutally dispossessing the innocent Palestinians. And still popular was the classic "Patience, O Yasser," designed to bolster the president's spirits as he endured in the besieged Muqata. "The occupation is defeated. . . . Our death is life," the male vocalist asserts amid "Sharon = Hitler" banners, pictures of Israeli tanks confronting Palestinian Red Crescent ambulances, and shots of bloody Palestinian bodies born aloft on stretchers, intercut with the voice of Arafat declaring that while the Israelis "want me persecuted, my answer is to be martyred."

Abu Ayyash's presentation was fascinating in that he provided insights into one of the dynamics at the heart of this Intifada—the relationship between Arafat and his Fatah faction, now returned to the armed struggle, and the Islamists who were using the selfsame methods against Israel and were competing with him for Palestinian public support. "Hamas and Islamic Jihad are rejecting dialogue" with Arafat, Abu Ayyash lamented, a reference to intermittent meetings between Arafat's Fatah loyalists and Islamic leaders. In the official Palestinian Authority narrative, Arafat's peace-minded loyalists had tried in these talks to persuade the evil Hamas leaders to put a halt to attacks on Israelis. In the real world, Arafat had on some occasions used these meetings to try to co-opt Hamas to his government and on other occasions to have Hamas accept his authority as to when to call temporary Intifada cease-fires, when to limit bombings and attacks on occupied territory, as well as when to engage in such violence inside Israel. All such efforts had failed, as Abu Ayyash, still clinging to the official narrative, nevertheless acknowledged. "They reject Fatah's rule. They don't want Arafat to rule them."

Raising his voice to underline the chutzpah of these extremists, he revealed: "They are ready to coordinate—but from a position of equality! They say they'll stop the military actions"—the term he used for the deliberate killing of Israeli civilians—"on three conditions: if Israel leaves the West Bank areas it has reentered since September 28, 2000, if the [Israeli] assassinations [of Intifada leaders] stop and if Fatah consults with them before any political steps. That won't work." Indeed it wouldn't: Under Sharon, Israel would pull back and stop targeting Intifada kingpins only if the terror stopped, not the other way around. And Arafat, of course, would never voluntarily cede his decision-making monopoly to his Islamic rivals. The outrage Abu Ayyash reflected without acknowledging it was that Hamas, at a time of "national struggle," had the impudence to make any demands of Arafat at all.

Our host tried to inject a note of optimism. "I don't think it is too late," he declared. "It's never too late for something good. I don't know how many people we will lose, how many friends we will have, but peace will come."

"It's too late for Arafat as far as most of Israel is concerned," I suggested. "There's nothing Arafat could do now to win back the Israeli public."

Absentmindedly drawing lines again, Abu Ayyash was undeterred: "Both our peoples have had bad luck. . . . We must get rid of this deteriorating situation—on the security and political level. If people see hope on the horizon, they will be ready for concessions. But if they see everything gloomy, they make the other choice—suicide bombings and military operations—because they have nothing to lose. . . . The solution is to go back to the [negotiating] table. Barak got to [offering] 96 percent of the West Bank. Let's start from there. Pull out from the occupied territories. Your extremists want a big Israel, ours a big Palestine. We each mistrust the other. Israel can destroy a [Palestinian] city. But the Palestinians can send ten thousand martyrs. Israel can kill a million Palestinians, but that will still leave six [*sic*]. . . . There is no bulldozer solution."

"But do most Palestinians believe Israel has the right to exist," I asked, "as a Jewish state, in its pre-1967 borders?"

"Absolutely. For one hundred years, a million years," Abu Ayyash assured us. "I'm not interested in throwing Israel into the sea or sending the people back to Europe. I'm from Jaffa originally. And I can't change where I come from. But I live in Ramallah; I have a job here, family here. If I go to Jaffa, I might get killed. I accept the price [of coexistence]. We have no choice. Yes, it's hard for me to see the Israelis enjoying Jaffa. I don't like the surgeon. But there is no choice but to have the operation."

. . . • . . .

Abu Ayyash, of course, acknowledged that Barak had offered 96 percent of the West Bank to Arafat. But while the TV chief knew it, he had helped to ensure that most Palestinians did not. On Arafat's orders, his TV stations had offered a very different version of events.

I will never forget an NPR radio interview I did late in 2000, when Barak was still in power but the conflict was already in full swing. I was in a studio in Jerusalem, and a passionate, earnest young Palestinian journalist was speaking from Gaza, and at one point in our long exchange, she tried to illustrate, for listeners a world away in East Coast traffic, how awful life had become for ordinary Palestinians. The way I remember it, the conversation ran like this: "Things are so bad," she noted, "that the mothers of Gaza are ready to sacrifice their daughters for Palestine."

"Why?" I asked. "Why are the mothers of Gaza not sending their daughters to play with my sons in the back garden?"

"What are you talking about?" she fired back in anguished disbelief. "How can we do that? You will never live in peace with us."

"What are *you* talking about?" I retorted. "This Israeli prime minister was elected by Israel precisely to make peace with you. He wants to work with your leadership to establish the state of Palestine on almost all of the land we captured in the 1967 war."

"No, that's not true," she said wearily. "You will never let us have a state. You will never end the occupation."

This from a journalist, supposedly well informed.

. . . • . . .

With the same passion I use to cite terrorism as the root cause of the collapse of the peace process, self-described Palestinian moderates cite the settlement enterprise. They rightly point out that while Rabin put a halt to most of the expansion at settlements in the West Bank and Gaza Strip, the building boom took off again under Netanyahu and positively soared under Barak. Had a deal been reached at Camp David, such construction would have been irrelevant; Barak would have ordered the dismantling of almost all the settlements, allocated compensation to enable as many settlers as wished to move back into sovereign Israel and relocated the rest into the small blocs of settlement where Israel would have expanded its sovereignty. But meanwhile, all ordinary Palestinians saw were more and more homes going up on the land they had been told would be coming under their sovereignty. Ironically, it was Palestinian laborers who were building the homes. And when the Camp David talks collapsed, Arafat could point to the constant process of settlement building to convince his people that the Israelis had never been serious about ending the occupation.

There was a valid domestic Israeli political imperative for Barak to keep sanctioning more building even at settlements he intended to evacuate: Had he halted the construction before the Camp David summit, he would immediately have found himself in head-to-head conflict with the political right. It was far simpler not to provoke that conflict until a final accord had been signed, when, he hoped, he would have the overwhelming support of the Israeli mainstream for the wide-scale dismantling of settlements, a relatively small price to pay for the full normalization of relations with the Palestinians and, ultimately, the rest of the Arab world. But such internal political subtleties meant next to nothing in the Palestinian street, where the vague, discredited promise of an eventual reversal of the settlement-building process was set against the reality of more building and more arrivals, including Russian immigrants, converts from northeast India and "rediscovered" Jews from Peru.

Quite apart from the disillusion the settlements have broadened among Palestinians, and despite the fact that several of my relatives live in them, I think that history will show the unbridled, nonblueprinted post-1967 settlement enterprise to have been one of Israel's most catastrophic steps. Had successive governments adopted a firm program of building in a few limited areas, solely for reasons of boosting security in our sliver of land alongside the sea, we could have won the understanding, even the support, of much of the international community. Nine miles wide at its narrowest point, and relentlessly attacked from the West Bank, Israel would have had a strong case for broadening that narrow waist by establishing communities just across the Green Line border, and, similarly, for reestablishing what had been Jewish communities in areas adjacent to and protective of Jerusalem, and for settling on the Jordan Valley border—a buffer, most especially, against the Iraqis and Iranians farther to the east.

Instead, however, the post-1967 Labor governments proved unable—in fact, unwilling—to prevent activists from building homes all over the West Bank, often right up against Palestinian population centers. The incredible Israeli military success of the 1967 war prompted an upsurge of Israeli Jewish messianism—it was seen as confirmation that the divine power looked kindly on the Jews' return to their homeland—and a desire to take long-term physical hold over the areas "liberated" in those six days of battle. Clearly, the prospect of a "return" to places of such biblical and historical significance as Hebron, Bethlehem and Shilo resonated deeply with the largely secular Labor party, too, deeply enough to overwhelm any concerns about the democratic and demographic implications of laying claim to this territory. And the post-1977 Likud governments, consumed by the ideal of restoring a biblical Greater Israel, hugely encouraged the enterprise. In his second term as prime minister, in the 1990s, Rabin drew a distinction between the logically located "security settlements" and the troublesome "political settlements" in the heart of the West Bank. But in his first prime ministerial incarnation, two decades earlier, he, too, had failed to limit settlement to areas his security advisers considered essential to maintain. And, ironically, it was Shimon Peres, later to position himself significantly to Rabin's political left, who had frequently undermined him on this, effectively supporting the establishment of numerous settlements he would, years later, under the Oslo accords, be pressing to evacuate.

In the second Intifada, these political settlements, liberally distributed throughout the West Bank, came to constitute everything but an asset. Although I would strongly support their dismantlement under the terms of a peace accord, to have evacuated them unilaterally in the midst of a terrorist onslaught would have indicated to Palestinian extremists that their strategy had paid off, and would thus have led to a further intensification of attacks on Israeli targets. Moreover, any effort at unilateral evacuation would have sparked terrible internal feuding between the settlers and their supporters, on the one hand, and, on the other, those who believed we shouldn't be there. Such internal dissent would likely have been fierce and dangerous even if we had reached a peace deal—a sovereign Israeli government ordering a retreat from what many regard as God-given land. Dismantling settlements in the absence of a deal, to the delight of a onetime peace partner now trying to kill us, would probably have brought something akin to civil war. The violent scuffles we witnessed in October 2002 when the army was sent to evacuate one of dozens of illegal settlement outposts—the Gilad Farms, erected, without government approval, to commemorate Gilad Zar, a West Bank settlement security officer murdered in May 2001—would have been child's play by comparison. There are some strange and dangerous forces flourishing in some of the most extreme settlements: people like the gang from the Bat Ayin settlement who were caught in the act of planting a bomb outside an Arab girls' school in East Jerusalem in April 2002, and those who claimed credit, in the name of a right-wing extremist group, for the murders of three members of the Tmeizi family in a drive-by shooting outside Hebron in July 2002, and half a dozen other fatal attacks on Palestinian innocents. For the most extreme settlers, there are no means that cannot be employed to justify maintaining their hold on the territory. A settler underground in the 1980s was exposed as it plotted to blow up the mosques atop the Temple Mount. And the killing of a prime minister was a small and entirely worthwhile price to pay for the retention of territory the Lord promised Abraham.

Yet because the settlers were there, many of them honestly believing that their presence was keeping all of us safe, we could not properly protect sovereign Israel from the bombers. The various Sharon-led coalitions dragged their feet for as long as possible over building a protective fence along anything resembling an Israel–West Bank borderline, fearing that it would be seen as precisely that, a border, something the Israeli right, with its commitment to Greater Israel, was ideologically opposed to erecting. The sheer volume of suicide bombers pouring across the nonexistent border—in stark contrast to the failure of more than a handful of terrorists to infiltrate from fenced-off Gaza—gradually forced Sharon's hand. But the farther the West Bank fence extended, and the harder it got for the gunmen and bombers to target Israel, the more, inevitably, they would focus on the more vulnerable settlements. That would mean more Israeli soldiers would have to be dispatched there to defend the indefensible—200,000 Jews living in the midst of 2 million Palestinians—and more soldiers like Keren Yaakobi would pay the heaviest price for the folly. Yaakobi, nineteen, was shot dead by Palestinian gunmen in Hebron in December 2002. Earlier, she had been attacked by some especially hardline Hebron settlers as she sought to prevent them from attacking Palestinians, her parents said. "I believe that life is holy, life is holy before the land," said her father, Yigal. "They [the settlers] are maniacs, fanatical with religion. If they want to live there, it is okay with me, but they must guard themselves."

After Dror Weinberg, a father of five with a pregnant wife, was killed by Palestinian gunmen in Hebron, along with eleven other soldiers and security men, the front page of *Yediot Ahronot,* Israel's biggest-selling daily, featured two commentators battling out the dilemma with the familiar non-nuanced absolutism: settler champion Aryeh Eldad urging that we "declare Hebron part of Israel, along with anywhere else from where they kill us," and the dovish Bet Michael demanding that we relinquish all the settlements and describing the Intifada as a war Israel was fighting solely "for the well-being of the settlers."

Soon after the Gilad Farms clashes, a very senior army officer, in a one-on-one briefing, set out some of the dilemmas posed by the rash of illegal outposts, dozens of which had sprung up in recent years, some of which had been "retroactively approved" by the government, others of which were maintained in open breach of the law. "We have a legal obligation to protect every Israeli, everywhere," he noted, "even if they are somewhere illegal. For us, protecting lives supersedes even the law. For them [the illegal settlers], land supersedes the state, the law, democracy, the will of the people and even life. You have these settler youths who have no concern for the state of Israel. They don't even heed their own leaders or rabbis. They are out of control and it is unacceptable, wherever you stand politically.

"These dozens of outposts are a security nightmare," the officer went on, "prime targets for terrorism. There have been numerous cases of people, soldiers and security officers, dying as a consequence of them. There are currently several hundred soldiers guarding such settlements. And it's a big problem for us in the army: We have to take a reservist and explain to him that he has to do reserve duty, dangerous reserve duty, to guard people who are breaking the law. Also, we look terrible internationally, even to our friends. We pledged that we would establish no new settlements. So if we don't stop them, if we don't confront these flagrant lawbreakers, even our friends will say we are turning a blind eye to new settlement building. Evacuating them, however, gives us these horrible, heartwrenching confrontations, of soldiers and cops battling civilians. Dozens injured. Unacceptable."

This senior officer expressed the conviction that several young settlers who had been arrested in the wake of the violent scuffling at the Gilad Farms, their actions captured in TV footage, would be put on trial and punished, and that this would reinforce the fact that Israel was a country where the rule of law held sway. "Those responsible will be prosecuted," he said, adding, as though to reassure himself, "I believe it will happen. They've got the film." He was wrong. No charges were brought.

To those questioners in American Jewish audiences who tell me that Israel needs to hold on to the settlements, and encourage more and more people to live there, I suggest that the security implications, the moral implications and the demographic implications require a certain survivalist pragmatism. And to those questioners in American Jewish audiences who tell me how troubled they are by the settlement enterprise, and ask me why Israel has never followed a sensible, self-interested policy on the issue, I have no answer. The settlements in the West Bank and Gaza Strip were not the root cause of the second Intifada, but they were a key factor in our inability to reduce that conflict unilaterally.

"I always thought you Israelis were crazy but admirable," a soft-spoken Palestinian academic told me well into the second Intifada, "to return here after two thousand years. But now I worry for you, and for us. I have always spoken out against the militarization of the conflict. . . . But even if we are saints, Israel will continue the settlements. By continuing settlements, Israel has marginalized peaceful forces on the Palestinian side. It is such an extremely stupid policy that it's just amazing to me that Israel would follow it."

. . . • . . .

In the same vein, many's the Palestinian who has assured me that if only the assassinations of key Intifada orchestrators were to stop, so, too, would the attacks on Israelis. (I wasn't persuaded.) To quote the same academic, "If Israel ends the assassination policy, even Islamic Jihad would end the suicide bombs inside Israel for at least a truce period. Assassinations breed a desire for revenge, and revenge against soldiers doesn't hurt," he asserted contentiously, "so they want revenge against civilians." This man said he had himself witnessed one such Israeli hit—the killing in Ramallah in August 2002 of Muhammad Saadat, brother of Abu Ali Mustafa's successor as chief of the Popular Front for the Liberation of Palestine. "I am still traumatized by it. I'm not saying Muhammad wasn't involved in stuff, but he definitely never injured or killed an Israeli. He ran a small shop. I remember his smile. . . . I heard the shots and ran to look. I couldn't approach him for twenty minutes, the red laser was on my forehead"—presumably the sights of an Israeli gun. "There were five bullets in his body. I was so angry. Today it is impossible to write as I did against the militarization. Because if we decide to stop, then Sharon wins, and the people don't want that. They don't want to surrender."

Many's the Palestinian, moreover, who has insisted that Sharon deliberately ordered the killing of high-profile Intifada activists, terrorists, precisely to ensure "revenge attacks" on Israel and a rapid end to any period of calm, to dash any hint of optimism, to ensure he was never dragged back to a peace table. And Sharon could not go back to the peace table, they went on, because he would immediately be exposed as one of two things: as a hawk with no readiness to compromise, to be reviled by the international community and rejected by those Israelis he had hitherto fooled; or as a dove with real willingness to compromise, to be ousted by the rightist camp and its supporters, who had sustained him in power. That was an assertion that mounting evidence rendered rather harder to dismiss.

To cite the most dramatic instance, I remember going to bed one Monday night in July 2002 feeling mildly and most unusually optimistic. After a brief lull in violence, Shimon Peres, still the Israeli foreign minister at the time, had been meeting with various Palestinian ministers, notably Arafat's two American-urged recent appointees, Finance Minister Salam Fayyad and Interior Minister Abdel Razak Yehiyeh. The former is an ex–International Monetary Fund official, who was trying to centralize all PA funding into one transparent account. And the latter is a septuagenarian ex-guerrilla, who nobody believed would possibly be allowed by Arafat to fulfill his declared goal of reforming and streamlining a dozen-plus security networks into a lean, mean antiterror hierarchy (and who, it turned out, survived in the job for only a few months). But Peres was nevertheless telling the nation how impressed he was with the duo, and it was being widely rumored that Yehiyeh was meeting with various Tanzim and Hamas murderers, trying to get them to cease and desist.

And then I woke up on Tuesday morning, July 23, to learn that an Israeli F-16 had dropped a one-ton bomb on an apartment bloc in Gaza City, successfully eliminating the intended target, Salah Shahada, the commander of the Hamas military wing, which was responsible for a string of attacks on Israeli. But the bomb killed more than a dozen other Palestinians as well, many of them very young children—including a two-month-old baby—who had the misfortune to be living, and sleeping at the time, in various makeshift homes adjacent to the targeted bloc.

Sharon initially called the air raid "one of Israel's greatest successes," which would have been a spurious claim even had Shahada been the only fatality. But coupled with horrifying footage of the panicked bomb zone—parents screaming; children pulled from the rubble in their nightclothes; that baby, the next day, wrapped in a Palestinian flag, only his expressionless face exposed, carried at the head of a funeral procession joined by hundreds of thousands of inflamed Gazans—it gave the Palestinian media a natural opportunity to indict Sharon for committing premeditated murder again, convicted by his own satisfied phrase, and thus to whip up the anti-Israeli sentiment a few notches higher than the apogee to which the bombing would in any case have raised it. Hours later, Sharon, Peres and the army were all publicly backtracking. They said there had, of course, been no intention to kill civilians. If such a death toll had been anticipated, the operation would have been aborted. Four times—no, six times—no, eight times, declared Defense Minister Benjamin Ben-Eliezer, his estimates escalating plaintively, recent plans to eliminate Shahada had been scrapped because there were civilians too close to him. Shahada had been "in the crosshairs" of an F-16 just three days earlier, Sharon was now saying, but the pilot had held his fire because of the locals nearby.

Yossi Sarid, leader of the Meretz opposition party, asked sourly what Sharon had expected might happen when he sent an F-16 to drop a bloody great bomb on a residential area. "When you send an F-16 to blow up a block of flats, you have to know that there will be civilians hurt, children hurt," Sarid said. "Where else would they be in the middle of the night?" But I don't doubt for a second that the civilian casualties were an unpleasant shock to Sharon and Ben-Eliezer, two ex-generals who had placed fatally exaggerated faith in the assessments of their military planners, who, in turn, had not checked their reconnaissance photography with sufficient scrupulousness. What I do doubt are Sharon's motives in approving the hit at that particular time—one more in a series of such strikes that coincided with, and thus shattered, occasional faint cease-fire hopes. Serious American-led efforts to broker a cease-fire were indisputably smashed in late August 2001, when Israeli pinpoint missiles killed Abu Ali Mustafa. It was a similar story in January 2002, when Raed Karmi, the Tulkarm terror chief, picked up the receiver to make a call from a public phone booth he often used in the city and was blown to smithereens. Government officials justified the Mustafa assassination by arguing that the PFLP had recently carried out a spate of car bombings in Jerusalem—which, by good fortune alone, had caused no fatalities—and was planning many more, with Mustafa personally directing the bombers. Likewise, the Karmi elimination: Here was a known killer who was promising a great deal more death and destruction. And Shahada was plainly bent on carrying out more attacks. True, all true. But was their elimination specifically timed to rupture peace efforts?

For all the certainty with which Sharon's critics insist that the answer is yes, and all the vehemence with which his defenders say no, I suspect that no one but Sharon can offer a definitive answer. The Sharon government was following an open policy of what it preferred to call "targeted strikes" against alleged Intifada kingpins. Military intelligence and the Shin Bet security service were charged with accumulating information on the movements of such designated targets, and reporting to the cabinet when an opportunity arose to eliminate one of them. Sometimes the hits were approved. Sometimes they were not, for innumerable reasons that were never publicly discussed—naturally, given that the targets remained targets.

But perhaps all of this misses the point. Perhaps the questions we Israelis should be asking ourselves concern whether our government and "defense forces" should be in the hit business at all.

First of all, what does it do for us, morally, to be eliminating our enemies on a strategic basis? I have no moral reservations when Israel blows up someone who is on the point of murdering one or more of my people, or is dispatching or arming somebody else to carry out the crime. I cannot quibble with a policy that has had Israel relentlessly killing what are called "ticking bombs," a suicide bomber or gunman en route. If you somehow found out that a gunman was on his way to wreak murderous havoc in your child's school, wouldn't you want him thwarted, and feel absolutely justified in so doing? As you raced to the school to try to save the life of your child, wouldn't you want to be sure that your government, however liberal and tolerant, was putting aside any legal restrictions that might prevent his interception? Wouldn't you be furiously demanding that any and all means necessary be employed to stop the gunman? In the case of a so-called ticking bomb, most of us feel that our government has not merely the moral right but also the moral obligation to kill before we are killed.

But that's the easy part. The challenge is in laying down the moral borderlines for those who fall short of the "ticking bomb" designation. A bomber en route? No question. A known bomb maker building the explosives in his factory, deep inside Palestinian-controlled territory and thus, far beyond our reasonable powers of arrest? Yes, still a legitimate target, I'd say. But what about a proven recruiter and indoctrinator of suicide bombers who usually takes extraordinary precautions to avoid capture and whom the military say they have a rare opportunity to target in a remote area? That's already a slightly harder call, although most of us would probably still endorse his killing, seeing it as a guaranteed way of saving innocent lives. But where does one draw the line? Where does morally acceptable assassination end and state terrorism begin?

And then there's a second question, one concerning what the mathematicians might call "the security cost-benefit equation." In the long term, do these assassinations make us safer, or the reverse? Killing a bomber en route clearly saves lives. But, to get specific, what about the killings of Mustafa, Karmi and Shahada? Inarguably, the assassination of Mustafa cost the life of Tourism Minister Ze'evi, who was gunned down as he walked back from breakfast to his room at the Hyatt Hotel in Jerusalem one morning two months later—in a revenge attack by the PFLP, allegedly orchestrated by Mustafa's successor as secretary-general. And the PFLP participated in numerous further attacks on Israeli targets. The Shahada strike was followed by another spate of bombings and shootings. And the assassination of Karmi had, arguably, the most devastating consequences of all. Prior to his killing, his Al-Aqsa Brigades tended to involve themselves principally with the murder of Israelis traveling on the roads of the West Bank. Bad enough. But in the immediate aftermath of Karmi's death, the Al-Aqsa Brigades began orchestrating suicide bombings inside Israel as well, for a while even eclipsing the Islamic terrorists of Hamas and Islamic Jihad, who had hitherto monopolized such actions.

Opinion polls during the second Intifada told us that an overwhelming majority of Israelis, in full knowledge of the potential for such actions to go awry and for civilians to die, and in full knowledge of the thirst for vengeance they provoke among Palestinians, nevertheless strongly supported the targeted strikes. Even Ze'evi's bereaved family never queried the Mustafa killing, an event that plainly triggered their own tragedy. And much of that support, I would venture, stemmed from the widespread sense that Israel had little alternative but to carry out the hits as part of its wider patchwork of policies designed to thwart the suicide bombers. Ideally, the PA's innumerable security networks would have spared us the dilemma. That, after all, is precisely why Israel, controversially and, we must now acknowledge, unwisely, armed the PA in the first place, providing it with the weaponry with which it was supposed to ensure public order and confront the radicals. But Arafat was never prepared to make a concerted effort to take on the killers. And because Israelis didn't believe the Palestinian assurances that a halt to the hits would bring a halt to the bombings, and because of the profound fear that any letup in assassinations would give the bombers the confidence to move around freely and prepare further attacks, support for the targeted strikes consistently extended from the far right deep into the center left of the Israeli political spectrum. Over time, though, I fear, such assassinations became rather more than a method of last resort. A necessary evil veered close to becoming a counterproductive norm.

6.

Yussuf

Yussuf is waiting by the side of the road, just past the tunnels that lead through the hills south of Jerusalem on the route out to Bethlehem. It's 7:30 on a Friday morning about two years into the second Intifada and he's on his fourth evil-smelling cigarette of the day, which he kindly puts out as he takes the passenger's seat and I firmly decline his offer to puff along with him. A bookkeeper by training and plumber by default, he's a friend of a friend, and though I've interviewed him previously by phone—he lives at the Al-Arub refugee camp, outside Hebron—we've never met. I'm struck immediately, as anyone would be, by how thin he is—Kate Moss, runway-model thin, though for reasons a culture shift away from fashion. As he'll tell me later, matter-of-factly, he's worked one month in the last thirteen, and out of that meager, unreliable income, he's supporting his wife and four children, his parents, his brother and his sister-in-law and their two kids.

I pick him up in a kind of no-man's-land that is outside Israeli-claimed sovereign Jerusalem but on the very outskirts of the West Bank. Israelis occasionally get killed here; Palestinians get stopped at the local roadblocks designed to prevent their entry into Jerusalem.

The café where we've decided to sit and spend the morning talking is a kind of no-man's-land café, a Palestinian-owned combination grocery and extremely rudimentary coffee shop, situated just before the roadblock that leads back into Israel and the small town of Tsur Hadassah. Outside, fat black grapes ripen on vines that climb over the entrance, supported by wooden trestles. Inside, signs in Hebrew and Arabic advertise Coke and cookies and the services of the garage at the back of the building. In the course of the four hours and countless coffees we'll spend at Habayit Haboded (the Solitary House), young ultra-Orthodox men, Palestinian builders and farmers, and Israeli border policemen will pass through, all evidently on familiar terms with the sprawling family members who spend their time alternating between tending the cash register and watching Friday's scenes from a mosque and Koranic readings on the color TV bolted to the ceiling. Some of the ultra-Orthodox men will even take a seat on one of the two sofas, beneath the cheaply framed hammered-metal relief of the Dome of the Rock, and gaze up at the TV imams, perhaps recognizing a distant kindred spirit.

Ideally, we'd have been meeting where I'd have understood Yussuf's life the best, at his home in Al-Arub—three rooms of rudimentary breeze-block walls and concrete flooring, 800 square feet serving as home to twelve people. His is a corner property and thus something of a palace, Yussuf tells me, with windows in two of the walls. In theory, it's only a twenty-minute drive from the corner where I rendezvoused with him. Except that it took him two hours to get to me, and there's no telling how long it would have taken me to get to him, or whether I'd have made it at all. And if I had, whether I'd have made it back out again. Fifteen thousand Palestinians live in Al-Arub, and not all of them are prepared to pour out their hearts to Jewish, Israeli journalists. When Jerusalem's Moment café was blown up in March 2002, killing eleven young Israelis, the suicide bomber, Fuad Ismail Hourani, twenty, turned out to have traveled in from Al-Arub. He had had no record of Islamic extremism, no known Hamas membership. "I knew who he was," acknowledges Yussuf, "but I'd never have dreamed he'd become a bomber. He was single. He'd studied in Ramallah, I think. Just a quiet, unremarkable guy." There are plenty more quiet, unremarkable guys at Al-Arub and everywhere else in the West Bank, quiet guys with no money, no food, no hope, but with a surfeit of bitterness and, in many cases, plenty of personal loss to avenge; quiet guys who, if word got out that Yussuf was hosting an Israeli journalist for the morning, might seize the opportunity. "Next time," says Yussuf, late in our conversation, "you'll come to my house."

"Inshallah," I say, hoping so, but doubting it. I'm content to ride into

the West Bank in one of the bulletproof jeeps from which the daily reporters cover this conflict, and to spend an hour here and an hour there at an interviewee's house in one or another town. But I'll drive my own Israeli car across the border only if I know exactly where I'm going and it's not too far in. For now, I draw the line at a prolonged sit-down chez Yussuf, deep in Al-Arub.

Vast numbers of Palestinians have variations on Yussuf's life story, and, apart from the dead and the maimed, they are the most pitiable victims of the fifty-plus years of conflict. I'd say victims of the Arab leadership's dead-end vision. Yussuf would be more charitable to his own leaders and less so to mine.

His parents used to live in Kiryat Gat, a small town at the northern tip of the Negev desert, where a state-of-the-art Intel plant today manufactures microchips in ultrasterile conditions but which before Israel became Israel was home to Yussuf's grandparents as well. His father earned an honorable living as a builder. Jewish-Muslim relations were harmonious, Yussuf says, and the family stayed put through the War of Independence in 1948. But when that war was over, and Israel had survived the Arab world's effort to strangle it at birth, "the army came and asked them to leave."

And so Yussuf's parents found their way to nearby Hebron, and a tent at Al-Arub, anticipating a brief exile before the Arab troops regrouped and liberated their occupied homeland. But liberation never came. The tents were replaced by semipermanent structures that were expected to be needed for five years at the most. Five years turned to decades, and there Yussuf's parents and thousands more like them still live, fifteen thousand people in an area about a half a mile by sixteen hundred feet—the size of a few Ikea superstores.

There they live in crowded, squalid repression, all these generations of refugees and refugee descendants, telling anyone who asks that peace can't come without a "right of return." According to Yussuf, though, most of them are actually long since reconciled to the fact that the dream is dead. Liberation is not around the corner. The Israelis aren't going anywhere, and they aren't about to welcome them back, either. "In the past, they really did believe they'd go back. And even today, they still hope so," Yussuf says of his parents. "But after 1967, they realized it wasn't about to happen. That's when those people who could afford to and had the space started adding rooms to the homes."

Yussuf is thirty-six, and the refugee home in Al-Arub, he confirms over the morning's first polystyrene cup of muddy Turkish coffee, is the only place he's ever lived. Eli, the friend who introduced us, whose Tsur Hadassah home Yussuf helped build, believes that, in other circumstances, Yussuf could have been an academic, or anything he wanted to be. Yussuf himself might have chosen accountancy—he studied bookkeeping in Ramallah after high school. He's strikingly self-aware and unmistakably smart. But his real life got in the way.

Arrested in Ramallah during the first Intifada—he says he was "in the wrong place at the wrong time"—he spent four months in an Israeli jail, detained without trial. And then, having helped out from age fifteen on the building sites where his father was working, he found employment where he could as a plumber, which is pretty much what he's done ever since—whenever, that is, he can both find work and physically get to it. He's practiced his trade just about everywhere in Israel and the West Bank, he says, earning between twenty and sixty dollars a day, and losing all kinds of preconceptions along the way. "For example, I've worked in Kiryat Arba"—the settlement alongside Hebron, from where Baruch Goldstein set out in February 1994 to gun down Palestinians at prayer in the Cave of the Patriarchs—"and I had thought they were all extremists there. But they're not. There are plenty who simply moved there because it was the only place they could afford." Much of the time, he has essentially been working for the enemy—in the settlements. "I don't think of it as building homes for settlers," he says. "I think of feeding my family." Most of his employers were honest, although five years ago he worked eighteen days for a contractor at Tsur Hadassah, and the man refused to pay him a shekel, taking advantage of the fact that Yussuf didn't have a valid permit to work in that area at the time and therefore had no legal recourse. "He abused me. He did the same to lots of people. I tried to call him, but he never came to the phone." Yussuf shrugs. "There was nothing I could do except forget about it," or perhaps loathe us all the more, which he says he refuses to allow himself to do.

Until the summer of 2000, work in the West Bank and inside Israel was fairly plentiful overall. Then came the second Intifada, and Israel, attempting to thwart the bombers, canceled the permits that had enabled so many Palestinians to work legally inside Israel (and barred entry, too, to those who had hitherto worked without permits but with the tacit, turn-a-blind-eye support of the authorities). That massive workforce was the mainstay of the Palestinian economy, its exclusion a case of Palestinian gunmen shooting us in the head and themselves in the foot. Yussuf asserts that "none of the workers with permits ever carried out an attack" and that the restrictions imposed on them are thus vindictive rather than vital. But this is untrue. The most horrific case that comes to mind is the incident in February 2001, when Khalil Abu Ulbah, thirty-six, a Gaza City father of five, plowed the Egged bus in which he had legally been ferrying Palestinian workers to and from the Strip for five years into a group of Israelis waiting at a bus stop south of Tel Aviv, killing eight of them (an attack, incidentally, that Arafat publicly dismissed as "a traffic accident").

His family, Yussuf says, gets no money or assistance whatsoever from the Palestinian Authority, or anyone else for that matter. "Every few months, we get a fifty-kilo bag of flour from UNRWA"—the United Nations Relief and Works Agency, which is responsible for humanitarian aid to the refugees—"but that's it." So how did his family manage through the long months when he had no work? I ask. He shrugs. "I sold my wife's jewelry. And people help one another. We have next to nothing, but we'll all share what we have."

Even though the Palestinian Authority has received colossal sums of money down the years for its people, Yussuf has no complaints about the PA's failure to alleviate their poverty. Between 1967 and the early 1990s, when Israel maintained a full military occupation, he says, nothing was spent on the camps. There were no phones, no sewage infrastructure, only the most spartan school buildings. During the years when the Oslo process moved forward, by contrast, "Arafat started to build infrastructure. They put down concrete where there had just been packed earth for roads. The PA enlarged the school, although there's still no heating. They built a sewage system. They installed phones. I used to have a phone"—matter-of-fact shrug—"only it's cut off now because I couldn't pay the bill."

Never mind improving camp conditions; why didn't Arafat and the oil-rich Arab world knock down the camps and finance new housing for people like Yussuf decades before the Oslo process? It would have required only a few days' Saudi oil revenues. My answer is that Yussuf and the rest of the hundreds of thousands in the refugee camps are the abused playthings of their own and the region's Arab leaders, a festering wound that Israel can be usefully blamed for not healing. Yussuf, of course, disagrees. "It wasn't the responsibility of the Arab world to solve our problem. Israel, which caused the problem, had to lead the way. Remember that Germany began making payments to the Jews. And it wasn't the job of the Palestinian Authority to build homes for us. That's not what its money was for. Its money was to fix the schools. The refugee problem is an international problem, and needs an international solution. But Israel and the rest of the international community refuse to address it."

Indeed, the architects of Oslo consciously left the refugee question, and the other thorniest issues, to the end of the process because they hoped that by then there would be enough mutual trust (what a hollow phrase nowadays) to enable a solution. That never happened. But, again, Yussuf won't hear of Arafat's culpability. "In 1996, Peres [then prime minister] was asked, 'How did you stop the terrorism?' And he said, 'I spoke to Arafat.' The bombs only go off because there are no talks. How many times lately has it been calm, only for that calm to be shattered because Israel assassinates somebody?"

So now here we are, barely half an hour into our conversation, knee-deep in the blame game. I point out that the bombers flourished even in the Rabin years, when, if Arafat had been genuinely committed to peacemaking, his every interest would have demanded that he stop them.

Yussuf counters with Baruch Goldstein as the first suicide attacker. (This is not true. Hamas had carried out its first suicide bombing the previous year, in the Jordan Valley.)

I argue that Arafat's refusal to tackle the extremists—and specifically, the bombings in February and March 1996—was the root cause of Netanyahu's election victory that May, and the consequent paralysis of the peacemaking.

Yussuf retorts that those bombs were retaliation for that January's killing by Israel of the master Hamas bomb maker, Yihya Ayash.

So what were we supposed to do, I ask, allow Ayash to go about his explosive business untroubled, and why didn't Arafat stop him?

Arafat tried, claims Yussuf. But he couldn't do it right away. It took him a while to cement his authority after he was finally allowed to go from Tunis to Gaza in 1994. But then he did take on Hamas. People were killed in internal clashes between Arafat's police and the Islamists.

Arafat did make one or two halfhearted attempts, I allow. But there was no strategic decision to counter the terrorists, no follow-through on the fundamental Oslo commitment both to desist from terrorism and to act decisively to prevent it. Arafat used to laugh and pretend not to know whom Israel was talking about when the generals and the politicians listed the bombers and implored him to arrest them.

Wrong again, Yussuf insists. Look at the period from 1996 to 1999. Once Arafat had established himself, he did stop most of the terrorism. There were hardly any attacks in those years.

But then Arafat, put to the real peacemaker's test, walked away from the table at Camp David, slipped the reins and let the gunmen and bombers go to work again, I remind him.

No, retorts Yussuf, there was no Palestinian gunfire in the early days of this Intifada. It was Israel that fired first, on the Temple Mount, and against even its own Arab citizens, killing thirteen of them. And when the bombings started, Israel deliberately destroyed the PA, smashing its police stations and security headquarters, even though it was Hamas that was carrying out the attacks—simultaneously blaming Arafat while depriving him of the means to take action.

And on we go, around and around, the Israeli and the Arab, the Jew and the Muslim, two protagonists professing moderation and a desire for reconciliation, each convinced that his own leadership was trying to achieve it and that it was the other side that failed. It is a dialogue of the mutually disillusioned.

. . . • . . .

As we talk, Yussuf fills in the fabric of his tragedy, the Palestinian Everyman's tragedy: the parents who lost their home; the brother who can't find work; the grinding poverty that means he never has a few spare shekels to spend on a treat for his four young kids; his daily need to play cat and mouse with the border police to get to his current job at a building site in Har Homah, yet another disputed Jewish neighborhood not far from here. "Two weeks ago, the roads were closed off, so we were walking for three or four kilometers on the way to work. We got stopped by a border police patrol on one of the days. They made us sit in a pit for two hours, then sent us back home." (I've seen Palestinians locked up in similar circumstances elsewhere. Driving one summer through Modi'in, a small new city between Jerusalem and Tel Aviv and close to the West Bank border, I stopped at a police station to ask directions, and saw perhaps two dozen young Palestinian men sitting listlessly on the ground around the walls of a locked outdoor pen about the size of a double garage. I asked a policeman what they were doing there, and he said it was an everyday thing. These were the laborers arrested that morning for entering Israel without the necessary permits. They would be sent home—actually, dumped back into the West Bank—later in the day.) "It should take twenty minutes from Al-Arub to Jerusalem," says Yussuf. "I get up at five-thirty and, on the days when I make it, I get to Jerusalem at nine." He doesn't mention that he must also circumvent the Tanzim and other Palestinian militants, who don't want him working in Israel, either.

I marvel when he tells me that, after all these years, his home still lacks floor tiles and that its ceiling hasn't been plastered. "Listen, David," he says gently, "we can't just walk into the bank and take out a mortgage. So far, we've not had the money to plaster the ceiling." I empathize when he relates the appalling saga of the day his mother suffered a stroke, and what should have been a five-minute ambulance ride to the hospital in Hebron turned into an hour-long ordeal: "We couldn't go via the main road"—because of the checkpoints where they might be stopped and searched or turned back—"and it took forever to get there via the side roads." (Fortunately, the doctors told him, his mother's condition had not been worsened by the delay, and she gradually recovered.)

And yet, Yussuf insists he is anything but consumed by hatred for me, my people, Israel, the ostensible causes of his lifetime suffering. "Hatred?" he says, shrugging, almost apologetic. "No, I don't hate you. My father, of course, hated Israel for what happened to him. But hatred is for people who don't know any Jews themselves. For me, I know there are good and bad Jews and Arabs. If you look at the whole process," Yussuf says, "we got thrown out of our homes, and so did the Jews get thrown out of their homes, and worse"—he's talking Holocaust here. "The solution for the Jews was the state of Israel. And our solution could have been found years ago. There's no need for us to have lived in refugee camps all these years. We should have been given the choice to return or to make our lives here, in a new Palestine, with financial aid so we wouldn't have to start from scratch. And I, and most others, I believe, would have chosen to live here, in the place I know, and would say the same right now, rather than going back to Israel, where I know I am not wanted. Hebron is my home now."

Yussuf sounds like anything but an undereducated, stymied plumber from a refugee camp. In fact, he sounds like the most polished and subtle of moderate Palestinian politicians, speaking the reasonable language of coexistence that moderate Israelis long to hear: concern for his people, but also sympathy for the plight of the Jews; a desire to rebuild his life, but not at the expense of Israel. And as we bicker through the morning, clashing earnestly across the dirty plastic tabletop while the imams drone on the TV in the background, I keep asking myself, shabbily, Can this be for real? How can Yussuf really be this humane, this tolerant, this empathetic, this farsighted? Is he only telling me what he knows I want to hear? Would there really be any point? At some moments in our conversation, I even catch myself imagining a Palestinian propagandist looking over his shoulder and nodding approvingly at Yussuf's outlining of terms that might dupe Israel into new compromises, part of a phased plan for Israel's eventual destruction. How is it that Yussuf can sound so forgiving when so many others around him, from the same background, are so murderously hostile—that quiet neighbor who carried out the Moment suicide bombing; that majority of all his other Palestinian neighbors, near and far, who say they back the bombers and see the goal of this Intifada as ending not the Israeli occupation of the West Bank, Gaza Strip and East Jerusalem but the Jewish sovereign presence in the Middle East?

Reading my thoughts, Yussuf says, "People say one thing but believe another." Then he adds that many people have left the refugee camps over the years—those who had the money, the better-paying jobs. Israel doesn't need to worry about them anymore, he intimates. They certainly won't want to roll their lives backward and uproot themselves to live in hostile Israel. So all we're really talking about, in the West Bank at least, he asserts, is the 200,000 people in the camps. (He doesn't mention the 500,000 in the camps of Gaza, the 110,000 in the camps in Syria, the 210,000 in the camps in Lebanon and the 280,000 in the camps in Jordan.)

It's dishonorable, and worse, of me to question the integrity of the slender man with the cigarettes across the café table. It's a reflection of how low I have sunk these past few years, how mistrustful I have become. And it's no defense to say that most everybody else feels the same.

. . . • . . .

Yussuf says he defines himself as an Orthodox Muslim and, as such, as a man religiously opposed to the killing of civilians. "All religions oppose killing," he says breezily, almost daring me to contradict him with my stereotypically Western, terror-filled conceptions of his faith. I oblige. I say it seems that many of the most prominent spiritual spokespeople for Islam advocate the widespread killing of non-Muslims, by suicide attacks if necessary, in an unrelenting, brutal campaign to impose Islamic rule across the planet. Yussuf professes horror at this characterization. "When the prophet Muhammad sent his people to war, he told them not to kill civilians, not to kill children, not even to uproot trees. He urged that all people be treated as equals. In Islam, all men are equal. Islam brought equality to the world."

So the suicide bombers, and those who encourage them, are breaching the foundations of Islam? "You can't kill innocent people, under any circumstances," he says. But who are the innocents? Are soldiers on duty innocent? Off-duty soldiers? Settlers? Where does Islam draw the line? Where does Yussuf draw the line? "Fighting soldiers can be acceptable," he says. "But someone who goes on a bus or at a university or a café? I condemn it."

And yet your neighbor, I say, the Moment café bomber, posed for the customary farewell video and told the world he was off to kill some Israelis in the sacred name of Islam? "Islam didn't make him do it. Life made him do it," says Yussuf, chillingly. "The pressure. The poverty. The hopelessness. David, you just don't get it. You can't get it. When we were kids, my mother would be searching for scraps of fabric to make clothes. The rain poured into our house. As a married man, I don't have a shekel to give my children for food. They want toys. I can't buy them. A computer? Forget it. Even some heating in the schools is beyond us.

"Why did my neighbor commit suicide? Why are Palestinians lining up to commit suicide? Listen, plenty of people kill themselves anyway, all over the world. So here our suicides think, Why not kill not only themselves but also some of the people who've ruined their lives at the same time? It's so easy to understand: If someone already wants to die, it's no big deal to kill some of the Jews, too. And this way, he dies a hero. And his family gets all kinds of financial help, too."

Precisely. The family gets help, and exalted status. He's the hero, for killing Jews. And all the rest of the neighbors pile into the mourning tent outside the family home to tell his mother and father how proud they should feel of their son and his heroic sacrifice. And the religious leaders who inspired him now come to praise him. What kind of a culture is that?

Unusually, Yussuf is briefly speechless. Then he says slowly, "Some people think like that. Some think he is a hero. And some think like us, that the only solution is peace. No more war and bloodshed. That only peace can let us live like human beings. The family of Hourani is one of the last that would have wanted this kind of thing. They would never have supported it. Yes, they set up a mourning tent, but that does not mean they endorsed the bombing. By Islamic law, you have to have a mourning tent, even if you are opposed to how someone died. It's to comfort the parents. And I don't think they took any money—from Iraq, or the Saudis, or anyone—as reward for his act." (Israeli officials insist that almost every bomber's family accepted such payments.)

I persist: But doesn't Islam preach holy war against Jews, Christians, other faiths? Yussuf sighs, then seeks again to defend his faith: "If someone comes to your house to fight, you don't sit quietly. In our case, that means opposition to occupation is legitimate. But not, as I said, killing civilians, innocents."

But doesn't Islam hold that any territory that was once controlled by Islamic rulers, such as today's Israel, has to be restored to Islamic rule? Yussuf looks sheepish, smiles wanly and concedes: "Yes, it is all Islamic territory; you are right. Personally, I can compromise, temporarily, and accept a Palestinian state only in the West Bank and Gaza Strip. But, religiously, there can be no permanent compromise on that basis." He tries to win me back: "You Jews are the same," he says. "You want all of the land of Israel"—biblical Israel, from the Mediterranean Sea to the Jordan River, and beyond.

And, indeed, some of us do, and some of us even invoke the Jewish God to claim a divine right to all such land—but not the most prominent and respected interpreters of our faith, our mainstream spiritual leaders. They don't insist that compromise is blasphemous. They understand God's will to value life over land.

. . . • . . .

Partway through our conversation, Eli, our matchmaker, shows up. He has spent the earlier part of the morning delivering various children to various schools, and staying on at one of them for a ceremony to mark the seventh anniversary of the assassination of Yitzhak Rabin. And he can stop for only twenty minutes or so now, he tells us, because he has a whole host of Sabbath-eve errands to run. So he speaks fast, filling me in on the details of his relationship with Yussuf, whom he first met as "that scumbag Shimon's worker"—referring to the dishonest contractor who gypped Yussuf out of eighteen days of wages. Shimon and Yussuf had been doing the plumbing for Eli's home in Tsur Hadassah, and Shimon had cheated Eli, too, disappearing, the work left unfinished. Eventually, Eli hired a new plumbing contractor, who, coincidentally, hired Yussuf. Yussuf's brother Majid also wound up working with him, as did his cousin Khaled.

Eli is a big, warm, passionate man. He is also obsessed with the news. North American–born, he's lived in Israel for the past twenty-one years, having moved here as a Zionist, a man who believes emphatically in the Jews' right to live in their homeland. When he first arrived, he had right-wing views. He did his time in the army and reserves, and his service in the first Intifada changed him, gradually drawing him into the peace camp. At that time, he says, he saw the isolated humiliations soldiers visited on Palestinians, and the day-by-day, drip-by-drip process by which occupation breeds hatred; the way that, if one people rules over another, force inevitably has to be used, innocent people are hurt, emotionally and physically, and how, when that happens to someone close to you—a father, a grandfather, a child—the seeds are planted for a new generation of hatred, more violence and a cycle that goes on and on. But Yussuf is the first Palestinian he ever really got to know properly, and clearly the relationship, now five years old, has been a revelation.

Eli has four young children, and he is convinced that if those children, and others, are to have a future spared of bloodshed, Israelis and Palestinians will have to find a way to live peacefully alongside one another on the land they both covet. They must get past the fact that each side believes it is right and defuse the hatred and hostility—"however clichéd that may sound," he says apologetically.

One day before the second Intifada began, when heavy rain brought a temporary halt to building work, he and Yussuf, who had gradually been having longer and longer conversations about themselves, their families and the "situation," spent several hours at a Jewish friend's house down the road, where Yussuf had also been working. Here they had a heart-to-heart talk about Eli's army experiences, Yussuf's first Intifada experiences, Eli's thoughts on Arafat (never favorable) and peacemaking (hitherto optimistic), Yussuf's on Israel's leaders and attitudes to peace. A friendship was born. "I had fears based on ignorance," Eli acknowledges. "And

Yussuf shattered some of that ignorance. Me and him, the thin guy from the refugee camp, who, to put it mildly, didn't move in the same circles, formed a connection. It evolved. His life has been lousy. In other circumstances, he'd be a university lecturer. He'd be at the dentist as often as I am."

Yussuf, it seems to me, became a kind of focus of Eli's decency, and, to some extent, the (deserving) beneficiary of Eli's sense of guilt. Eli had a new house, a wonderful family and was more than happy with his lot. And Yussuf, just as smart and motivated, had far less. Was the starting point of their friendship Eli's discomfort that reality had turned this man, his equal, into his plumber? "Absolutely," says Eli. "That's why I wanted to make it better." So Eli gave as much work to as many members of Yussuf's family as he could. Eli prevailed upon his father, a pharmacist, to send medicines for Yussuf's ailing father on a regular basis. When Majid was arrested in Jerusalem for allegedly stealing a pair of spectacles from a woman in whose house he was working, Eli went to the police station and did what was necessary to get him released. After the building work on Eli's house was completed, he continued to deliver the medicines, and he was hoping to find a sponsor who might enable Yussuf to travel abroad.

But then came the second Intifada, and the world tilted. Getting together was not simple anymore. This no-man's-land café became one of the few places where they could meet without undue risk. Two months into the Intifada, Eli asked Yussuf to rendezvous with him at the gas station just down the road, where he handed over a package of groceries—meat, candies, coffee, cigarettes—correctly assuming that Yussuf and his family would be struggling. "He didn't know what to say," Eli recalls. "He was a mixture of gratitude and of swallowed pride at having to accept such booty." Yussuf neither confirms nor challenges this description. Eli goes on: "I said, 'Don't say thanks. But let me walk away thinking you'd do the same for me if the tables had been turned.' "

As Yussuf sits silently beside him, a light, benevolent smile sometimes playing across his features, Eli muses that, in a better world, "I would have been able to expose Yussuf to the things I know he wants; to find a way forward and not have him be my plumber or building worker. I wanted to get him a computer, connect him to the Internet so that he could hook up to the world. That was then. I gave what I could. I don't think Yussuf has any complaints against me. But the world has changed so much now. The mutual faith has so collapsed. And things can't go back to the way they were when we first met. I wish they could. I always wished that Yussuf and I could just be friends, taking our families out together to a museum in Tel Aviv or for a coffee in Hebron, with our backgrounds an irrelevance. The way things look now, that's not going to happen. But the most important thing I think I've done is to have related to Yussuf as an equal. He knows I respect him. I respect him for who he is, far more than I would respect someone who hadn't come from that cursed, miserable background, from that undemocratic culture, with no freedom of speech."

Perhaps for my benefit, perhaps for his own, Eli takes the opportunity of our meeting to put to Yussuf theories I assume have long been germinating as their friendship has flourished. In the Arab world, he suggests for openers, there are two elements you cannot ignore: honor and the need for revenge when that honor is violated. He says that he has learned enough of Muslim culture to know that their attitude to death is different from ours. He heard from workers on his house about the feuding between their families over perceived slights, which could lead to so-called honor killings and revenge killings. If Palestinian Muslims are so patently ready to kill their own people for such "crimes," not to mention murdering hundreds of their own kin these past few years for alleged "collaboration" with Israel, Eli says, he has to assume that they will forever seek to murderously avenge the conquering of their land, the Israeli claim of sovereignty over their holy places. And he fears that in this Intifada, spurred on by the claims of Hezbollah leader Sheikh Hassan Nasrallah in Lebanon that Israel is like "a spider's web" that can be swept away, the Palestinians are going for broke, trying to rid the region of the Jews, fulfilling what Nasrallah calls their "duty" of liberating Palestine.

Yussuf says that is all a misreading of the Palestinian and Muslim mind-set. "Respect, yes. Revenge, no," he demurs. "I can take you to meet people who have lost children in the Intifada but have good relations with Jews."

And would Yussuf's belief in good Jews survive the death of his own child, heaven forbid? Wouldn't he be pushed over the edge, provoked to seek revenge? "Absolutely not," he says. "I'd hold my faith and hope even if I lost a son. Otherwise, you cannot carry on. The hope has to stay."

Eli asks Yussuf a question he says he's asked him many times before: Where are the "Palestinian Peace Now" agitators ready to defy their mainstream to demand reconciliation and peace, immediately, with Israel? "I see Jews holding vigils outside the defense ministry in Tel Aviv, demanding a commission of inquiry into this or that alleged Israeli atrocity in Gaza or the West Bank," says Eli. "I see the Women in Black [far-left activists] gathering every week to demand an end to the occupation. Where are their Palestinian equivalents?"

Yussuf says they are out there, that there are many people as peace-minded as he is, waiting for their moment.

"I don't believe him," Eli says to me. "I don't see them marching outside Arafat's headquarters and pleading for a halt to the killing of Israeli civilians, carrying placards calling for an investigation into Arafat's sponsorship of terrorism. What I see is eleven innocents killed in Meah Shearim, and eleven at Moment, and twenty-nine in the Park Hotel in Netanya on Passover, and delighted demonstrations of support in Ramallah for the bombers; and spontaneous, genuine, heartfelt celebrations after the Twin Towers; and the joyous, frenzied lynching of two Israeli reservists. Never chants of 'Stop the pogroms. Stop delegitimizing the Jews.'

"For a long time, I didn't understand why people like Yussuf couldn't take control out there, leading the marchers, leading the opposition to Hamas and the bombers and Arafat. I'd think of Yussuf, and I knew he knows we don't drop poison candy from planes to kill Gaza schoolchildren, or use depleted uranium bombs and spread AIDS and mad cow disease and all the other dreadful things Arafat and his coterie despicably tell their people that we do. I'd wonder, Where is Yussuf, and all the other Yussufs he claims are out there?" Eli admits. Yussuf smiles but says nothing. "But I know now that he can't do that. He has to stay out of trouble. He's hunted by Israeli border policemen, who are angry and frustrated, and he has to risk his life against them to get to work and try to feed his family. Who am I to expect him to put his life on the line to lead peace rallies? He has children and two sick parents to support. But I want to hear all the Yussufs he says are out there. I need to hear them. And I hear nothing."

With the air of a man observing an appalling, anticipated reality gradually come to pass and being powerless to prevent it, Eli says he's watched as first Arafat's refusal to compromise and then the bombing campaign have gradually radicalized Israel, and seen Yussuf suffering the escalating repercussions—the lost work permits, the life-threatening journeys to work, the financial hardships. And yet, to Eli's intense frustration, Yussuf just won't see it his way, won't blame Arafat, won't acknowledge how and why the deterioration began and what needs to happen to reverse the process. And, most significantly, Yussuf won't champion a more moderate position than Arafat's. When the Camp David summit collapsed, Eli remembers, he asked Yussuf what more Arafat honestly wanted, what more he thought he could get. And Yussuf told him that while Arafat could compromise over a small proportion of the territory, and allow Israel to maintain a few concentrated blocs of settlement, he couldn't compromise over Al-Aqsa—the Temple Mount had to come under full Palestinian sovereignty. Eli asked Yussuf if he shared that position, and Yussuf said that he did. (Yussuf will later tell me, "The Western Wall is for the Jews. But Al-Aqsa is given to me by God. The Temple Mount is the property of the Muslim world. That's what Arafat said at Camp David. And he would have needed the approval of the entire Islamic world to say any different. He couldn't compromise on the Temple Mount." Does Yussuf acknowledge a Jewish connection to the Temple Mount? Does he think there was a Temple there in biblical times? "There's no historical proof, but no proof to the contrary," he says generously. "Each man to his own faith.")

"So now I know," says Eli, "that even my friend Yussuf, who is prepared to give up on the dream of returning to his father's house, and who doesn't pray five times a day like the other, most devout Muslims who worked on my house, will watch all hope of peace drain away into a war of religion. A war in which the most prominent leaders of his religion believe Jews have no right to live here. Are we Jews going to give up on the Temple Mount and change our history to say that we were not from this land? Of course not. So now we face nothing but a religious war. No winners. And my children will suffer, and so will Yussuf's. And it's happening day by day. And I cannot forgive the other side for instilling so much fear in my children, and watching their fear turn into a hatred that was never there before."

Yussuf, recalls Eli, "didn't believe Sharon would win the elections of February 2001. He thought the Israeli media was lying. He couldn't see how Arafat's positions, how the Palestinian delegitimization of Israel, were affecting Israelis. I felt sorry for him, and worried for him. A week before the suicide bombing at the Park Hotel in March 2002, I told him, based on nothing but my own sense of the government mind-set, that if there was one more big bombing, the army would be ordered deep into the West Bank to stop the bombers. Again, he didn't believe me. And of course I was right: The bomber struck, killed twenty-nine people who'd gone out for the festival meal, and we launched Operation Defensive Shield, and now we've spent months out there in the cities and the camps, making their lives hell. Yussuf always returns to the same sentence: 'You know that I educate my children differently.' But I know a dreadful, undeniable fact as well, that on either side of him are people who want to kill me. And because of them, we'll all go on suffering. I don't want Sharon's bulldozers to come and knock down his home and force his family to flee into Jordan. But that's where we'd be headed. And the only hope for his son Mustafa and my kids to be friends and escape this is for Yussuf to harness more Yussufs to prevent the disaster."

Throughout this impassioned outburst, Yussuf sits and smokes, not looking sad or patronized so much as wistful. And after Eli has hugged us both and driven away, Yussuf tells me he's sorry to see and hear how "a leftist like Eli has lost his faith and hope in peace. If you and he were on my side of this conflict, if you were living where I live, believe me, you'd see things very differently."

Alas, I'm still convinced that people like Yussuf have been misguided and manipulated by their leaders, by their media. And he *knows* that it's *we* who are misguided, because he is living the misery, watching as our reoccupation boosts the extremists, seeing ordinary, quiet, unremarkable people turn into cold-blooded killers who will deliberately take down a dozen young Israelis at a coffeehouse. He asks me how Palestinian leftists can possibly stand up and clamor loudly for reconciliation, as Eli wants them to, when Israeli forces have retaken even the meager 42 percent of the West Bank that had been relinquished, when the curfews and closures and roadblocks have created an occupation more oppressive than ever. "When, although there was never a gunshot in two years fired from Al-Arub, we had tanks on the main road outside the camp for months. When kids threw stones and got machine-gun fire in response. In the first Intifada, the army used tear gas and rubber bullets to disperse stone throwers. Now it's all live fire." Never mind the absence of a Palestinian Peace Now, he says. "Where is the Israeli Peace Now, really? Why is it quiet? Why hasn't Peace Now protected the Palestinian people? Why didn't they prevent the reinvasion?" (The following morning, coincidentally, a Peace Now activist would be injured by gunfire from militant settlers while out in the fields together with other Israeli leftists, not far from here, helping Palestinians get in their olive harvest.)

Perhaps, I venture, it is because most of the Israeli moderates have been alienated, and because, even on the Israeli left, given Arafat's refusal to take on the bombers, few people see any way to thwart the attacks other than by encircling Palestinian cities and trying to track down the killers. How easy does he think it is for Israeli leftists to stand up and clamor for reconciliation, I ask him, when men, women and children are being blown up throughout the country, and when the partner they thought wanted to make peace with them is hailing the martyrs?

"Well, as the occupation returns," says Yussuf, "there's just no way that a Palestinian leftist can stand up alongside the tank you've now put outside his home and demand that his people not resist the occupation. That's impossible. When Israel kills a dozen children by dropping a one-ton bomb on a Gaza neighborhood, that rips the ground away from beneath the Palestinian left. If terror alienates your leftists, think what your reinvasion of the entire West Bank, and destruction of the Palestinian Authority's ministries and police stations, does to ours. The occupation is the obstacle. If it goes, the leftists will return. And stand up to Arafat."

Welcome back to the deadlock.

. . . • . . .

I pay for the coffees. A tall man in his early twenties stands at the cash register. "Who is he?" he asks Yussuf, raising an eyebrow in my direction. I answer for Yussuf in my halting Arabic: "A journalist. Jewish. Israeli."

"I hope there'll be peace," says the man at the register.

We walk back into the car. Suppressing a ridiculous urge to peer under the chassis for explosives, I unlock the passenger door for Yussuf. Parked alongside us is a jeep with border police on a break. An ultra-Orthodox man is having his car fixed at the adjoining garage, blithely defying the oft-repeated military instructions to citizens not to trade their safety for the few shekels saved on a Palestinian mechanic.

Out on the main road, we pass the mainly ultra-Orthodox settlement of Betar Illit to our right, where Yussuf helped build the synagogue. A little later, we drive by the Arab village Husan on the left, where Palestinian youngsters used to gather in front of the mosque to stone Israeli cars before the army built a high metal fence dwarfed only by the minaret. (Eli was driving past one day when one such barrage smashed through the windshield of the car in front of him, sending its driver screeching off the tarmac. For a while, his wife pleaded with him to use the alternate route from Tsur Hadassah into the city, circuitous but inside sovereign Israel. But Eli reasoned that since nowhere is remotely safe, such a prolonged diversion would constitute what you might consider a false prudency.)

At Betar Illit, I say, "You built the synagogue even though you don't think they should be living there."

And Yussuf says, "But even Barak said he would dismantle Betar Illit."

"So you didn't mind building there because you knew whatever you put up was only temporary?"

"Yes, life has to go on. People have to live—the residents of Betar Illit, and me."

At Husan, I say, "It's late Friday morning. In that mosque, they're probably preaching to kill Jews, right now."

And Yussuf says, "Not all of them preach that."

"I've seen them on TV."

"Not all of them. And not all of those in the audience believe them. I've seen the Israeli demonstrations where they shout 'Death to the Arabs.' I know not all Jews believe that. Not even all those at the demonstrations believe that."

I drop off Yussuf near the tunnels where we had first met. His journey to Al-Arub will likely take an hour or two. Mine is ten minutes, if that, through the Gilo–Beit Jala battlefield: past the roadblock, with the curt assent of the soldier on duty, into tunnel one, onto the bridge that leads to tunnel two, a once exposed stretch where Israelis were frequently fired at by Palestinian snipers, fatally in at least one instance, and where the army has therefore erected concrete and metal barriers at irregular, apparently haphazard intervals. Any Palestinian gunman in the houses on the hillside above could still take potshots. Old posters are glued to the concrete: THEM THERE, US HERE. For "them," read "Arabs." For "there," read "Jordan."

That Yussuf is prepared to settle for life in Hebron rather than in Kiryat Gat is insufficient for the Israeli far right, the people behind the posters. They want to see him on the other side of the river.

. . . • . . .

Postscript: Two weeks after our coffee morning at Habayit Haboded, the army bulldozed half of the building, acting on a court order that deemed it to have been constructed illegally.

7.

Anatomy of an Attack

At first, it was only on Sunday mornings. But as the second Intifada rolled relentlessly on, I—in common, I think, with many Israelis—woke up almost every day before I needed to, before the alarm clock, in an absolute reversal of a lifetime's anathema to rising early, initially puzzled by the heavy feeling in my stomach. Then I'd remember: I live and am raising my family in Israel, and several of my all-too-near neighbors—you can bet on it—are hoping today will be the day they get to kill us.

It began with Sunday mornings because, for most of the 1990s, Sunday morning was the preferred time for the bombers to strike. An unusually high proportion of soldiers would be returning to bases on Sundays when they blew up our buses. So our nation would go to bed on Saturday night with a sense of dread.

After September 2000, though, the killers weren't so picky. Soldiers, husbands, wives, grandmothers, children, toddlers, Filipinos, Arabs—they were all fair game. So why strike when the defenders were expecting you? Why restrict yourself to Sunday morning if you could hit a young girl's bat mitzvah party on a Thursday evening (the David's Palace hall in Hadera, northern Israel, on January 17, 2002; six dead)? Why not blow up a billiard parlor on a Tuesday (the Sheffield Club, Rishon Letzion, on May 7, 2002; fifteen dead)? How about destroying a beachfront disco on a Friday night (the Dolphinarium at Tel Aviv beach, on June 1, 2001;

twenty-one fatalities—almost all of them recent young immigrants from the former Soviet Union)?

Since every minute of every day was potentially bomb time, we always awakened with the reasonable fear that something terrible had happened while we were sleeping. Again like most Israelis, I'm sure, I developed a dismal morning routine: wake up uneasy, remember why, disarm the redundant alarm clock, restart the computer, turn on the television. If Channel 1, state television, is showing bizarre 1960s-style children's programming, featuring glove puppets and wobbly scenery, start to relax. If Channel 2, commercial TV, features a hostess with eyeball-searing flame orange hair loudly interviewing a morose chef nursing a panful of undercooked eggplant, relax further. (I'd turn to Channel 1 first because its coverage tended to be less hysterical; Channel 2 tended to be quicker with the news of a blast, however.) Then check the answering machine—hoping not to hear the messages from overseas relatives or requests for interviews from foreign radio stations that signified overnight drama of some kind. And finally, my slumbering computer having resuscitated itself, log on to one of the Hebrew newspaper Web sites, which report even the most minor of bombings and shootings. If after that I'd uncovered no calamities, I'd give a sigh of relief and head for the shower.

Except that the relief could be premature. As I got out of the shower on the morning of Tuesday, June 18, 2002, Lisa called to tell me that she had not been in the Patt Junction blast, which had just rocked the nation.

. . . • . . .

When a bomber succeeded, there was a whole other, infinitely more miserable routine that unfolded, too. Take November 21, 2002, one of the dozens upon dozens of examples. Another bus has just been blown up—the number 20, they're saying on the radio, packed with schoolkids, ten minutes from my home, in the Kiryat Menachem residential neighborhood of West Jerusalem. Lisa and the kids have only just left, so although they'll be heading vaguely in that direction, I know they're safe. Discarding my anxious-father mind-set and entering journalist mode, I grab a notepad, pull on a T-shirt and a pair of pants, then head off to the scene.

The traffic, predictably, is backed up all the way—normal morning rush hour, complicated by bomb-related road closures and legions of ambulances fighting their way through. I try to use back streets so as not to exacerbate the problem. As I edge closer, the radio documents the worsening casualty toll—two dead bodies, one of them that of the bomber. Not too bad then, I allow myself to hope, but it's still early. Now there are three bodies. Now a sickening jump to eight. Then nine, ten, eleven. (The first, lower figures, I imagine, reflected those bodies that were thrown clear, whole or in pieces. The leap upward came when the police began removing corpses from inside the vehicle.) Several of the dead are presumed to be schoolchildren. The station broadcasts mothers screaming wordlessly for their children, some of whom are dead, others mutilated. Tomer, an eyewitness, says he saw a body hanging out of the bus window, as well as dismembered "flesh, hands, feet," and describes "the unimaginable smell of flesh burning." I speak to Lisa on the cell phone in her car; she's holding it to her ear, off the speakerphone—in breach of the law—so that the kids won't hear the conversation. With her real estate agent's encyclopedic knowledge of Jerusalem, she directs me to Mexico Street, where the bus has been hit. She's told the kids there's been an attack, and given Josh the bare details, which have been absorbed with fatalistic nods and sighs.

In the cars alongside me, too, radios are broadcasting from the bomb site. Drivers are staring grimly ahead, jaws clenched. I see one man whose knuckles are glowing white from the force of his grip on the steering wheel. Another is running his hand through his hair over and over again, front to back, front to back, eyes partially closed. He catches my gaze; we shake our heads slowly at each other.

I park at the end of the street, where yellow police tape and crazily abandoned patrol vehicles have blocked it off. I'm a couple of hundred yards away from the bloodied arena, and I'm already crunching on broken glass. Not many journalists have arrived yet, but there are dozens upon dozens of policemen.

There are two more lines of tape, and policemen checking my press card, and now I'm approaching the bus from behind. It is perfectly parallel-parked at the stop, beneath an awning of gently swaying trees. At a distance, it looks quite unharmed, obtrusive only because of the frantic attentions all around it of the blue-uniformed cops, the plainclothesmen with yellow plastic covering their shoes and the bearded, skullcapped men of the Orthodox organizations who heroically collect every scrap of violated, broken bodies for Jewish burial. Closer, though, the appalling reality is all too apparent. Windows are smashed. Parts of the plastic roofing lie in the road. There are bloodstains on the tarmac. Two or three bodies are under plastic sheets on stretchers. Through the shattered double doors at the center of the bus, a single black sneaker is visible. There's a child's backpack, some school notebooks. The purple-and-pink upholstery is bloodied and torn, the white stuffing emerging. Bits of window frame are hanging down over the election poster, eerily intact on the side of the bus, in which an elderly sage urges voters to choose his Shas ultra-Orthodox political party on Election Day.

The mayor arrives. Surrounded by a handful of reporters, he holds court alongside a parked black Opal marked "Checked 21.11.02" in chalk on the windshield—the police inscription that certifies the vehicle as booby trap–free. The mayor is, as ever, commendably soft-spoken. He praises the heroic performance of the police in preventing so many bombings and notes that "barely a day goes by" without an attack or attempted attack. He urges curiosity seekers to stay away and Jerusalemites to go about their daily business and not capitulate to the terrorists, even though "no one should delude themselves" that this is anything but "a war of terror." He is moved to anger only when lamenting the deliberate killing of ordinary citizens, many of them presumably young children, and castigating "the murderous Yasser Arafat" for "setting the tone" that encourages the attacks. Taking a shot at one of his Likud party rivals, former prime minister Netanyahu, he adds that "now is not the time for panicked actions"—a reference to Netanyahu's repeated calls for the expulsion of Arafat—but, rather, for "strategic policies" to defeat terrorism, via the partnership between Israel and the Bush administration.

As the mayor concludes his impromptu press conference and heads off to telephone the prime minister with an update, the next act in what has long become an achingly familiar performance gets under way: the police briefing. Looking like a pair of glum bouncers who let the thug into the nightclub but must remain on duty outside, Shlomo Ahronishky, the national police chief, and Mickey Levy, his Jerusalem commander, stand side by side—bulky black-haired men, chests out, Levy with fingers clasped in front of his waist, Ahronishky with hands on hips—and prepare to repel what has by now become a pushing madhouse of perhaps two dozen print, radio and TV reporters.

Positioned with the broken green bus behind him, so that the TV cameras can show it as a backdrop, Levy goes first, stolidly reciting the facts of the bomber having "entered the bus and detonated a powerful blast," resulting in many deaths and dozens of injuries. The tone is deliberately dispassionate. If you ignore the content, he could be a village constable describing a minor burglary. But the body language—the tightness of Levy's mouth, the worry lines in his forehead, the flexing of his clasped fingers—betrays the anguish. Levy is a dedicated, honorable man in his early fifties, who well knows the fatal consequences of every failure and demonstrably lives his relentless work: Ten months ago, overseeing the rescue and initial investigation at a bombing in downtown Jerusalem, he became a casualty himself, rushed to the hospital after suffering a heart attack. Earlier this morning, on arrival here, he was filmed hugging a panicked local woman, who was crying into his chest.

Ahronishky, too, florid and solid, is a very human face of the law; he flushes with suppressed anger when denying a rumor that there was a specific warning of an attack in this neighborhood (a local mother has been screaming that the cops were searching house to house for two hours the night before). "We have prevented a great many attacks," he says, reining in the ire and sticking to the script. "To my sorrow, this attack we were unable to prevent." On the TV news tonight, an Israeli correspondent will cite this as the ninety-fourth suicide bombing of the Intifada; the BBC, typically, has a lower figure—eighty-five. Whatever the number, Ahronishky says what he has said at dozens of bloody scenes like this, week after week, month after month: "Facing up to such attacks is very complex. . . . This is a difficult period. . . . There is no single solution. . . . We are doing our best, but nothing we can do will guarantee 100 percent prevention. . . . We are deployed throughout the city, but Jerusalem is a prime focus for attacks and attempted attacks." Behind him, as he talks, bodies are being carried away on stretchers, and metal barriers are dragged in to keep back the mushrooming crowds of onlookers, a few of whom will soon begin to clamor for "Revenge, revenge" and "Death to the Arabs."

Camera crews have sprung up by now on an elevated clearing facing the bus. Neighbors and eyewitnesses are giving interviews, some plainly overcome by the horror of what they have witnessed, others clearly struggling to hide an unacceptable pleasure, given the context, at their fifteen seconds of fame. Chen Weingarten, a rescue worker, his black hair falling lankly across his wearied features, belongs firmly in the former category. "We've had preparatory courses," he tells Israeli state TV, "but nothing can prepare you for this. A body without legs. It's unthinkable. I won't be a human being now for days." A blond, cigarette-smoking mother who lives nearby falls into the latter: "Now we can't even take the bus," she shouts to the assembled media crews, successfully attracting their attention. "We can't send the children to school. We'll have to kick the Arabs out of here. Every morning, we're dying with fear." The Hebrew-speaking correspondents back away; they're looking for genuine eyewitnesses, not ranting neighbors. The foreign press drift off, too, more reluctantly, when it emerges that she speaks no English. Behind us, on the roofs of the nearest three-story apartment buildings, I notice, pairs of soldiers have now been deployed, impassively watching the growing throng below and—a lesson sadly learned—looking out for a possible new bomber, a second murderer sent to detonate among the crowds so agitated by the first.

By the time I get back to the car and head to work, we know the bomber's name—Nael Hilail, twenty-three, from Bethlehem, who turns out to have been single, black-haired, and sporting a faint mustache. His father, Azmi, producing a photograph when the camera crews come calling later, is impassive. (The next day, though, he is quoted in the press as saying, "Our religion says we are proud of him until the day of resurrection. This is a challenge to the Zionist enemies.") His mother clutches a similar snapshot to her chest, wailing with grief, which is not a reaction we often see. Many such mothers in recent months have rejoiced in the heroic martyrdom of the fruit of their loins, publicly at least. (The eighteen-year-old bomber who blew up a baby and her grandmother in Petah Tikva in May 2002 had phoned his mother shortly before self-detonating and received her blessing.) Hamas is praising the "operation" as "part of our continuing resistance to the Zionist occupation and crimes."

At the city's hospitals, the slightly injured are telling their tales. "I climbed out of the window," says Meir Kimche, a schoolboy in his early teens.

"I always check who gets on when I'm traveling back from work," says Tami Revivo, a blonde in her mid-thirties. "But in the morning, on the way out of the neighborhood, I'm not usually so worried. Today, I was reading my book of Psalms."

Herzl Shai, the driver, who survived only because the bomber had the poise to wait a while and detonate his device toward the center of the bus rather than at the entrance, insists that he looked like a schoolkid and that no amount of security could foil such attacks. "I thought it was a road accident," Shai says, explaining, however incredibly, that his initial response to the bang was that someone had unwittingly driven into his vehicle. "So I stopped the bus. Then I saw the bodies everywhere."

As of midnight, the death toll has halted at eleven. At least seven more of the dozens injured are in serious condition. Four of the dead are sixteen or under, including an eight-year-old boy killed along with his grandmother. The bomb is being described as only moderate in size, hence the relatively intact shell of the bus, a contrast to the usual mangled metal skeleton. But the device contained a murderous dose of steel pellets. Every man, woman and child aboard bus number 20 was killed or injured.

"They got up this morning, decided what to wear, made their plans, set off," my colleague Netty says to me at the office later, "and then—click—like that, it's over."

"Awful, and unthinkable," I agree dully.

"And no matter how many times it happens, it doesn't get any less agonizing." She sighs.

"Actually," I say, "I think it gets worse and worse."

. . . • . . .

Such was the nature of this conflict that within days the dead were buried, the injured were forgotten and the media spotlight was turned elsewhere. There were times when, by 7:00 p.m. on the day of a morning attack, the on-the-hour radio news didn't even mention it because so many other developments had superseded it. At one time, television station managers would automatically break into programming when news broke of a violent incident; not anymore. There had to be loss of life, or the fear of fatalities, to "justify" such interruptions. (One Saturday night, Channel 2 descended to extremes of programming as usual and went to a split screen when a terrorist attack—eleven killed by a suicide bomber at a bar mitzvah in Jerusalem's ultra-Orthodox Meah Shearim neighborhood—coincided with an important soccer match, an editorial judgment that sparked a national outcry.) And the days when the radio stations would play hour after hour of Leonard Cohen–esque somber Hebrew balladry in the wake of a blast or shooting were long gone, too.

Nothing will erase the feeling of hopelessness and impotence created by the four Islamic extremists' bomb blasts in February and March of 1996, in which sixty Israelis were killed. Those blasts, battering away at a country that was mourning its own extremist's assassination of Prime Minister Rabin, savaged Israelis' faith in the peace process. There were atrocities in the course of this terror campaign, too, that stand out for one reason or another: the Dolphinarium blast, because of the number of young immigrant fatalities; the bombing of the Park Hotel on the first night of Passover in 2002, because of the high toll—and the symbolism—the targeting of families celebrating the festival of freedom, or attempting to. But there were so many attacks, so many horror shows from the scene and heartrending services at the cemeteries, so many newspaper front pages turned into passport-photo collections, with their rows of innocent, unknowing faces, the toll of the newly dead. Simply because of that sheer intensity of killing, the inconceivable became the familiar, and the atrocities merged into one another, causing few people to remember the names or even the faces of the victims. The Kiryat Menachem blast came only six days after the twelve soldiers' and security guards' deaths in Hebron, creating new wrenching sagas of bereavement to move those earlier ones aside. Just as the Hebron killings came to overshadow the horrific killing by a Palestinian gunman of a mother and her four-year-old son and five-year-old daughter in their bedroom at a northern kibbutz only five days before that. And just as, a week after the Kiryat Menachem blast, it was overtaken by the failed missile attack on an Israeli passenger plane from Mombasa, and the simultaneous car bombing of the Israeli-owned hotel there (with three Israelis, two of them children, among the thirteen victims), and hours later by the Palestinian shooting spree that killed six Israelis at the bus station and at the Likud party headquarters in Beit She'an as Likud members voted to retain Ariel Sharon as their party leader. On and horrifyingly on it went. We have a feature in *The Jerusalem Report* called "14 Days," a minichronicle of the most significant events of the biweekly period covered by each issue of the magazine, usually ten or so items in capsule form. Many times, all the space was taken up with the bare details of the latest atrocities, and there was hardly enough room to list the names and ages of the dead.

But while, for those of us mercifully not directly affected, one attack could merge into another, there is no forgetting for the injured or the bereaved—not for those people, those hundreds of people, whose terribly burned faces and bodies, and sometimes severed limbs, can never be fully repaired; not for those hundreds of people who will never see their loved ones again, like the family of Yoni Jesner.

8.

The Killing of Yoni Jesner

This is the story of the senseless death of Yoni Jesner, nineteen, murdered on September 19, 2002, in Tel Aviv, as recounted to me by his eldest brother, Ari, four days later. It stands for no other death. And it stands for all the other deaths.

The Jesner family emigrated to Israel from Glasgow in 1984. "My father said he used to watch me leave the house at age seven to play football, and I'd slip off my *kippa* and put it into my pocket," remembers Ari, the eldest of the four children. "That was it for him. He decided to give Israel a try." In Israel, an Orthodox Jew might remove his *kippa* to play street soccer if he worried about losing it in the heat of the game. But he wouldn't have to remove it to avoid the curiosity, or the taunts, of his playmates.

The Jesners stayed for four years, but then the parents divorced and mum and her children returned to Scotland, while Yoni's father stayed in Israel. They'd keep coming back to Israel for their holidays, though, and as the children grew up, they each came out alone, taking off a year or two before going to university. Yoni, a boy with fresh, inquiring features and short, thick brown hair, was the youngest of the four. He had planned to spend one year at the Har Etzion yeshiva in Alon Shvut, a settlement in the West Bank's Etzion Bloc, south of Jerusalem, before taking up a place at medical school in London. But he so enjoyed himself that he deferred his medical studies a second time and began a second year in yeshiva in

September 2002. That the yeshiva was in the West Bank was not significant for Yoni, who was not especially politicized. It was an institution with a fine reputation for challenging its students, and Yoni felt fulfilled there, examining his Judaism—"asking questions," says Ari, "about what life was all about, and God's role in it."

On that terrible Thursday, Yoni and his first cousin Gideon, also a student at the yeshiva, set out for Tel Aviv, where they were to spend the weeklong Succoth festival with Gideon's family, who were visiting from the United Kingdom, in the Tel Aviv Hilton. The two teenagers were traveling on the number 4 bus on Allenby Street, one of Tel Aviv's busiest thoroughfares, standing near the exit doors in the center of the bus, when a young man got on at the front. Immediately, this man detonated the explosive device he was carrying—not a very large device by suicide-bomber standards, perhaps eleven to fifteen pounds of explosives, but one supplemented by bolts and nails. Its impact was further reduced by the fact that he detonated it before the driver had even closed the doors and pulled away from the stop, so the bus wasn't sealed. But even this smallish charge in the unsealed bus was so devastating as to kill six people and maim dozens more. Among the dead were the driver, Yossi Memstinov, a thirty-nine-year-old father of four, and Yoni. Gideon, dazed by the force of the blast, remembered nothing but a boom and the sight of glass and metal flying down the bus. He recovered, to find his cousin, who had been standing behind him, lying on the floor, his eyes rolled back; a bloody wound on the right side of his head marked where a bolt had entered, plowed through his brain and lodged in his brain stem. Yoni was lifted clear of the smoking wreckage of the bus, and medics strove to resuscitate him. He was taken by ambulance to the hospital, Gideon alongside him, but although his heart was still beating—he had been placed on a life-support machine—he had effectively been brain-dead from the moment of impact.

Ari was at work, as usual, in his law office in London when his father-in-law phoned to say there'd been a blast and that Yoni and Gideon had apparently been injured, Yoni seriously, Gideon less so. Ari tracked down his mother, who was out shopping in Glasgow, and later made contact with his father, who was already on the way to the hospital. As the medical updates came in and they rapidly realized how gravely Yoni had been wounded, the family members overseas made plans for the quickest possible journey to Israel. They arrived the next day, to be met by the British ambassador, and went straight to the hospital. "We knew what to expect," says Ari, "but we were still hoping for a miracle, thinking that if anyone could pull through, it would be Yoni."

But there would be no recovery. When they entered Yoni's room, "he wasn't there," says Ari. "He was alive, in a sense, to us. But he wasn't there. We were aware that in these bombings, there are limbs and other bits of people flying all over the place. I remember someone seeing a heart lying on the sidewalk. So there was relief that he was in one piece. We could hold his hand in the hospital and talk to him. And there was relief that he didn't suffer any pain, didn't know what had happened. But he wasn't there anymore."

There was no time for lingering farewells. Under Israeli law, a team of doctors who have not treated the patient are required to rerun various tests to confirm and pronounce death. Once that determination had been made, religious law then provided for an immediate burial, before the Sabbath. The family had decided that Yoni, who had intended to emigrate permanently to Israel on the completion of his medical studies—should be buried in Jerusalem. "It was obvious," says Ari. "He died here; he loved it here." And that left little time before sundown, the start of the Sabbath.

But before the process could begin, the hospital's transplant staff asked the family whether any of Yoni's organs could be made available for donation. "We hadn't considered it," says Ari, wryly stating the obvious. "It's not something you think about."

Their instinctive reaction was to say no. "You're preparing to bury someone you love and you want them to go whole." He sighs. "But then we all thought more about Yoni, about what he would have wanted. This was someone who had a place to study medicine at University College Hospital in London, who planned to come back here as a doctor and save people's lives. How could we not donate his organs? It would be the most fitting tribute to him to help someone."

Having secured the family's assent, the doctors then raced against time to remove kidneys, liver and spleen before the body had to be transported to Jerusalem. "It was almost like they stripped the body," muses Ari. "You're losing life; you're saving life—it's all such a mess. . . . But later that afternoon, as I stood at the side of the grave and they were lowering Yoni into it, I realized the decision was a hundred percent right. It would have been such a waste not to donate his organs. They're burying Yoni and he's gone, but he's saved some other people. And I looked around the cemetery and thought, How many more people could have been saved?"

. . . • . . .

As I talk with Ari, so soon after his brother has been killed, he clearly hasn't even begun to grapple with the loss—and he knows it. Yoni had been back in the United Kingdom just a few weeks earlier, attending Ari's wedding, but for more than a year, the family hadn't seen him on a daily basis. He'd been here in Israel; they'd been over there. And therefore although they knew, intellectually, that he was dead, it wasn't as though their norm had shifted. "So I know it still hasn't sunk in yet that we're not going to see him again, ever," Ari says—that Yoni wasn't going to be phoning, or coming to meet them at Ben-Gurion Airport, or walking toward any of them across a room.

As I said earlier, I had spoken to Ari briefly at a press conference he had convened the day before, at which he had stressed Yoni's love for Israel, tried to convey the family's terrible sense of loss, and explained the decision to offer his organs for transplant and the pleasure that appropriate recipients had been found. We'd arranged to meet again a day later, today. And no sooner do we shake hands and sit down face-to-face—across a small bare table in a corner of the lobby at the Jerusalem hotel where his family are staying—than we start talking freely and candidly. There is no small talk. Neither of us offers the other coffee.

I know that for me, discussing the death of a young British man, not long in Israel and just starting out on his life, has a particular relevance. Twenty years earlier, I'd come to Israel from England at about the same age, similarly wide-eyed and energetic, though quite evidently less Orthodox, lazier and incomparably duller academically than Yoni with his straight *A*'s. And I think that for Ari, there is a certain relief, or comfort, to be talking openly with someone whose writing he's read and who comes from a not dissimilar background.

We talk at first, not unnaturally, about the waste—the dreadful waste of a bright nineteen-year-old life. "He was an amazing kid," says Ari, smiling in acknowledgment that he's saying what every older brother would say of a younger sibling, but adamant nonetheless. "I'm trying to be objective, and the fact is that he wasn't your average nineteen-year-old. He was all our family's best qualities and strong points rolled into one. I thought I kept pretty busy when I was his age, but Yoni . . . He was a straight-*A* student, though my mother couldn't understand how he did it, since he was never at home studying. He ran Bnei Akiva [the Orthodox

Zionist youth movement] in Glasgow. He ran the city's Jewish Youth Council, an umbrella group for Jewish youth organizations. He was in charge of sending Jewish delegates to the Scottish Youth parliament. He helped our rabbi with the children's services at synagogue and led some of the main services. He volunteered in the local Jewish burial society—at eighteen! When he got to yeshiva, he was seen as a bit of a joker, because he was so energetic and upbeat, and there were some who thought he'd drop out, that he wouldn't be able to cope with the rigors of study. But, of course, he coped fine; he was putting in more hours than anyone else. And before he left for Israel, he'd spent a month writing up two years' worth of material for use in Jewish assemblies in schools in Scotland, material for kids in non-Jewish schools who come out of the main morning assemblies and have a separate program of Jewish-related material.

"So, yes, to lose someone like him, it's terrible. Just terrible. I suppose it happens all the time in Israel," Ari continues, pushing his rimless glasses higher up his nose and sucking in his lower lip, "but here was somebody who was so young. He wasn't married. He didn't have a family. So it's the cutting off of a whole branch. He was still an individual, on his own. I just hope we can take this and make the most positive thing we can out of it. And do things in his memory."

In this, our longer conversation, as at his press conference, Ari is startlingly composed—sure of what he wants to say, emphatic in his choice of words. Although his background is Orthodox, he describes his views on religion as "not classically Orthodox" and is adamant that, generally and in the case of the killing of his brother, "I don't view things as happening because God causes them. I believe human beings are responsible. God is a concept, an idea, a force, maybe, but not someone upstairs pulling the strings."

So he isn't blaming God, or fate, or destiny, for Yoni's death. Nor is he blaming religion in general, or Islam in particular. No. Specific, murderous human beings assembled the evil device and dispatched its brainwashed detonator. The suicide bombers have to be "one of the most horrific and savage things devised by man," he says, "a concept so far removed from Western norms as to be incomprehensible."

Even to the Americans? I ask. Even after September 11?

"Yes. Of course, the United States understands the impact of September eleventh"—the impact of the attack itself, the strike against its symbols, the horrific death toll, the unprecedented use of jet fuel–filled airliners to wreak maximal devastation—"but not the concept." That, Ari asserts, is something the West is simply not equipped to absorb and comprehend: "Not the notion of an educational process that teaches children that it is the will of God, a positive deed, an advance for the cause, to kill oneself and take innocent victims—civilians, not even soldiers—with them. Bear in mind," he goes on, "that in the case of these bombings, in Israel, the attackers know that Israel has more than a million Arabs among its six and a half million people. So when they turn up on a bus and kill, they're going to kill Muslims, Christians and Jews. The amount of hatred and brainwashing required to do that is beyond comprehension. And the West has not come to terms with the Arab, and I include the Palestinian, mentality. We project a Western approach—that if only *we* do this, *they*'ll do that. We turn a blind eye to where they're coming from and what they're thinking."

Does Israel bear any responsibility? I ask him, meaning any responsibility for the growth of the hatred, the failure to offer hope to the Palestinians, the expansion of settlements on land cherished by the Palestinians—the perceived root causes, among those with such sympathies, of the Palestinian suicide-bomb phenomenon? Ari interprets the question differently than I had meant it, looking for an answer from within the internal Israeli debate as to whether the pro-Oslo left and center left brought down this plague upon our house, whether Rabin, Peres and Beilin set in motion the process that has now culminated, for the Jesners, in the death of their son. And he is forgiving: "The dream of the 'New Middle East,' " he says, consciously echoing Peres's idealistic vision in the halcyon early days of the Oslo accords, "is a dream we all justifiably aspire to, but it was dreamed recklessly. Yet that's easy to say with hindsight, and I don't want to criticize. It was a good dream, but I don't know that the evidence for it existed. Israel turned a blind eye to the fact that the Palestinians were talking in English about peace and in Arabic were educating toward jihad and holding summer camps for suicide bombers. There were warnings all along. The language being used by Palestinian leaders didn't change. The bombings didn't stop." He includes his then teenage self in the ranks of the fools: "These were things that naïvely we thought would all pass away."

And now, how do we find a way out of this blood-drenched alleyway, this dead end? I ask this, thoroughly unreasonably, of a twenty-six-year-old who lives abroad and who has no pretensions to political wisdom, simply because his brother, whom he spoke to by phone a week before, now lies buried in Jerusalem. And, of course, he can offer no solutions that have escaped the attention of cabinet ministers and peace brokers and spiritual leaders. But he does offer the common sense that continues to elude many of them. "There is no short-term solution. You can't solve a conflict that has been running for decades in the space of a few years."

Could Israel have done something different to prevent Yoni from being killed? I ask him, going back to the earlier question. And for the very first time in our conversation, Ari pauses, seems ready to essay an answer, pauses again. "I don't know if Hamas"—which has claimed the credit for the murders on the bus—"could ever have been restrained." He shrugs finally. "Arafat should have dealt with them, though—just like the Israeli Shin Bet deals with the minute extreme right wing in Israel, making sure they don't get out of hand." (Actually, the Shin Bet has a dire record of dealing with the extreme right, having failed, as of the end of 2002, to make a single arrest in relation to the murders of several Palestinians in attacks apparently perpetrated by Jewish assailants. It was a failure that maintained the inglorious tradition of incompetence that saw Yigal Amir, who bragged openly about his plans to kill the prime minister, and whose bragging was reported to the Shin Bet, twice attempt to assassinate Rabin and then succeed the third time without attracting the attention of the security service.)

No, I persist, leave Arafat's words and deeds aside. What could Israel have done differently? Should it have killed, arrested or exiled Arafat, done the same for Hamas's spiritual leader, Sheikh Yassin? Should it have sent more troops into West Bank cities, or used greater force against Palestinian targets? Should it have long since completed a fence to seal off the West Bank the way that Gaza is sealed? That might have been enough, in and of itself, to have stymied the man who murdered Yoni. Should we have rehabilitated Arafat in the first place? Was that the original sin that ultimately cost Yoni's life and all those other lives?

"Israel had to try to speak to the other side," says Ari. And the other side was Arafat.

. . . • . . .

As it turned out, the best match for one of Yoni's kidneys was Yasmin Abu Ramila, an Arab girl from East Jerusalem, who had been on dialysis

9.

On the Second Battlefield

Given the atmosphere of efficient authority they generally manage to convey, overseas television bureaus are often startlingly chaotic environments. As long as the narrow area shown on-camera appears to be calm and neat, it doesn't much matter what is going on off-camera, or how messy the rest of the room may be. The Jerusalem bureaus of CNN, the BBC and the innumerable other global TV channels that operate out of a single high-rise building on the Jaffa Road are no exception. When a hot news story is breaking—that is, most days—producers are frantically combing through towering piles of newspapers in search of basic facts and figures, phoning potential interviewees and passing news updates to correspondents, who are often in the midst of a live report. Phones are ringing nonstop and fax machines beeping weirdly and less predictably. Each of several televisions is broadcasting a different channel. All of which constitutes only the first and most minor of challenges facing a guest interviewee thrust into this melee, scheduled to do a "two-way" with the station's anchorman or anchorwoman in the main studio in distant Atlanta, London or wherever.

At the BBC, such guests are seated demurely behind a low desk, sometimes with a huge backdrop photo of an Old City skyline. The area is curtained off and the disturbances minimized. Interviewees in the CNN bureau, one floor below, by contrast, are planted on a rather precarious elevated bamboo chair, itself perched on a wooden box, worryingly adjacent to the huge waist-high and frequently open window at the far side of the room. On Jaffa Road immediately beneath, buses screech noisily to a halt along a row of bus stops before pulling as noisily away again, taxis sound their horns and, all too often, ambulances careen, sirens wailing, to victims of terrorist attacks or other medical crises. In both bureaus, above the camera line in front of the interviewee, dazzling sun-bright studio lights illuminate the guest's otherwise pasty features. Frequently rather too close for comfort to the scheduled commencement of a live interview, a minimicrophone atop a thin black wire is hurriedly inserted between the lower buttons of the interviewee's shirt by a harassed technician, then laboriously extricated to attach to the tie or upper shirt. A pale pink plastic earpiece is shoved into the appropriate orifice and secured to the back of the collar, leaving the interviewee terrified to move his head, for fear of dislodging it and thus losing the only link to the interviewer's voice. At the BBC, the camera tends to be focused by remote control a minute or two before the interview is scheduled to start. At CNN, the cameraman casually positions himself beside the camera, located some ten feet away, only seconds before a voice in the interviewee's ear warns that show time is approaching.

Although the guest may be able to see him- or herself on one of those television screens, it is a cardinal rule that, however tempting, the impulse to look must be resisted: If the interviewee is glancing at a screen off to the side, by definition he or she is not staring directly into the cold glass eye of the camera, and so appears shifty to the viewers at home. In many cases, there is no screen showing the anchorperson with whom the guest is speaking. His or her only contact with the interviewer, then, is through that precariously planted earpiece, and there's no way to see the smiles or grimaces this or that comment may be provoking. There's usually a certain amount of interference on the line carrying the questions into the ear, and it takes some practice to master the art of finding a volume level, via a little control panel theoretically within reach of the guest's left hand, that is not so loud as to distort the interviewer or so quiet as to render him inaudible. On a show with more than one guest, and especially where interviewees are arguing with one another, these routine technical problems of hearing what is being said, nuances and all, and responding quickly and eloquently present a still greater challenge.

As you may have gathered by now, I've sat many times behind the demure desk and atop the bamboo chair, doing my best to hear the questions and respond intelligently. I don't hear too well at the best of times, and the match between my left ear and the standard earpieces is one emphatically not made in heaven. I am perpetually terrified that the earpiece is about to fall out, and that, embarrassingly, I'll have to attempt to reinsert it in mid-interview. I also generally find myself unable to judge whether I am holding my head straight or tilted ridiculously to one side.

None of which would matter in the slightest were I being called in to offer analysis or comment on, say, marginal domestic Israeli political issues. But I'm generally invited into the studio to give viewers overseas an insight into Israeli public opinion, or Israeli government policies, relating to the conflict with the Palestinians. And with the advent of the second Intifada, it was often in the immediate aftermath of a major incident. (I sometimes drove to the studios one way down Jaffa Road while ambulances were heading the other way to evacuate victims of a bombing.) And in contrast to my lecturing duties as a reservist, I felt, when Jim in Atlanta or Lyse in London asked me the first question, and I was live on the air, that I was on something akin to the front line. This was a conflict, after all, that was being fought on two battlefields: the real one, on the ground, and the virtual one, via the print and electronic media. And I believe that the latter was enormously significant, because it so influenced public opinion and policy making and therefore shaped future developments. What had happened in Jenin or Jerusalem was important; so, too, emphatically, was what ABC or NPR or Al-Jazeera said had happened there.

Prior to the outbreak of this conflict, I'd commonly be asked to offer analysis from both sides, to assess both Israeli and Palestinian thinking. Presumably, I was regarded as a sufficiently fair minded and well informed journalist to fulfill that role. But once the second Intifada began, the networks no longer asked Israeli journalists for insights into Palestinian thinking and trends and policy making. When they called me, it was for the Israeli angle only. When they wanted Palestinian insights, they asked a Palestinian. This was not unreasonable. Who could blame them? We had a war going on.

As an Israeli journalist, I revel in the freedoms I enjoy. I know I can say whatever I consider to be true, whether it is pleasing or infuriating to the government. More than that, I love the fact that, in contrast to politicians, government spokesmen and diplomats, I am neither bound by any guidelines nor enslaved to any dictated message or position. I'm also acutely conscious of the power of television. I write a "From the Editor" column in every issue of *The Jerusalem Report,* and I'd like to think that readers take it seriously, whether they like it or loathe it. But the magazine is generally read by people who are fairly well informed and passionate about Middle Eastern affairs. When I'm on TV, I'm aware that I may be speaking to people who have only a sketchy knowledge of the region, and that I have only the briefest time to try to impress upon them what I deem to be the critical issues, positions and truths. I've also registered the impact of these TV appearances. My columns generate a few e-mails. A five-minute interview on CNN can provoke hundreds, and results in dozens of phone calls. I had someone come up to me as I was staring into the sun in a park in Tel Aviv, holding on to a safety rope and watching Adam painstakingly ascend a sixty-five-foot climbing wall. He asked me if I was David Horovitz, then told me that a friend in Antigua had sent him an e-mail with a downloaded excerpt of a three-minute clip of me on CNN. He wanted to shake my hand; I proffered it, then quickly returned it to the rope.

That sense of the need to express myself clearly and effectively was deepened by my profound belief that Israel did not always receive fair treatment from the overseas journalists covering this conflict. I shrink from using the word *bias.* I did not personally encounter a single foreign journalist based here who deliberately set out to distort and misrepresent events to Israel's detriment (or that of the Palestinians, for that matter). But there were certainly factual errors, and I do think there was frequently a lack of balance. I don't think Israel can afford to feel entirely proud about how it handled this conflict, but it was infinitely more sinned against than sinning. In an ideal and thoroughly unrealistic media universe, I'd have wanted every TV news clip to begin with something like "Two years and five months after Yasser Arafat rejected Israel's viable offer of Palestinian statehood and resorted to orchestrated violence, today in the West Bank . . ." Of course, that was not about to happen. But the absence of sufficient context to enable viewers to interpret footage from the conflict was often deeply distorting.

Let me offer an example from a CNN Q & A half-hour show on which I was interviewed in early April 2002, at a time when the briefly energetic Bush administration special envoy Anthony Zinni had visited Arafat in the Muqata, which was surrounded by Israeli troops. CNN's visiting "fireman," Michael Holmes, a non–regional expert who had been flown in to cover this particular escalation, came closer to the Muqata entrance than the Israeli troops had allowed the press, and they fired stun grenades, hitting his vehicle. Around the same time, Israeli troops also searched the offices of CNN and other news outfits in Ramallah. The Q & A segment of the day was entitled "Is the Full Story Being Told in the Middle East?" When the CNN researcher called me at home to see whether I might make a suitable guest on the show, her first and, as it turned out, only question to me was "What do you think of the Israeli army's treatment of the journalists in Ramallah today?" I began to answer by saying that I thought it was appalling that reporters were not free to go about their duties. Although I was coming to a "but," she'd apparently heard what she thought was enough. She asked me to present myself at the CNN studio at the designated hour (not on the usual rickety bamboo chair this time, but on a balcony at a temporary second crisis studio in the King David Hotel).

When I was interviewed for real—by Jim Clancy in Atlanta—I began my answer in much the same way, although I got to the "but" this time. I said I thought it unfair and misleading that while CNN had been highlighting the office search hour after hour, it had failed to inform its viewers that in the past Palestinian bombers had hidden explosives belts beneath the supine forms of ailing Palestinian children in ambulances. It was therefore not beyond the realm of possibility that bombers might be hiding out, or might have hidden explosives, in the offices of CNN. I noted that while CNN had, again hour by hour, been making a huge fuss about the stun grenades fired at a press vehicle that had encroached into what the Israeli army had designated a closed military zone, and was now repeatedly asking analysts what Israel was "trying to hide," that kind of limiting of journalists' movement hardly compared to the terrifying climate of fear in which journalists often had to work when covering developments in areas under the control of the Palestinian Authority, developments such as the lynching of the two Israeli reservists in October 2000. Numerous camera crews were on hand that bleak day, but they were either forced away from the mob scene or made to give up their film at gunpoint. Only the gutsy Italian and Israeli crew of an independent Italian television network managed both to film the awful murder scene and to escape with the footage—the only reason we know for certain what unfolded there. After it was screened, every Italian television journalist fled the country in fear for his life, and the local bureau chief of Italian state television wrote a letter of apology to the Palestinian Authority for the damage the footage had done to the image of the Palestinians.

Conscious that my time on the show was limited, I didn't mention that CNN and other networks might do a fairer job if, while critiquing Israeli press freedoms, they were at least to recall on occasion the events of September 11, when TV crews had been barred by Arafat's forces from filming the spontaneous celebrations that erupted as news of the terrorist atrocities in America reached the West Bank, or to mention that journalists had been physically prevented from filming more recent events in a Jenin courthouse, where three Palestinian convicts had been shot dead by a gang of gunmen.

I did have time to point out, however, that CNN seemed to be reporting the Israeli siege of Arafat's headquarters in tones of sympathy for his plight—as Israeli aggression against an unfairly maligned would-be peacemaker—while underplaying the suicide-bombing attacks on civilians that had led Israel to reinvade Ramallah in the first place, many of them carried out by Arafat's own Fatah loyalists. It also wasn't highlighting Arafat's role in exhorting "a million martyrs"—in this context, a fairly blatant euphemism for suicide bombers—to give their lives in the battle for Jerusalem, spreading hatred via his own speeches and via the Palestinian media he tightly controlled. I even said that I thought CNN had consistently failed to put the entire second Intifada conflict into context, rarely reminding viewers that the fighting had erupted five years after Israel had voluntarily withdrawn its forces from all the major West Bank cities, leaving more than 90 percent of the Palestinians living in areas under Arafat's control, which meant that they had to leave the cities and go looking for the army, the absolute opposite of the first Intifada. The entire conflict, I noted, was routinely described as the "Palestinian Intifada against occupation." This terminology implied acceptance of the Palestinian claim that this was a dispute solely over the West Bank, Gaza Strip and East Jerusalem, an assertion that did not square with the fact that so many of the suicide bombings were being carried out not in the territories but deep inside sovereign Israel.

To Clancy's credit, he promptly turned to another guest on the show, an Egyptian journalist speaking from Gaza, and asked her whether she had seen inciteful material broadcast on Palestinian TV, and when she said that she had not, he gave me the opportunity to suggest that, in that case, she had been neglectful. To CNN's immense credit, they invited me to appear on a second show, only a few days later, and gave me more time to detail what I regarded as some of the contextual failures of their coverage and that of other networks, and they invited me to appear on numerous subsequent occasions.

Later that spring and summer, CNN scored a remarkable triple feat of antagonizing Israeli viewers: First, in its coverage of the May 27 suicide bombing at an outdoor shopping parade in Petah Tikva, in which Chen Keinan lost both her fourteen-month-old daughter, Sinai, and her fifty-six-year-old mother, Ruth, a tally of screen time showed CNN to have devoted three times as many minutes to its interview with the bomber's mother, in which she attempted to justify the crime, as to that with the bereaved Keinan. Soon after, on June 18, the network's founder, Ted Turner, mused in a British newspaper interview as to who the Middle East's terrorists really were: "The Palestinians are fighting with human suicide bombers, that's all they have," he told the *Guardian.* "The Israelis . . . they've got one of the most powerful military machines in the world. The Palestinians have nothing. So who are the terrorists? I would make a case that both sides are involved in terrorism." And finally, in its initial reporting on that same day's suicide bombing at Patt Junction, with dead bodies still being removed from the scene, the CNN correspondent found it essential to point out that Gilo, where most of the victims had come from, is considered an "illegal settlement" by the Palestinians.

When as a result of all these developments a minicampaign arose in Israel to have CNN removed from the basic satellite and cable packages, the network sent two senior executives to meet with a host of officials and journalists, myself included, and sought to undo some of the damage by screening a series of special reports on Israeli terror victims and set out guidelines for more appropriate coverage of such attacks, in which there would be less or no emphasis on bombers' relatives and their attempts at justification for murdering civilians.

Not all CNN correspondents were unfair, by any means. But the network, so widely viewed worldwide and such an influence, seemed to foul up or lose balance often. I was personally sneered at on-screen by a CNN anchor when detailing the Israeli perception of what had happened at Camp David, and told that I was spreading "a myth" that "most people actually involved in Camp David" had long since debunked. I saw reports from Gaza, in which a tank, churning up dust as it moved through the

Strip, was contrasted to black-masked Palestinian gunmen, seen in a series of romanticized interviews as they took their leave of a comrade in the cemetery and prepared to die if necessary in resisting the Israelis. No Israeli was interviewed, and there was no suggestion that Palestinian gunmen had been involved in anything other than defensive actions. During the Beit Jala clashes, CNN International ran another story with no Israeli "side," this one on foreign activists taking up residence in Beit Jala to serve as "human shields" against Israeli aggression. I watched Paula Zahn, the network's star morning anchor in the United States, ask a UN official standing in the Jenin refugee camp, days after the fighting there in April 2002, whether there was any truth to the Israeli allegation that the camp was a hotbed of terrorism. Jenin refugee camp! From which some two dozen suicide bombers had been dispatched, and where posters extolling these dead martyrs hung from all the walls and shutters.

On the BBC, for that matter, at around the same time, I saw an Israeli official spokesman being asked by the supposedly evenhanded anchorman in London, in tones dripping with venomous cynicism, whether the Jenin fighting was "the latest" in Ariel Sharon's series of massacres. This was patently an effort to try to link what had been a ferocious gun battle, during which Hamas fighters had bragged in telephone interviews that they were "surprising" the Israeli soldiers with murderous ambushes, with the massacre by Christian gunmen of hundreds of Palestinian refugees in the Beirut Sabra and Shatilla camps in 1982, for which Sharon, as Israeli defense minister, was later found by an Israeli commission of inquiry to bear indirect personal responsibility.

For hours after other networks were reporting precise details of suicide bombings, I saw the BBC continue to refer to such attacks as "explosions," with no hint of who the aggressor might have been, or even that these were deliberate acts of aggression—just "explosions" in which Israelis had been killed. December 27, 2002, for instance, saw four Israelis killed in a West Bank settlement. From the BBC World TV headlines that night, you'd never have known that a Palestinian gunman had been involved. Just another rash of these mysterious cases of spontaneously dying Israelis.

Particularly memorable was an interview conducted by the BBC's venerable silver-haired foreign editor, its doyen of overseas correspondents, John Simpson, in the West Bank during the summer of 2001, with Marwan Barghouti. In the clip that ran on the hourly news, Simpson chose not to ask why Barghouti's Fatah-Tanzim were openly targeting Jewish settlers in murderous drive-by shootings, but whether he thought that Yasser Arafat and his colleagues were resisting the Israeli occupation with sufficient force. Harshly tested by such forensic interviewing, Barghouti thought long and hard before responding, "No." Simpson saw fit to label that disclosure "unusually frank." And if it were your children, in your country, who might fall victim to such "resistance," Mr. Simpson, would you be asking the same question then?

Many of the overseas TV channels, not only CNN and the BBC, were guilty, within hours of a bombing, of making the attack itself the secondary item, reported only after a lead item that detailed how the Palestinians were bracing for Israeli attack. When the twelve soldiers and security guards were killed in Hebron in November 2002, the question of how Israel might retaliate rapidly displaced details of the attack itself as the opening element of the reporting on several channels. On March 29, 2002, two days after the Passover blast at Netanya's Park Hotel, with the death toll from that attack still rising as more victims succumbed to their injuries, both the BBC's World TV and CNN International carried unusually lengthy reports of the launch of Israel's Operation Defensive Shield military response. Fair enough—it was a major military incursion. But neither the Netanya bombing nor even that very day's suicide bombing of the supermarket in Jerusalem's Kiryat Yovel neighborhood, with its two Israeli fatalities, figured prominently in those news packages, and while Palestinian spokespeople were afforded long minutes to castigate Israel's militarism, Israeli spokespeople were allocated much briefer appearances and questioned much more aggressively. Unbelievable as this may look in print, one British TV network, shortly after the November 28 attacks in Mombasa, actually asked an Israeli Foreign Ministry spokesman what Israel was going to do to change the circumstances that were prompting such attacks. Not only were Israelis being blown up when vacationing overseas, but it was their fault, too.

. . . • . . .

Early in the Jenin crisis, even before the controversy over Israel's falsely alleged mass killings of Palestinians gathered pace, UN Secretary-General Kofi Annan asked, in that mild, devastatingly damning way of his, "Can the whole world be wrong?" That spring, the UN Human Rights

Commission passed a resolution advocating the use of "all available means, including armed struggle," to establish a Palestinian state. A short while earlier, the European Parliament had voted to impose trade sanctions on Israel, and the Council of Europe had expressed support for sanctions (declarative positions that prompted no practical policy changes). Archbishop Desmond Tutu called for divesture of holdings in Israel. So, yes, of course the whole world can be wrong. No reasonable, properly informed mind could even begin to grapple with an official EU stance that would have punished Israel for trying to thwart bombing attacks while European taxpayers' money was being siphoned off by Arafat's PA, without EU protest, to buy the explosives and pay the bombers. My point here is that if it is misinformed, the world *will* be wrong.

Jenin is a quintessential case in point. At the height of the fighting there, Israel was roasted internationally because of the Palestinian claims that it had massacred five hundred or more of the camp's thirteen thousand residents. Though furiously denied by the army and the government, the massacre allegations were initially impossible to prove or disprove, because the government prevented journalists from entering the camp. Reporters could and did speak to camp residents and soldiers, but their testimony could hardly be regarded as impartial. Most fair-minded reporters, in their print articles and broadcasts in early to mid-April, therefore, cited the impassioned Palestinian claims and the equally impassioned Israeli rejection of them, and made plain that there was no way for them to ascertain who was telling the truth.

In the United States, as the camp opened up, the reports began to tend to the skeptical, with the *Washington Post* on April 16 noting that "no evidence has yet surfaced" of massacres or executions, and *Newsday,* the same day, citing "little evidence" of the Palestinian-alleged mass killings. But in quite obscene contrast, several British newspapers, at around the same time, accused Israel of crimes up to and including genocide. "We are talking here of massacre, and a cover-up, of genocide," claimed a columnist in the *Evening Standard,* the London tabloid, on April 15. The next day, the very same day as the American papers were beginning to dismiss the false massacre claims, the London *Independent*'s correspondent here, Phil Reeves, having finally entered the camp, reported, "A monstrous war crime that Israel has tried to cover up for a fortnight has finally been exposed." He went on to say, "The sweet and ghastly reek of rotting human bodies is everywhere, evidence that it is a human tomb. The people say there are hundreds of corpses, entombed beneath the dust." The paper's large-lettered front-page headline screamed AMID THE RUINS, THE GRISLY EVIDENCE OF A WAR CRIME.

This and other British newspapers alleged mass killings, executions, thousands of disappeared Palestinians, and drew comparisons between Israel and the Nazis, Al-Qaeda and the reign of the generals in Argentina. The *Daily Telegraph,* widely accused of an overall pro-Israeli sympathy, carried a headline asserting HUNDREDS OF VICTIMS "WERE BURIED BY BULLDOZER IN MASS GRAVE." In several of the British newspaper accounts, prominent coverage was given to the allegations of a camp resident, one "Kamal Anis," who claimed to have witnessed a particularly horrific act of cold-blooded killing by the Israeli troops. In the *Independent*'s account, he saw "Israeli soldiers pile 30 bodies beneath a half-wrecked house. When the pile was complete, they bulldozed the building, bringing its ruins down on the corpses. Then they flattened the area with a tank." The London *Times* ran a similar version of these allegations. These were not opinion pieces, but purported objective reporting from the scene.

And again on the very day, April 16, that the most emotive of these unfounded reports occupied page after page of the "serious" British broadsheets, Gerald Kaufman, a senior member of Britain's governing Labor party, stood up in the House of Commons to denounce Ariel Sharon as a "war criminal" and his government as "repulsive," and asserted that "Sharon has ordered his troops to use methods of barbarism against the Palestinians," actions that were "staining the Star of David with blood." As Tom Gross would later note in an article for the *National Review,* in which he collated and critiqued some of these and other examples of what he called the often "malicious and slanderous" coverage of Jenin, Kaufman's Labor colleague Ann Clwyd, newly returned from a "fact-finding" trip to Jenin, demanded that European nations recall their ambassadors from Israel. Kaufman, who might well have become Britain's foreign secretary had Labor ousted the Conservatives a few years earlier than it did in 1997, had long proclaimed himself a friend of Israel, but Jenin—or rather, the coverage of Jenin—prompted a volte-face.

A few months later, coinciding with the Jewish High Holidays, Kaufman presented a self-scripted documentary on BBC-TV in Britain, entitled "The End of the Affair," in which he explained why his former infatuation with Israel had now cooled into disenchantment. I cannot testify to the depth, or otherwise, of Kaufman's former affection for Israel. But I had met him at a conference that brought together British and Israeli journalists, politicians, diplomats and others outside Jerusalem a few years earlier, and he was plainly happy and at ease to be in Israel at the time. I cannot prove that it was the reporting he'd read in the British press from Jenin that pushed him over the edge from friend to withering and prominent critic of the Jewish state, but he referred to that coverage in his April 16 speech. Incorrectly believing it to be credible and accurate, he noted, "Today's *Daily Telegraph* accepts the Palestinian estimate of hundreds killed. The *Times* today describes the 'stench of death' in Jenin, and the *Independent* calls what happened there a 'war crime.' " But that coverage contained much that was false, and much that was known to be unreliable even as it was being written, as some of the British newspapers—albeit with far less prominence—would subsequently acknowledge.

There were no hundreds of dead, no mass killings, no thirty cold-bloodedly executed Palestinians, no mass graves. It has been credibly documented that Israeli soldiers, trying to stay alive, were guilty of using Palestinian civilians as human shields, and that there was a subsequent grievous failure by Israel to allow humanitarian assistance to reach the camp rapidly. Moshe Nissim, who drove an army bulldozer in Jenin, gave a horrifying interview to *Yediot Ahronot* the following month: "For three days, I just destroyed and destroyed," he recalled. "Any house that they fired from came down. . . . They were warned by loudspeaker to get out of the house before I came, but I gave no one a chance. I didn't wait. I didn't give one blow, and wait for them to come out. I would just ram the house with full power, to bring it down as fast as possible. I wanted to get to the other houses. To get to as many as possible."

But Arafat's much-reported references to "Jeningrad"—Gross notes that 800,000 Russians died during the siege of Leningrad, and 1.3 million died in Stalingrad—were obscene. This was the heaviest battle of the conflict to date between Israeli troops and Palestinian gunmen. Fifty-two Palestinians were killed, most of them gunmen, twenty of them civilians. Twenty-three Israeli soldiers were killed, many of them reservists, fathers who had been called into this arena of conflict precisely to ensure that there was no military adventurism, no willful harming of civilians, even in this hotbed of Islamic extremism. Thirteen soldiers died in a single ambush. "This was a massacre of the Jews, not of us," an Islamic Jihad fighter, Abdel Rahman Sa'adi, told the *Boston Globe.* Egypt's *Al-Ahram* newspaper would later quote "Omar," an Islamic Jihad bomb maker, explaining, "We had more than 50 houses booby-trapped around the camp. We chose old and empty buildings and the houses of men who were wanted by Israel because we knew the soldiers would search for them. . . . We cut off lengths of water pipes and packed them with explosives and nails. Then we placed them about four meters apart throughout the houses—in cupboards, under sinks, in sofas. . . . The women went out to tell the soldiers that we had run out of bullets and were leaving. The women alerted the fighters as the soldiers reached the booby-trapped area." Israel could, of course, have bombed the camp, or at least the core of the terrorists' hideouts, and spared all its dead soldiers, but it shrank from the casualties this would have caused the Palestinians. The gunmen, of course, could have surrendered and saved everybody's spilled blood. Arafat, needless to say, could have sent his troops into the camp months or even years earlier to root out the bombers from what Israel called "the capital of the suicide bombers."

Six weeks later, on May 28, I was on a panel at a Tel Aviv University event, marking the inauguration of an Institute for the Study of Communication, with the then editor of the *International Herald Tribune,* David Ignatius, who remarked complacently that most people around the world now well recognized that there had been no massacre in Jenin, and that the misconceptions created by the initial unconfirmable, exaggerated reports had long been countered by the subsequently corrected reporting. I have my doubts.

Many weeks later, on August 3, 2002, the *Independent*'s Phil Reeves would acknowledge that "the debate over the awful events in Jenin four months ago is still dominated by whether there was a massacre, even though it has long been obvious that one did not occur." In his curious article, entitled, "Even Journalists Have to Admit They're Wrong Sometimes," Reeves persisted in describing the Israeli military action as "an act of collective punishment against many innocent civilians," but he apologized for his mistake in perpetrating the massacre falsehood, particularly because, he wrote, it had led to the overshadowing of other crucial issues such as "individual atrocities committed by the Israeli army, and the question of whether Israel's major military offensive in the West Bank was either a legitimate or an effective response to the (utterly unjustifiable) murder of Israeli civilians by Palestinian suicide bombers."

Those who are disposed to think the worst of Israel will not be deterred from recalling the "massacre" by the belated revelation that it never took place, and there's not much one can hope to do about that. But I fear that many open-minded people who read the screaming front-page headlines but missed the subsequent smaller-print clarifications and retractions still believe what was false to have been true. Kaufman, an extremely influential member of a governing party led by the man, Tony Blair, with probably more sway than any other leader on the world's most important decision maker, George W. Bush, may be one of them. As someone who grew up a good few decades after Goebbels's Nazi propaganda manipulations, watching the hatching of the falsehoods surrounding Jenin, seeing how they were disseminated and realizing how widely they were believed and were influencing both ordinary people and decision makers was for me the first real experience of the Big Lie. For the first time, I genuinely understood how reasonable and relatively well informed people can be misled by cunning propagandists and their witting or unwitting accomplices, then draw erroneous conclusions and so take inappropriate actions.

In early May 2002, undeterred by the fact that, mere hours earlier, a Palestinian suicide bomber had killed fifteen Israelis in a café–billiard parlor in Rishon Letzion—including Nawa Hinawi, an Israeli Arab woman who had two pregnant daughters-in-law; Edna Cohen, a sixty-one-year-old woman who had been celebrating her wedding anniversary with her husband, Avraham; mother of four Pnina Hikri, sixty; father of six Rafael Haim, sixty-four—the United Nations General Assembly voted, seventy-four to four, to condemn Israel for "the attacks committed by the Israeli occupying forces against the Palestinian people in several Palestinian cities, particularly in the Jenin refugee camp." The condemnation made no mention of the latest bombing, of the two dozen suicide bombers dispatched from Jenin, or of Palestinian attackers and Israeli victims of any kind. Yes, the whole world can be wrong.

Incidentally, news outlets that seem slavishly pro-Israel also do their viewers a disservice. Understandably, Fox News heavily outscores CNN as the cable channel of choice among American Jews, but its stance, which appears to be fundamentally supportive of Israel, carries its own disadvantages. When Arafat came under siege again after the September 19, 2002, Tel Aviv bombing, I watched Fox, CNN, the BBC and Al-Jazeera for the latest developments. CNN and the BBC underplayed the reasons why Israel would want to make life difficult for Arafat in the first place.

But Fox, with a series of invited guests whose common theme was to urge the U.S. government not to intervene and to let Israel handle Arafat however it wished, gave the viewer no indication that there could be any downside for Israel or for moderation. As it turned out, this installment of the siege, which Sharon had ordered without apparently first deciding whether it would be the moment he would try to force Arafat into exile, strengthened the Palestinian leader. In prior weeks, Arafat had appeared to be a figure in eclipse, increasingly marginalized and coming under unprecedented domestic pressure to reform his government and possibly appoint a prime minister. Now, down to his last couple of rooms and with the missiles flying all around him, he was center stage again, the object of the dreadful Sharon's attentions, and thus the adored hero of his people. In the weeks ahead, the reformists would lose momentum, and talk of a new prime minister would recede, albeit only temporarily. Viewers watching Al-Jazeera might have been able to anticipate some of this; it showed Palestinians marching through Ramallah that first night carrying posters of Arafat. The Western cable networks did not.

. . . • . . .

Bigger and smaller lies, conveyed via the media from the outbreak of the second Intifada, played their part in creating a situation in which Israel, to borrow a phrase from the former deputy foreign minister Rabbi Melchior, was being singled out as the new global human rights Antichrist: Witness the late-summer 2001 Durban NGO and UN conferences, ostensibly dedicated to battling racism, which turned into a festival of Israel bashing.

Israel must be held accountable for its actions, but it must not be held exclusively accountable, while other and worse human rights abuses—by the Palestinian Authority, and by other regimes around the world—are ignored. Israel has been marked as being among the most evil nations on the planet—if not, in some forums, as the most evil of all—and condemned and threatened accordingly. This is ridiculous. The lies and distortions helped create a situation in which Sharon was "routinely equated with Hitler" in Britain, according to James Purnell, a rising young member of Parliament from Blair's Labor party, with whom I lunched in Jerusalem in December 2002. This was acompanied by a rise in anti-Semitism, which saw synagogues vandalized by racists and left some of the people I grew up with afraid to wear yarmulkes when walking in parts of London. Pro-Palestinian protesters shouted "Death to the Jews" as they marched in Canada. And if it was far milder in the United States, it was immeasurably worse in some other European countries, including France, Belgium and Norway.

So deficient, indeed, was the moral compass in a country like Norway, disappointed broker of the Oslo accords, that Israel's very right to exist was no longer an automatic assumption there. And there's no doubting the pernicious influence unbalanced reporting has had. I think the breadth and accuracy of what was reaching the good citizens of Oslo from here might best be summed up by the senior editor at state TV, who told me, when I visited in September 2002, that "of course we show both sides of the story: We interview Palestinians and settlers." The anti-Israeli atmosphere in Oslo was such that members of the Jewish community said there had been several attacks on people wearing clothes or jewelry with Hebrew lettering. A pro-Israel demonstration some weeks before I visited had required a massive police security operation to protect the Jewish marchers. A subsequent pro-Palestinian demonstration went ahead with no need for significant police supervision. The Israeli embassy is a high-security center, all bulletproof glass, with buzzers and steel doors and metal detectors at the entrance, and concrete barriers to thwart would-be suicide car bombers on the road outside. With acid humor and more than a hint of alienation, one Oslo Jew quipped to me that "Norway is a bit like Saudi Arabia, isn't it? Dodgy monarchy, colossal oil revenues, disturbing sympathy for terror groups."

I was invited to Oslo by Irene Levin, a professor of social work and social research at Oslo University and founder of Info-Middle East, a pro-Israel organization set up by members of the tiny Jewish community to grapple with the implications of Norway having what Melchior described as the most anti-Israeli media in Europe. (The Danish-born Melchoir, onetime chief rabbi of Norway and someone who still visits often, ought to know.) This doubtless stemmed in substantial part from the fact that Norway was occupied by the Nazis during World War II, and *occupation* is therefore one of the dirtier words in the Norwegian vocabulary. It may also have stemmed from a psychologically complex process, similar to that undergone in France, whereby Norway's own guilt at having failed to protect its Jews sixty years earlier was somehow alleviated by the inaccurate but extremely convenient depiction of Israel as behaving no more impressively as regards the Palestinians.

Our depressing reality was anything but black and white. But in the Norwegian version of the conflict, things couldn't have been clearer: Arafat was the hero, Israel the villain. Arafat sought peace; Israel slapped him away. And the duplicitous President Clinton—with an eye on his wife's future Senate campaign, anxious to avoid alienating the crucial New York Jewish vote—simply lied in publicly branding Arafat the culprit. Arafat was the worthy Nobel laureate (albeit the only Peace Prize winner, I suspect, to be photographed happily clutching an assault rifle); Shimon Peres, according to awards committee member Hanna Kvanmo, should have handed back his prize. (Kaare Kristiansen, another member of the awards committee, who had resigned in protest at the award to Arafat in 1994, was a laughingstock.) Norway had given the name of its capital to a viable peace process; Israel had systematically ensured its collapse. Survivors of concentration camps were invited by Norwegian TV documentary makers to revisit the site of their persecution, then asked how they felt about Israel doing to the Palestinians what the Nazis had done to them. Israeli goods were on sale in supermarkets, but no thanks to a trade union movement that had made energetic efforts to impose a boycott.

Norway derided the Israeli argument that Barak attempted to end the occupation at Camp David; that the Intifada was a conflict Israel had tried to avoid; that the military incursions into Gaza and the West Bank cities were the only tools it had to counter the suicide bombers; that the path to peace was blocked by the refusal of the Palestinian leadership to keep urging an end to all attacks and signal genuine readiness for coexistence. The Palestinian narrative had been accepted and internalized so thoroughly as to leave no room for doubt. There was no Israeli narrative in the media. Shortly before my trip, when former Palestinian Authority parliamentary affairs minister Amr published his landmark article castigating Arafat for having rejected President Clinton's bridging proposals, the Norwegian public barely read about it. When Amnesty International excoriated the Palestinians for deliberately targeting settlers, that was barely reported, either—in stark contrast to the prominent coverage of other Amnesty reports slamming Israel. Months earlier, when Melchior was asked during a trip to his old rabbinical stomping ground why Israel didn't simply put an end to the occupation, he replied that Israel had tried to do so at Camp David. The state TV interviewer responded by inquiring, with deep cynicism, as to how much longer the rabbi would be trying to pass off that empty mantra.

At the request of Irene's group, I spent the day talking with local print and electronic-media journalists. The limit of my ambition was to make them aware that there were two narratives, and to ask them to consider whether they were investigating and presenting the fullest possible picture of the conflict. It was hard going: That senior editor I met at state TV appeared to have little sympathy with the very fact of Israel's existence, and she persisted in referring to pioneering Israelis as "settlers"—and by "settlers," she meant not those who had made their homes in conquered territory since 1967, but those who had lived in pre-state Palestine and built the modern sovereign state.

At the day's main event, an evening gathering of the Oslo Journalists Club, I was joined on the panel by a local journalist, a professor of media studies and Ahmad Kamel, the Brussels bureau chief of Al-Jazeera, who was born in Syria but is of Palestinian origin. He was somewhat hampered by the fact that he insisted on speaking French, which was laboriously translated into the perfect English that all Norwegians seem to have mastered. He was even more undermined by his attempts to prove Western media discrimination against the Islamic world, referring to an article in a Spanish newspaper carrying a headline about the "Islamic bomb." Why does the West go on and on about fears of an Islamic bomb? he complained. Why is there never talk of the Jewish or Israeli bomb, or the Christian bomb? The local journalist, sitting between me and Kamel, leaned over to look at the offending piece. Evidently able to read Spanish, he promptly pointed out that the headline, rather than being anti-Muslim, was actually a quotation from an Islamic leader in Pakistan discussing the Muslim moves toward nuclear self-sufficiency and that this leader happened to have mentioned specifically both the "Christian" and the "Jewish" bombs. But Kamel did win a certain amount of sympathy in the smoke-filled club when he talked about purported pro-Israeli bias at CNN, his competitor. (I suppose CNN would appear to have pro-Israel sympathies when viewed by a journalist from a network that calls suicide bombers "martyrs" and murderous gunmen "freedom fighters.")

Responding to his catalog of CNN grievances, I mentioned that most Israelis consider some parts of the Western media, and certainly CNN International, to be downright anti-Israeli—an observation that prompted a gale of laughter. When the mirth had subsided, I suggested that if most Israelis believed something that they, Norway's journalists, found hilariously improbable, perhaps their alarm bells should be ringing. And that perhaps, too, as the fortunate residents of a country with barely two-thirds the population of Israel but considerably more land, colossal oil, gas and fishing revenues, so much national wealth as to have eschewed membership in the European Union for fear of being asked to share it, next to no experience of coming under terrorist attack and a singular absence of rapidly arming hostile neighbors, they might want to reexamine some of their preconceptions regarding our conflict and consider how their world might change if they faced the threats we face, and how their leaders might act.

Two months before my host, Irene, was born, her pregnant mother had been forced to flee from Norway to neighboring Sweden to escape the Nazis. Norway had been conquered by the Germans in 1940—beneficiaries of the energetic preparations of local fascist leader Vidkun Quisling, who was promptly installed as premier—and the Nazis then began intensifying their efforts to round up the Jews. Of the eighteen hundred–strong prewar community, barely half survived; hundreds, including Irene's grandfather, great-grandmother and numerous aunts and uncles, perished in Auschwitz. But Irene's mother made good her escape, and she, her baby daughter and much of the family were able to return from Sweden after the war and rebuild their lives, reopening the family's clothes store in Oslo. Quisling was tried for high treason and shot. (His name, a byword for *traitor,* is said to be one of the two words Norway has contributed to the English vocabulary; the other is *ski.*)

If the wartime trauma left an abiding instinctual revulsion for occupation, it also left Norway with a certain desire to do right by its Jews. In 2001, the government allocated $5 million for the conversion of Quisling's wartime four-story mansion into the Center for Studies of Holocaust and Religious Minorities in Norway, which is set to open in 2005. Located on prime real estate on a peninsula southwest of Oslo, the vast building bears an eerie resemblance to the railway-line entranceway at Auschwitz-Birkenau, with a peaked tower rising from the center of its upper floor. It also features a newly rediscovered bunker, complete with a HEIL HITLER sign. Irene is one of the team involved in the planning for the museum, and she has nothing but praise for the government's commitment and assistance, and her compatriots' support. She has rather less praise for the prevailing attitudes to Israel. Irene's mother would have been forgiven for thinking that the dark days for Norway's Jews were over, soon after the war, when Maria Quisling walked into her revived clothes store and she was able to tell the disgraced wife of the man who had opened the doors to the Nazis, "I'm sorry, but I won't serve you in my shop." But while direct comparison with that era is misplaced, the anti-Israeli climate was now producing dark days for Norway's Jews again.

. . . • . . .

I encountered a surprising amount of ignorance among journalists covering this conflict—not among the veteran reporters, but among "firemen" parachuted in for a few weeks at a time, some of them the star reporters for their networks and newspapers, who tour the world's hot spots and conduct the star interviews but who don't have a deep familiarity with this region or any other. Several labored under the misapprehension that the West Bank and Gaza Strip had been sovereign Palestinian territory prior to 1967. There were also layers of conventional wisdom, and to resist such views required newly arrived journalists to display a strong antipathy to peer pressure. A prime conventional wisdom among European journalists, for instance, was that Sharon was a wicked man and a war criminal, and that, as a rule of thumb, when Israelis and Palestinians were offering contradictory accounts of Intifada developments—that is, most of the time—a reasonable course was to assume the worst of the Israelis, given the perceived perfidy of their leader. Another widely held belief in the journalistic community was that while both sides were culpable, the Israelis were clearly the primal sinners, since they were indisputably retaining territory to which even they themselves did not stake a sovereign claim. A few months into the conflict, a British reporter remarked to me, "If you end the occupation, you'll get great press coverage." To which I responded, "Yes, but if we do so without a sustainable peace agreement, it'll be short-lived."

I also heard from more than one foreign correspondent that Israel, as a democracy, must be "held to a higher standard" by the media, whatever that was supposed to mean. Perhaps, for instance, that when an Israeli soldier, in the course of a firefight with Islamic extremist gunmen in Jenin, accidentally killed a senior UN official there (in November 2002, thinking the cell phone in his hand was a grenade, according to the official army response), it was only right that Israel suffer day after day of hostile international media coverage. Whereas when Palestinian gunmen deliberately killed two members of the international force deployed in Hebron (in March 2002, a Swiss and a Turkish representative), the coverage was appropriately muted and attention quickly refocused elsewhere, with many reports not even stating that, as was unequivocal almost right away, it was Palestinian rather than Israeli fire that had been to blame.

Then there was the fact that some countries have historical biases in favor of the Arab world, and none has a historical bias toward Israel. And, of course, there was the lauded instinct among civilized folk to sympathize with and support the "underdog"—perceived here not as Israel, despite its vast and widening demographic disadvantage vis-à-vis the Arab world, but the Palestinians, because of their military inferiority. Put all that together (and decide for yourselves the degree to which plain old anti-Semitism might have been a factor), and I think you begin to understand why Israel might not always have been getting the fairest play in the international media.

. . . • . . .

Another critical element in the jigsaw, however, was the skill, or absence thereof, with which officials on the two sides used and abused the world's journalists. You might think that decades of statehood, an immensely more prosperous economy, every technological advantage and a reservoir of immigrants fluent in dozens of languages would have guaranteed that Israel's official "information" effort would consistently outmaneuver that of the Palestinians. You'd be wrong. It is my firm contention that, from the very start of this conflict, the Israeli spokespeople and their various hierarchies were criminally, even murderously incompetent, and I use those terms with full awareness of their weight.

One of the factors behind the heightened effectiveness of the Palestinians in impressing a watching world with the justice of their cause was a handicap I've referred to earlier and which I'll willingly have Israel carry: We're a democracy; they're not. (They did have elections, in 1996, but Arafat's only rival was a seventy-two-year-old social worker, Samiha Khalil, a mother of five from al-Bira. Her odds were not good.) So when the networks looked to prominent Israelis to comment, assess and argue, they might invite into the studio extreme right-wingers, extreme left-wingers and/or anyone anywhere in between. And given the accuracy of the cliché about three opinions for every two Jews, dissonance was guaranteed. I spent three of the most uncomfortable hours of my life in the elegant Pasha's Room at the American Colony hotel, the favored journalists' retreat on the "seam" between East and West Jerusalem. The occasion was an Australian television debate. I was one of the twelve Israeli panelists. The opposing panel was comprised of twelve Palestinians. I'd had no idea it would be a three-hour ordeal when I said yes to a friend who was the producer. But it was not the protracted nature of the show that made it so nightmarish; it was, rather, the composition of the panel.

The Palestinian team, which included several highly intelligent academics who had served as legal advisers to Arafat and his delegation at Camp David, spoke with one clear voice: They only wanted peace, and they really didn't mind how they got it—either by Israel withdrawing to its 1967 borders or by the establishment of a single binational state from the river to the sea. They were affable, eloquent, infinitely reasonable. They condemned terrorism, expressed pain at the settlers' theft of their land and insisted that Barak had not offered genuine peace terms at Camp David (because otherwise their leader would have accepted). They would probably have won over uncommitted or uninformed viewers even if the Israeli side had also spoken as one.

We did not. Seated immediately to my right was a member of the Women in Black—the far-left protest group—who had lost her husband in the Yom Kippur War. She spoke with passion about Israel's deep complicity in the decades of violence and placed all blame for the ongoing bloodshed firmly at the feet of her leaders. Seated immediately to my left was a member of the Women in Green—a far-right protest group. She emphatically defended Israel's divine right to build homes for Jews throughout the territories and ruled out territorial compromise or Palestinian statehood. Also present were two largely incoherent spokespeople for another pro-settler group and another far-left group. With this quartet dominating the Israeli responses, the Palestinians really didn't need to be there at all. It fell to a dignified and earnest father who had lost his daughter in the suicide bombing at the Sbarro pizza restaurant to try to stake out some kind of reasonable middle ground, and to me to try to offer an assessment of the thinking of the unrepresented Israeli mainstream.

Israelis are argumentative, passionate, unfocused and frequently self-defeating. Whenever, by contrast, the TV producers called in Palestinian talking heads, they got, with very few exceptions, spokespeople who peddled a single line, the slavishly pro-Arafat line: the one with all the repeated buzzwords about the "Israeli game plan to reoccupy the West Bank," and the "Israeli massacres and aggression against our people." For the first two years of the conflict, producers moaned off-camera about the impossibility of finding Palestinians willing to criticize Arafat publicly. But the viewers at home knew nothing of this. All they knew was that the Israelis spoke with many diffuse voices, while the Palestinians seemed to have a straightforward argument, which penetrated and resonated through repetition.

So be it. It was a small price to pay for the privilege of freedom of speech, most especially at this fraught time of war. I, personally, was never approached by any Israeli official and asked to highlight any particular point next time I was invited on TV. Meanwhile, Palestinian journalists got death threats for writing what they believed, and Palestinian officials and academics got death threats for speaking their minds.

The small democratic "disadvantage" could easily have been overcome had the official spokespeople been more competent. But the eruption of the violence caught Israel unprepared in that department, partly a consequence of former foreign minister Peres's dismantling much of his ministry's information hierarchy in the Rabin era amid assertions that Israel didn't need to worry about public relations since it was so clearly doing the right thing. And, scandalously, petty bureaucracies, infighting, inflated egos and erroneous priorities combined to prevent much of an improvement. The consequences were grave not only because of Israel's failure to win over its critics but also due to its failure to bolster support among international policy makers, and to alleviate some of the unease and defensiveness felt by Israelis and Diaspora Jews, as well.

The army's chief spokesman at the start of the Intifada, Ron Kitri, was a former high-school principal and knew little about the way the media worked. I was sitting alongside him on a panel, before a supportive visiting Jewish audience, when he confessed his complete mystification as to why, months after the start of the conflict, the world's dailies had not made front-page news out of the army's belated and inconclusive investigation into whose bullets had killed Mohammed al-Dura, the twelve-year-old boy shot dead at Netzarim Junction in Gaza at the very start of the second Intifada, who had become a Palestinian symbol of the conflict. It was the good-natured Kitri's own panicked department, early in the Jenin fighting, that had erroneously announced there had been hundreds of Palestinian casualties, fueling and giving false credibility to the Palestinian massacre claims. His office became notorious for failing to respond to inquiries about the circumstances in which Palestinian civilians were killed, leaving journalists with little choice but to follow their reporting of unconfirmed Palestinian assertions with the bland one-liner they'd received from Kitri's office, to the effect that the "Israeli army is investigating the incident." Kitri was finally replaced, almost two years into the conflict, by the media-savvy Ruth Yaron, a former spokeswoman at the Israeli embassy in Washington, who understood the deadlines and other pressures on working journalists but who had to grapple with a bureaucracy and a leadership echelon of macho, decidedly non-media-savvy generals, many of whom, when interviewed, spoke in the language of threats and ultimatums, lacked competency in English and bristled with disdain for the media.

The Foreign Ministry, meanwhile, maintained its own, entirely separate hierarchy, and when Peres was Sharon's foreign minister, it peddled a line entirely contradictory to that of the prime minister, talking up the need to keep on working with Arafat even as Sharon's aides were stressing that there could be no further contact with him. Though blessed with numerous individuals whose native language was English, its information unit under Peres and his successors was overseen by officials who insisted on becoming prime interviewees even though their English was not fluent. Never were these deficiencies as rudely exposed as on the night of the suicide bombing at the Dolphinarium discotheque on June 1, 2001, when these officials popped up on several networks, attempting to explain that Israel was going to act with restraint, despite the loss of more than twenty young lives, in the hope that its nonretaliation would finally bring home to the international community precisely who the aggressors were. This was a brave and possibly laudable government policy but, at least partly because the spokespeople were so incapable of effectively explaining it, an unsuccessful one. Not only had those youngsters lost their lives, but the official Israeli spokespeople of the day were not equipped to explain properly who was to blame for their deaths.

As for trying to reduce the anti-Israel sentiment in the Arab media, the ministry, again while blessed with those who speak Arabic, at one stage sent a fresh-faced, blond, inexperienced young diplomat, speaking heavily accented Arabic, into the Arab TV den, with predictably underwhelming results. This despite the screamingly obvious fact that the way this conflict was being perceived in our region would affect the degree to which passions became inflamed, determining, in turn, how many people protested how angrily in Amman and Cairo, which itself would influence the actions taken by the Abdullah and Mubarak regimes, always vulnerable to their public opinion.

Over at the prime minister's office, the official PR campaign was led by Ra'anan Gissin, nicknamed "Mad Dog" by smirking foreign correspondents because of his propensity to start each interview barking at ten on the volume dial, and then ratcheting up from there. Gissin is well informed and likable, but even off-camera conversation is best conducted with him on one side of the room and you on the other.

On top of all this, Israel suffered from an abundance of politicians with egos the vastly inflated size of the lacunas in their English vocabulary, who grabbed any opportunity for exposure, even overseas exposure, but who wouldn't have dreamed of taking one of the Foreign Ministry's excellent courses for diplomatic cadets on effective media performance. Watching them shout, bluster, stumble and gratuitously offend on the foreign networks, I sometimes mused that the army would be well advised to deploy troops to prevent some of them from ever reaching the studios.

Inept individuals aside, there remained an acute lack of coordination between these hierarchies, and a scandalous absence of professionals with real media expertise—the kinds of people who would have realized, say, that on the last day of Colin Powell's visit to the Palestinian areas and Israel in April 2002, with the secretary of state giving a press conference, and Arafat giving an impromptu briefing of his own from the sandbagged entrance to his battered Ramallah HQ (in which he complained to "His Excellency President Bush" that "I can't go outside the door" without risking death by Israeli fire), Israel ought to have organized some sort of media event of its own. The most evenhanded TV news editor that night simply had to show Powell's ponderings and Arafat's rantings, but much as he or she might have wished to balance things up with a clip of someone representing Israeli officialdom, the Israelis had not provided any footage.

Israel needed the kind of people who would have known better than to send an extremely nervous and inexperienced spokeswoman, immediately after a suicide bombing, into CNN's studios carrying a captured suicide bomber's (empty) explosives jacket. The producers, who marveled to me about this later, assumed it was her own jacket and that she had forgotten to put it down, and they tried helpfully to take it from her seconds before she went on the air. But she held on to it and then raised it up for the camera. It wasn't immediately clear that it did not contain explosives; the bureau people had no idea what was going on, and I'm sure at least some viewers were left wondering why an Israeli spokeswoman was trying to blow up CNN. Doubtless, the stunt seemed like a good idea at the planning stage—perhaps aimed at showing how easily such equipment could be brought into harm's way—but in practice, it reeked of gimmickry, and incompetent gimmickry at that.

Israel needed the kind of people who would have known better than to fly down legions of foreign reporters in drafty, uncomfortable transport planes to the southern port of Eilat, where they were to be shown the arms haul from the just-intercepted *Karine A* in January 2002. Having led them to the dock where the Katyushas, the antitank missiles, the assault rifles and much, much more of the $10 million weapons haul were laid out in orderly rows, the officials then left them waiting for ages outside in the wind for the press conference to begin. To top it off, Sharon, Defense Minister Ben-Eliezer and Chief of Staff Mofaz then conducted almost all of the press conference—Israel's most graphic opportunity to demonstrate to the world the contradiction between Arafat's fine words of peace and his quiet preparations for murder—in Hebrew, without translation.

Even more critically, Israel needed the kind of people who would have long since absorbed the fact that Israel does not enjoy the "benefit of the doubt" at times of heavy conflict, and so would have realized that—in contrast to the United States during the Gulf War, say, or Britain during the Falklands conflict, when much of the media allowed itself to be managed and massaged by the military spokespeople—when the fighting was at its height in Jenin, the worst possible move was to ban reporters and cameras from the battle zone. Israel should not have been actively inviting reporters to what might well have been their deaths. But, after issuing all the appropriate warnings, it should not have prevented those who wanted to document the conflict firsthand from doing so (and just think what kind of material embedded reporters, traveling with the army, might have sent back). The world's media would not, then, have been so vulnerable to the mendacious Palestinian massacre claims. The cameras would have filmed bloody close-quarter fighting, and that, rather than the rubble and devastation they were finally allowed to film long days later, might have been the image the world would have remembered and drawn conclusions from. At the very, very least, why wasn't an army spokesman's unit sent into Jenin to provide footage of the clashing forces? It might have run on CNN with the disclaimer "Provided by the Israeli army spokesman's office." But it would have run. And it would have shown two sides in close combat, and rapidly dispelled the massacre lie.

At the height of the Jenin controversy, some Israeli official spokespeople actually refused to be interviewed by the networks because they were scared they would be torn apart. Official spokespeople were telling the prime minister there was nothing they could say that could affect the devastating perception created by the footage of Israeli tanks on the move. Serge Schmemann, a former *New York Times* correspondent here, asserted to me during a winter 2002 NPR debate that the horrific images from the territories "speak for themselves." They do not. TV does not always show, explain or even refer to the cause. (And what's more, in the Palestinian areas, TV often provides only a partial picture: For their own safety, Israel bars its nationals from staffing camera crews for foreign networks there, and the Palestinian cameramen have a national interest in self-censorship, choosing what to film and what not to.) Of course there were things to say to explain why the tanks had moved into Jenin. An Israeli government spokesperson could have said something like this: "Does Israel have to lay out the corpses of the one hundred and twenty-six Israelis killed in acts of terrorism by bombers and gunmen dispatched last month alone [March 2002], from places like Jenin refugee camp, for the world to understand why we had no choice but to send in the army to try to do what Arafat had pledged to do—disarm the gunmen and dismantle the bomb-making factories?" That kind of question might not have radically changed thinking around the world, but it would have had some impact. It would have affected the way viewers looked at that footage. It could have influenced the tone and content of the anchors' questioning.

Around the world, what's more, Israel's cause was harmed by its propensity to appoint ill-equipped envoys to positions of the greatest sensitivity. David Ivri, Israeli ambassador to the United States at the start of the second Intifada, is a much-admired veteran of the defense establishment, a former air force commander, but he wasn't comfortable being interviewed on TV. His successor, Danny Ayalon, was about the fiftieth choice of both Sharon and Peres for the job, but he got it because none of Sharon's preferred forty-nine was on Peres's list, and vice versa. The ambassador in London when the Intifada erupted, Dror Zeigerman, and his successor, Zvi Shtauber, were political appointees who spoke imperfect English but who were chosen because of their loyalties to prominent politicians. Until the summer of 2002, the London embassy at least had an effective spokesman, D. J. Schneeweiss. But when he completed his term, he was replaced by a spokeswoman who did not speak perfect English and who got the job because of the admirable desire of the Foreign Ministry to advance female diplomats. A group of Anglo-Jewish activists came to Israel and begged the Foreign Ministry to reconsider her appointment. They, too, were ignored. And months later, only domestic political developments prevented the appointment of Dalia Itzik, a leading member of the Labor party, as the next ambassador to England; needless to say, her English was not strong, either. The editor of one of the British newspapers whose coverage had been most troubling to Israelis, the *Independent,* happened to be Jewish—Simon Kelner—and might well have been receptive to an eloquent and impassioned plea from the local Israeli ambassador and spokesperson for a reassessment of its reporting; the chances of those who spoke halting English advancing their case with the necessary subtlety were slim. "What have we done to deserve ambassadors like these?" a very senior member of the Anglo-Jewish community asked me at a time when Itzik's appointment was mooted. "Israel is being crucified here. We've lost the argument with the students, the teachers, the trades unions, the media and the lower-level clergy. And these are the people you send over to try and win them back?"

Similarly, in South Africa, which sets the tone for much of the continent's attitude to Israel, some recent ambassadors (prior to the South African–educated Tova Herzl, who took over soon after the second Intifada began), political appointees, too, were so unsuccessful that even the Jewish community tried to minimize its dealings with them. "Whenever we learned that he was going to be on the radio or the TV, we cringed with embarrassment," one South African Jewish leader said to me, referring to a recent envoy. "Nobody could understand much of what he was saying, and the Palestinian spokespeople made mincemeat of him." This in a country where Israel's struggle to get a fair hearing had been automatically rendered immensely difficult by the simple fact of the long-standing warm relationship between Arafat and Mandela. When Mandela hugged Arafat during the latter's visit to South Africa in the late spring of 2001, it didn't matter whether, in their talks, the South African icon distanced himself somewhat from his Palestinian colleague. The picture of that embrace conveyed an unmistakable, far-reaching message that Mandela, symbol of conciliation, warmth and integrity, a man extraordinarily devoid of personal bitterness, was Arafat's friend. Arafat was therefore perceived as a good man. And by extension, Israel was considered to be the guilty party in the conflict.

But Israel's cause was still not a lost one. I spent a few days in South Africa in late summer 2001, and accepted invitations as a guest on some highly popular radio call-in shows, one of them hosted by Jon Qwelane, the very mention of whose name set some Jewish leaders shivering. Urging me to cancel, they told me I'd be used as a punching bag for Qwelane's renowned anti-Israeli sentiments. I wouldn't be given time to speak. Callers would cut me apart, with the host applying the scalpel. They showed me transcripts of previous shows, in one of which Qwelane had steamrollered a Jewish caller who'd invoked the appellation "chosen people" to try to exculpate Israel from any criticism.

I was suitably nervous. But Qwelane proved to be well informed, unusually well read, properly skeptical, yet more than ready to listen, and he gave me more time than I needed to explain why I had decided to live in Israel, why the Jews deserved a state, why that need not prevent Palestinian independence, why it was wrongheaded to flatly accuse Israel of practicing apartheid (since the Palestinians were not second-class citizens of Israel, but the people next door, living on land over which, for the most part, Israel made no sovereign claim and whom Israel had earnestly attempted to partner toward statehood), and to express some of the Arafat-related despair I have set out in this book. I tried not to draw parallels or distinctions with South Africa, of which I am largely ignorant. Where I could, I talked from personal experience. Most of the callers were phenomenally hostile, several of them adamant that Israel should be wiped off the face of the earth. In parrying them, I honestly feel I opened some minds.

Similar official ineptitude ruled at home when dealing with visiting delegations. I had breakfast with a group of South African politicians in November 2002, blacks and whites, who were anxious to help Israel and the Palestinians resolve our conflict through the expertise they'd gained in resolving theirs. They had spent the previous day in Ramallah, being lied to. They had been told, among other things, that six thousand Palestinians and sixty Israelis had been killed by their respective enemies in the 1987–1993 Intifada. (The true figures, according to the credible Israeli B'Tselem human rights watch group, were 1,162 Palestinians and 160 Israelis.) And their program of meetings with Palestinians had served to underline their original conviction that the suicide bombers were a symptom of the peace process's collapse, not its cause. The cause was the occupation. If Israel had only ended that, if Israel only would do so now, the bombings would stop. "How would you expect people to react?" one of them asked me. I tried to prove to them that it was the bombings that had derailed the process—citing chapter and verse on the numerous 1994 and 1995 attacks, which had occurred even as Rabin was pushing forward toward a planned end of the occupation—but they would not be moved. At one point, when I was arguing against their contention that Israel was an apartheid state, one of the delegates, a former deputy law-and-order minister in the de Klerk government, interrupted me to say, "Of course you're an apartheid state. What we saw in Ramallah yesterday was as bad as anything that went on under apartheid."

My friend Peter, a former South African and an unassailable political dove, later told me I might have suggested to them that had the Palestinians taken a leaf out of the ANC book, and pursued nonviolent resistance, and had they been led by a Mandela-like figure, capable of emerging from twenty-six years in jail with his faith in man's essential goodness actually enhanced, they could have long ago reached the coexistence and independence they claimed to be seeking. I failed to make those points, however, or much of an impression, I fear. When I told them I considered myself a political moderate—because for all my revulsion I felt for Arafat and his acolytes, I was ready to back large-scale territorial compromise in negotiations with a genuinely peace-minded Palestinian leadership—they laughed, not rudely, but pityingly, at the extent of my self-delusion. And when I asked them whom they were going to be meeting with for the rest of their day in Israel, they said that, apart from Foreign Ministry officials, they didn't know, really, because the Israeli politicians their ambassador had lined up had all canceled at the last moment. So I think we can safely assume they went home unpersuaded of the justice of the Israeli cause.

The root of all this incompetence was the prime minister's office. Post–Camp David, Ehud Barak had so many problems simply holding on as prime minister, confronting the Intifada and making a final stab at peace at the Taba talks—in all of which he failed—that he may not have had much spare time to worry about public relations. But that's what his advisers were there for. And Ariel Sharon was caught up in a siege mentality, believing that much of the world, with the exception of the United States, was so firmly predisposed to hate him that no amount of effective public relations would ever make a difference. His often incompetent spokespeople fed that complex by performing so ignominiously while at the same time assuring Sharon they were doing the best possible job in impossible circumstances. And Sharon's rivalry with Netanyahu was another factor. In the final weeks of 2002, when Netanyahu was briefly appointed foreign minister, even as he tried unsuccessfully to oust Sharon as Likud party leader, the prime minister often sneeringly praised Netanyahu for the effectiveness of some of his public relations efforts. His tones seemed calculated to suggest that Netanyahu—still a skilled TV performer, though not the peerless force he had been a decade earlier—had been reduced to dealing with the most marginal of matters, while he, Sharon, was handling the real business of running the country.

. . . • . . .

Israel's critics might respond to all of this by saying that if Israel had used less force against the Palestinians, it wouldn't have needed more effective exponents to polish its message. I would respond that, yes, Israel's cause would have been immeasurably helped if fewer civilians (and ideally none) had been killed during military actions, such deaths had been investigated more rigorously, rogue soldiers had been punished appropriately and the world's media had been dealt with more openly. But it would have been helped still further if government officials had better explained to the world the circumstances in which Israel found itself. Look how effectively the Palestinians did so.

Palestinian spokespeople were strikingly soft-spoken and deferential—in stark contrast to the likes of Gissin—and so much more effective as a consequence. The PA didn't use very many of them, but those it relied on spoke first-class English and knew exactly what they intended to say—people like the urbane PLO Washington envoy Hassan Abdel Rahman; the former PA minister Hanan Ashrawi, a professor of English literature (in whose company I once commentated for the BBC on the pope's visit to

Jerusalem—this during happier times), who muted her criticism of Arafat to become one of his most effective defenders; and Saeb Erekat.

A peace negotiator turned PA minister, Erekat, who has a master's degree from the United States and a Ph.D. from England, was perhaps the most effective of all the Palestinian talking heads once the violence started. His finest tactic was his first and simplest one. Shortly before he went on the air, when the mike was safely affixed to his tie and the earpiece was in, he took the rudimentary step of asking the producer for the anchorperson's name. And then, when Jim or Tumi or Jonathan put their first question to him, he began his answer by saying, "Well, Jim," "Well, Tumi," or "Well, Jonathan," thus imperceptibly establishing himself as the anchor's friend. And that made him the viewers' friend, too, because the viewers were watching Jim, Tumi and Jonathan because they trusted and liked them. Immediately, that sense of friendship gave added credibility to everything Erekat had to say. (Contrast that to, say, the performances of Peres, far from Israel's weakest TV interviewee. I once saw him interrupt Tumi Makgabo at CNN and address her, most unfortunately, as "Dear lady.")

What Erekat had to say was not always the truth. He was at the forefront of the "five hundred massaced in Jenin" campaign (and initially even spoke of three thousand dead). He alleged falsely that the massive fence Israel was slowly building along the Israel–West Bank border would divide the West Bank into noncontiguous cantons (it was biting far into West Bank territory in many areas, but it was not severing it into distinct sections). And it was Erekat who, on May 1, 2002, alleged on live TV that Israeli troops were in the process of storming and burning Bethlehem's Church of the Nativity, an incendiary claim promptly co-opted by Arafat. Erekat happened to be in Jericho, not Bethlehem, at the time, so there was no danger of him allowing the lack of firsthand information to get in the way of his erroneous assertion when he phoned in to CNN.

Erekat was by no means the only Palestinian spokesman to play fast and loose with the truth. In early April 2002, I watched Leila Shahid, Arafat's representative in France, assure CNN presenter Clancy that when Yitzhak Rabin was prime minister there were "no terrorist attacks." Her point was that when Arafat had a more reasonable partner, he was able to thwart terrorism. Clancy did not refute the "no terrorist attacks" assertion for the lie it was—perhaps he didn't know—and allowed Shahid to continue uninterrupted. There were, in fact, numerous suicide bombings when Rabin was prime minister, after the Oslo accords had been signed—twenty-two Israelis blown up in Tel Aviv in October 1994; twenty-one more killed at Beit Lid in January 1995, to name just two of the worst atrocities. And Arafat's failure to prevent them was one of the factors that had sent Rabin's popularity in Israel plummeting, raising immediate doubts about the viability of the Oslo process and contributing to the climate of public anguish that ultimately produced Rabin's assassin.

The cynicism of Erekat's performances was brought home to me when, in December 2001, *The Jerusalem Report* ran a cover story on the heroic work done by Israel's hospitals in dealing with the victims of suicide bombings. The article, by Netty C. Gross, underlined that, the circumstances notwithstanding, Jerusalem's hospitals had, without hesitation, stuck by the ethics of the medical profession, providing treatment to all who needed it and giving priority to those in gravest condition, victim or bomber. Quite by chance, Netty had run into a Palestinian parent one day at the Shaare Zedek hospital, a man whose baby son had been born with a life-threatening disease. The son was being kept alive thanks to the devoted treatment and expertise of this hospital's staff. The father, it turned out, was a prosecutor at the PA's military courts in Ramallah, a man whose task it was to press charges against Palestinians who had collaborated with Israel, and who could face execution if convicted. I was struck by the awful irony: Here was the Israeli medical profession dutifully helping maintain the life of a child. And there was his father seeking the death sentence for those whose "crime" was to help Israel keep its civilians safe from the bombers. Far from honoring its Oslo commitment to hunt down the bombers, the PA was instead expending its energies trying to prevent other Palestinians from helping us do so. The saga was given added piquancy by the fact that, a few hospital floors away on the day Netty ran into this father/prosecutor, one such Palestinian collaborator was also receiving treatment, having been rushed in with gunshot wounds. But the ultimate piquancy was provided by the fact that the father/prosecutor, later promoted to PA judge, was Ashraf Erekat, brother-in-law and cousin of Saeb.

10.

Getting It and Giving It

Hours after two Islamic Jihad bombers slammed their explosives-filled jeep into the back of a bus at the Karkur Junction on October 21, 2002, killing fourteen Israelis, Lisa and I sat down for a little merciful light relief: the week's installment of *The West Wing,* one of the very few shows we'll do our best to watch, even letting the phone go unanswered, a true act of nerve.

It was an episode entitled "On the Day Before," and while the major plotline focused on a convoluted battle to prevent an override of the presidential veto of some new legislation, the simpler second strand concerned the fallout from a suicide bombing in Jerusalem. What a depressing coincidence, you might say, for the episode of *The West Wing* that dealt with a suicide bombing to be broadcast in Israel on the very day of a suicide bombing. But actually, several times we had been watching an episode of *ER,* the other must-see American import, and had realized with a jolt that the sirens of the fictional ambulances on TV were being drowned out by sirens on real ambulances rushing by on Hebron Road.

What was extraordinary about this episode of *The West Wing* was the suspension of disbelief its writers required of Israeli viewers. In the fictional blast, two American soccer players were killed, and President Josiah Bartlet and his chief of staff, Leo McGarry, earnestly discussed whether or not the United States should respond with some kind of military action. They eventually settled on the need to pressure Yasser Arafat into issuing a condemnation and arresting and handing over the head of the splinter terrorist group behind the blast. Such a story line might have been barely credible prior to the summer of 2000, when suicide bombings were not a weekly occurrence, though even then the notion of the United States responding militarily in any way would have been silly. But this was an episode written long after the second Intifada had begun, and first broadcast in the United States in October 2001. And watching the earnest to-ing and fro-ing in the fake Oval Office, immediately after the real nightly news had shown emergency workers in the real Israel scraping bits of a dozen dead bodies off the sidewalk, only underlined, for the umpteenth time, how even sophisticated and relatively informed outsiders, such as the writers of *The West Wing* presumably would think themselves to be, miserably failed to understand this conflict.

In the real world, our "routine" suicide bombings caused no crises at the White House, not even when American citizens were among the fatalities. Five American citizens were killed in the Hebrew University bombing of July 31, 2002, and I can promise you there was no frantic tête-à-tête between Bush and White House Chief of Staff Andy Card about possible military action. In the real world, Arafat never had a problem condemning anything in English, for administration and other consumption; such statements flowed as easily as the guns to Gaza via the underground tunnels from Egypt. Arafat wanted the Western world to think he honestly condemned such actions; it was what he said in Arabic, or didn't, that mattered. Indeed, Arafat quickly issued his standard English words of condemnation for that day's bombing attack: "The Palestinian Authority, as is known, opposes the killing of all civilians, be they Palestinian or Israeli." Moreover, there was not a single occasion on which Arafat handed over, to Israel or the United States, the head of any Palestinian group orchestrating terrorism. The most he did—and this was as the hugely reluctant concession to end weeks during which he was held immobile by Israel in his Ramallah headquarters in the spring of 2002—was consent to the British and American supervision of the imprisonment, in a Palestinian-controlled jail in Jericho, of the men who had orchestrated and carried out the murder of Tourism Minister Ze'evi.

The *West Wing* writers got it similarly wrong in their hurriedly concocted episode in the aftermath of 9/11, "Isaac and Ishmael," shown in the United States on October 3, 2001. Their slick-talking highfliers, always ready with the bon mot, were depicted asking a roomful of White House youngsters to try to make sense of the Bin Laden death cult. "Extremist Islam is to Islam as what is to Christianity?" was one question. And the answer they solemnly posited was the Ku Klux Klan. With all due repugnance for the murderous racism of the Klan, would that Al-Qaeda were a threat of comparable proportion. These people aren't merely dangerous, narrow-minded bigots. They want to kill any and all of us. And they lust for death themselves. It's an enemy of a whole new order.

I'd ask you to forgive my pedantry over what is, after all, only a bit of TV drama. But it is TV drama that takes itself highly seriously. It's TV drama that may well constitute the best insight tens of millions of viewers in the United States and worldwide have ever gained into the presumed workings of the White House—and, on this occasion, on the repercussions of, and reactions to, a suicide bombing. And the very fact that the writers of *The West Wing* could get things so wrong, notwithstanding the expert input of the ex–White House luminaries who serve as their advisers, reflected a nonfictional parallel: The real administration staffers and officials also had a hard time recognizing what was going on here.

. . . • . . .

Clyde Haberman, a former *New York Times* correspondent in Jerusalem, wrote an article in that paper on the day after 9/11, suggesting that Americans might henceforth better understand what Israel had long been suffering—as the terrorists' punching bag, petrified anytime and anyplace that an explosion may wipe away their families and friends, and the butt of international condemnation when it tried to protect itself. "Do you get it now?" he began. "It is a question that many Israelis wanted to ask yesterday of America and the rest of the finger-pointing world. Not in a smart-alecky manner. Not to say, 'We told you so.' It was simply a question for those who, at a safe remove from the terrorism that Israelis face every day, have damned Israel for taking admittedly harsh measures to keep its citizens alive."

"Do you get it now?" The answer I would have to give is that the Bush administration didn't get it at all until many, many months after 9/11, with terrible consequences for both Israeli and American interests.

However paradoxically, I really believe something positive for Israelis and Palestinians could have come out of the savage attacks of 9/11 had the Bush administration held firm, in the context of our conflict, to its admirable resolve to draw a firm distinction between good guys and bad guys, and to ally itself with the former to counter the threat of the latter. But rhetoric aside, it did not.

September 11 was a reversal of the awful routine for us in Israel: We watched, horrified, as terror struck thousands of miles away this time. Instead of our phones ringing constantly as appalled friends or relatives overseas called to ensure that we hadn't had the fatal misfortune of being in the wrong place at the wrong time, it was we who were frantically telephoning them. We shook our heads in uncomprehending disbelief as that second plane plowed into the second tower, instantly aware that what we were witnessing was an attack of such scale and symbolism as to dwarf everything that we had been enduring: a single unthinkable assault outstripping the weeks and months of smaller wickednesses visited upon us. And when our leaders made the politicians' equivalent of personal condolence phone calls, prime minister's office to White House, Foreign Ministry to State Department, the horror and sympathy and solidarity they expressed were heartfelt and genuine and unlimited. And they were doubtless perceived as such in Washington.

By contrast, I cannot know how widely the small but spontaneous demonstrations of delight that broke out in East Jerusalem and some West Bank and Gaza cities (in Gaza, joyful marchers held up pictures of Bin Laden) reflected ordinary Palestinian sentiment. Arafat, quick to recognize the danger, had his security personnel rapidly snuff them out, and camera crews were warned not to film them. In a gesture he ensured was more widely covered by the TV networks, he then organized a personal blood donation as a symbolic act of emergency support for the victims. But when Arafat contacted President Bush to express shock and distress and pledge Palestinian support for the new U.S. war on terror, he was lying. And yet, for all intents and purposes, however unaccountably, the administration gave every indication of taking him at his word, too: The Palestinians, just like the Israelis, were classified on the white side of the president's Kodachrome divide. And we all suffered as a consequence.

What the president failed to say when the "appalled" Palestinian leader came on the phone was, Prove it. Bush's post-9/11 distinction between those nations and organizations that would solve their disputes and advance their causes peaceably and those that would not was correct. "Every nation in every region" had a decision to make, I remember him saying.

"Either you are with us or you are with the terrorists." And the sheer dreadfulness of that day's terrorism offered him an unexpected opportunity, just possibly, to force Arafat to switch sides, and belatedly start to make good on the lapsed Oslo accord pledge to stand against terror. You want to be considered one of the good guys? the president could have asked him. Well, we need all the help we can get and we'd be pleased to have you with us. But you'd better start by sending your security forces to smash the Hamas and Islamic Jihad terror cells. You know who's involved; you've had most of them in your jails for a few days at one time or another. This time, keep them there. And tell those of your loyalists, in the Fatah Tanzim, the Al-Aqsa Brigades and their spin-offs, that loyalty to you, in the new era that just dawned, means putting down the machine guns and the hand grenades, shutting the bomb-making labs and taking another crack at negotiations.

Arafat might well have ignored any such presidential plea. But if there was ever a last chance of him heeding the call to renounce "armed struggle," this was it. The man who liked to whine to Western diplomats that there was only so far he could go against the will of his people might just have been shocked, at that precise juncture, into telling those people that terrorism simply wasn't going to fly anymore; that it was time to get humane; that however legitimate the "resistance," the days of pursuing it via rifle barrels and bomb labs were over.

But Bush let Arafat off the hook. And even though some of his security chiefs were urging the chairman to seize the moment to clamp down on those who would heed his word and to confront the Islamic extremists and the others who would not, Arafat took no initiatives, and the bombings continued. And a month later, after gunmen from the PFLP had fatally shot Cabinet Minister Ze'evi, avenging the assassination of their leader, Abu Ali Mustafa, two months earlier, the army expanded its West Bank operations to try to track down the killers, and we were all spiraling down into another sea of bloodshed. If Arafat had clamped down on the PFLP and the other militant groups, some of the bombings might have been halted, Ze'evi might have been spared and hundreds of thousands of Palestinians might not have had to endure the ensuing living hell of roadblocks and curfews and mass arrests for questioning.

Great Britain didn't distinguish itself, either. When Jack Straw, the foreign secretary, flew to Iran in late September 2001, he did not do so to read its leaders the riot act, or to tell them to stop advancing the elimination of

Israel as a central platform of government policy, or to stop recruiting, training and raising funds for terror groups, or to stop organizing terrorist attacks. (The bombing of the Jewish community offices in Buenos Aires in 1994, in which eighty-five people were killed, to give just one example, was initiated at a meeting of Iran's most senior leaders and supervised by its minister of intelligence affairs, Ali Fallahian, according to documentation released by the Argentinian government.) As ridiculous as it might seem, Straw went, rather, to try to woo Teheran into the antiterror alliance. In remarks deliberately timed for release during his visit, Straw lamentably intimated that terrorism against Israel could somehow be legitimized by what he called "the anger which many people in this region feel at events over the years in Palestine." Iran, unsurprisingly, rejected Straw's advances, but it happily co-opted his Palestine comments, turning reality on its head and declaring the Palestinians to be "the main victims of terrorism." This wrongheaded British expediency still prevailed at the end of 2002, in the run-up to the U.S. offensive against Saddam Hussein, when Britain played host to Syria's Bashar Assad, Iran's partner in facilitating Islamic extremist terror, many of whose prime exponents enjoy a safe haven in Damascus. Assad and his wife even got to meet the queen. I wonder, as he sat in her palace, if he was asked how far he kept the Hamas and Islamic Jihad training centers from his?

To many Israelis, myself included, it seemed that the U.S. administration compounded its post-9/11 failure by very publicly rapping Israel over the knuckles, in subsequent weeks and months, for entering Palestinian-controlled West Bank cities to try to hunt down the bombers. The first time a State Department official declared that the United States wanted Israel to "get out" of the Palestinian areas immediately and "never go back," Prime Minister Sharon publicly assumed that this was a lower-level official speaking out of turn. But the demand was repeated higher and higher up in the administration, until President Bush himself said the same thing, wagging his finger and insisting that "I meant what I said." This was music to the ears of the Palestinian bombers: Israel's greatest ally was trying to keep them safe. They had no fear of the PA, and now the United States was trying to ensure they need have no fear of Israel, either.

For those more moderate Palestinians who were urging Arafat to act against the bombers, it was a heavy blow: If the United States was telling Israel not to confront these assailants, why should Arafat risk the anger of his own people to do so? And in the Arab world, parts of Europe and, of course, parts of the media, the American position was manipulated to constitute a green light for the bombers: If the United States was telling Israel it had to absorb such attacks without response, that must mean, as Palestinian propaganda so often had it, that they constituted a legitimate response to Israeli occupation. (On October 7, 2000, the United States, I believe, made its original grave error by abstaining in the UN Security Council vote on the one-sided Resolution 1322: Adopted by a vote of fourteen to zero, it deplored the "provocation" of the Sharon visit to the Temple Mount and the "subsequent violence there and at other Holy Places, as well as in other areas throughout the territories occupied by Israel since 1967, resulting in over 80 Palestinian deaths and many other casualties." This was used to condone the armed Intifada from the very start.)

The U.S. stance was presented as confirmation that there were different categories of terror: the unjustifiable actions of Al-Qaeda against American targets and the state terror of Saddam's Iraq, on the one hand, which demanded an unrelenting counterwar until the threat was defused; and, on the other, Palestinian terrorism against Israel, which could be excused and tolerated because it sprang from a credible grievance that urgently needed addressing, and that could continue until that grievance was resolved. The administration was boasting of its success in bringing down one repressive, terror-fostering regime, the Taliban, and killing its most dangerous activists, while spearheading international protests when Israel attempted to limit the terror-inciting potential of another, the Palestinian Authority, and to eliminate the associated terrorist recruiters, bomb makers and gunmen.

Therefore, by failing to hold Arafat to his antiterror pledge, and restraining Israel from confronting the bombers, Bush undermined his own good-guys-and-bad-guys argument. He also allowed the Israeli-Palestinian conflict to heat up again, to the detriment of his preparations for war in Iraq and attempts to win support in the Arab world. And he also harmed the interests of ordinary Israelis and Palestinians, who were dragged down again into heavy violence. This is what inspired Sharon's tongue-lashing of the administration on October 4, 2001, in which he implied a comparison between Bush and Neville Chamberlain, warning the United States not to "sacrifice" Israel to "appease the Arabs. . . . Israel won't be Czechoslovakia. Israel will fight terrorism."

Eventually, though, the administration did get it. I've heard that well over a dozen drafts were written of the speech on the Middle East that Bush delivered from the White House on June 24, 2002, and that most of the earlier versions, where State Department wording dominated, would have received about as warm a reception at the prime minister's office as a UN fact-finding delegation. But Bush's envoy, Gen. Anthony Zinni, an ex-marine who evidently knew when he was being fed a line, had by now reported to the president that Arafat was pulling the wool over Western eyes with his English-language condemnations of each attack, while giving no Arabic-language orders to his security personnel to prevent the next one. Shin Bet had also persuaded the administration of the authenticity of documents, seized from Arafat's and other Palestinian officials' offices during the West Bank onslaughts of the spring, that showed Arafat personally authorizing cash payments to gunmen. And Bush had been given all the details of the *Karine A* haul—which included a consignment of C4 explosives large enough for dozens of bombs, perhaps even hundreds—and recognized that no undertaking of that scale would have been attempted without Arafat's personal assent. Bush redrew his line in the sand on June 24, and belatedly placed Arafat on the wrong side of it, branding him and his coterie of defenders as being "compromised by terror." Only when the leadership was changed, he said, could the Palestinians realize the aspiration for independent statehood that he, the president, and most Israelis, for that matter, endorsed. (Europe still didn't get it many months later. Joschka Fischer, Germany's foreign minister, was holding talks with Arafat in Ramallah on April 9, 2003, ironically, as jubilant Iraqis were tearing down statues of Saddam while American tanks rolled through Baghdad.)

The only trouble with demanding Arafat's replacement as a precondition for progress was, first, that the Palestinian chairman was extremely reluctant to go gently into that good night; second, that the inflamed Palestinian people were in no mood to ditch him in favor of someone Israel would find more convenient; third, that even if they were of such a mind, charismatic, courageous and peace-minded alternatives to Arafat were in short supply. It wouldn't get better so long as Arafat was in control, but his departure wouldn't necessarily solve much, either. Opinion polls had consistently shown that were Arafat to disappear, the favored successor would be someone of a similar mold, preferably Marwan Barghouti, the "mastermind" of this armed Intifada, the man indicted by Israel for alleged direct involvement in orchestrating several dozen murders. Indeed, surveys showed that in terms of popularity, the order of preference was Arafat, Barghouti and Ahmad Yassin, the paraplegic patron sheikh of the suicide bombers. The likes of Sari Nusseibeh and Nabil Amr barely figured. Neither did Abu Mazen, who would ultimately accept the nomination as the PA's first prime minister and attempt in vain to peel away some of Arafat's powers.

. . . • . . .

From very early in this conflict, I received invitations to lecture to visiting Jewish and non-Jewish groups, and to groups abroad, about what it was like to live here, how we had gotten into this mess and how we might get out of it. In my reserve duty, lecturing to the army, I'm required to be non-partisan: Even when, as is often the case, I'm asked to discuss something as politically divisive as the peace process, I'm not supposed to betray my personal sympathies and preferences, however unrealistic or challenging that may sound, and am told instead merely to give dates and details of accords and of disputes and of redeployments. This is constraining and challenging, but in terms of the army, it makes sense. The top brass want soldiers who are being sent out into the territories, and even those who are not, to have some sense of the process that brought us to the current stage of interaction with the Palestinians, but they don't want impressionable minds fed political ideology in the guise of education. Even in my non-army lectures, however, where no such formal constraints apply, I try to paint as fair-minded a picture as I can of our reality, to tell audiences what most Israelis think, what most Palestinians think, why the minorities disagree with that consensus. If pressed, I don't hide my personal views, but I try not to bludgeon people with them. In the hour or however long I have, I want to do my utmost to bridge the distance between Israel and wherever they live or have come from, to plunge them into the heart of our world as best as I can. In short, I want them to get it. Of course, as someone who has wanted to throw things at the TV set many evenings in impotent frustration at what I thought was the distorted picture being beamed out, I'm well aware that one man's imagined consensual portrait is another's wicked distortion. But I try.

I had one of my most entertaining experiences lecturing in the United States in April 2002, at the annual conference in Washington of the American Israel Public Affairs Committee, AIPAC, the influential pro-Israel lobby group. Rather than giving a formal address, I was invited to host a "town hall" meeting: to make the briefest of introductory remarks, then try to deal with anything the audience wanted to ask me. The crowd was good-natured and informed, an encouraging combination, and, it turned out, prepared to be self-deprecating, too—icing on the cake. The most interesting segment began when a man near the back stood up and barked out, "Why don't you just kill Arafat? That'll change everything for the better, won't it?"—or words to that effect. This earned considerable, though not universal, applause. Then someone else called out that, far from killing Arafat, Israel should be negotiating with him—this being the only way out. There was more applause, this from a different segment of the audience. And then there was a groundswell of self-deprecating laughter at the inherent contradiction. To offer a case study in conflict problem solving, I turned the suggestions back to the audience, asking them to imagine for a moment that they were Israel's prime minister, and to run through the options and likely repercussions vis-à-vis Arafat.

As I remember it, we first talked through the pros and cons of Israel eliminating Arafat—easily done, but sure to generate a torrent of international opprobrium, led by our shocked friends in the United States, and who knows what kinds of military and terrorist acts of revenge by our neighbors and their pet extremists. And in killing Arafat, we'd also be killing off any foreseeable hope of negotiation, since every Palestinian advocate of reconciliation would be discredited due to Israel's murder of the chairman.

From there, we turned to the possibility of dispatching him into exile, the "solution" favored by Netanyahu. This could not be so easily accomplished, we agreed, given Arafat's credible insistence that he would rather die a martyr than voluntarily submit to deportation—in which case, we'd be back at unhelpful option one. But assuming he could be enticed aboard an outbound plane, would that help? I asked. It might create a vacuum that a more reasonable figure might leap to fill, someone suggested. But not necessarily, I countered, given the fury Israel's deportation of their elected president would engender among Palestinians. And we would have to endure the sight of the aggrieved Arafat overseas, now liberated by Israel from any lingering responsibility to confront terrorism, and free to stir up as much anti-Israeli sentiment as he could.

At the other extreme, there was the choice of turning a blind eye to Arafat's terrorist recidivism and taking another stab at negotiation with him. That might yield at least some kind of a cease-fire, but how viable would such a course be, given the abysmal record of accords violated? And so we were left, we agreed, with what might be described as the least worst option, the one that the Sharon government had been pursuing: attempting to marginalize Arafat, refusing to deal directly with him and leaving him to fester in Ramallah until such time as the penny finally dropped for his abused people and they booted him upstairs or sideways, or he passed away naturally, and maybe, just maybe, somebody better would come along in his place.

While, unsurprisingly, we stumbled across no revolutionary ideas, the discussion that day did bring home some of the complexities that can get lost over the thousands of miles between here and there. These were people who, by virtue of their very presence at the convention, really cared about Israel, wanted to rally for Israel and, not unnaturally, also wanted to tell Israel what they thought it ought to do. But it's one thing to demand the ouster of Arafat, or his rehabilitation, for that matter, or any other dramatic new policy, from a vantage point a continent away. It's quite another when you have to live with the consequences if it turns out to have been a bad idea.

It doesn't always work out as well as it did at AIPAC. I had some depressing run-ins concerning Rabbi Michael Lerner, editor of an American Jewish magazine called *Tikkun,* who in the early summer of 2002 sent out an e-mail to I don't know how many addresses he had somehow accumulated, mine included, inviting "special people" to a gathering in California. Its aim, Lerner said, would be "to deal with a difficult issue: the Denial [he used a capital *D* for emphasis] rampant in the Jewish world about the role that Israel is playing inflicting pain and violating human rights in Palestine and the way Israeli policies are starting to generate all kinds of anger against the Jewish people."

Lerner wrote that he wanted Israel to survive as a Jewish state and noted that his own children had served in the army, but he went on to assert—from the safety of the United States, I should add—that "the people of Israel . . . really are not as vulnerable as they perceive themselves to be," and that he therefore sought to formulate "a strategy to break through the levels of Denial so that we can help the Jewish people acknowledge what is wrong in what Israel is doing."

As ill luck would have it, Lerner's e-mail landed on my work computer during a ten-day period that saw the suicide bombing by Arafat's Al-Aqsa

Brigades near an ice-cream parlor in Petah Tikva (May 27) in which Chen Keinan's mother and baby were killed; Albert Malul shot dead in his car in the West Bank (May 28); three teenage boys gunned down during a basketball game at the West Bank settlement of Itamar (May 29); and seventeen people blown to pieces by an Islamic Jihad suicide bomber at Megiddo Junction (June 5). So my sympathies for those who lectured to me from San Francisco to the effect that "the people of Israel . . . really are not as vulnerable as they perceive themselves to be" were not at their height. I wrote a withering column about Lerner in *The Jerusalem Report.* Specifically, since the rabbi, in his condescension and self-deception, was asserting that Israelis and their supporters didn't really know what was going on out here, I urged him to hold his get-together not, as planned, at a "retreat center" in the San Francisco area, but in Jerusalem or Tel Aviv—or, perhaps, in a marquee at the just-bombed Megiddo Junction.

The column generated a heated debate on our letters pages, with some forceful missives from assailants of the rabbi, and others, equally forceful, from his defenders, one of whom misrepresented my position as being that since Israelis are the victims of this conflict, "all of the violence we perpetrate is to be excused." My point was, and is, as I wrote at the time in suggesting that Lerner and his adherents gather here, that they and we should of course take note of what was occurring at the roadblocks and in cities under curfew—the daily humiliations imposed upon ordinary Palestinians. But they should also visit those whose loved ones had been murdered by Palestinian attackers, and hear briefings about the innumerable bombings thwarted by those roadblocks, and about the bomb factories destroyed and the lifesaving intelligence information obtained during the army incursions. And they should remember that the stringent security measures had not been in place before the conflict exploded in September 2000, when Barak was trying to make peace with Arafat, and that those measures would be ended, and hundreds of thousands of Palestinians could return to jobs inside Israel and start to heal their economy, the moment the attacks on our populace ceased—the moment the Palestinian leadership changed its strategy. Lerner should be reminded, in short, that the way to stop the futile deaths on both sides, first and foremost, required a simple end to terrorism, not a complex formulation of strategy.

I'm more than ready to accept that Lerner is a good-hearted man who was dismayed by the sight of Israeli tanks besieging Palestinian towns, and shamed as we all were by the frequent killings of Palestinian civilians by Israeli troops in the heat, and shade, of this conflict. And I fully understand the attractions for people like Lerner of arguing that the orchestrated terrorism employed against us was, fundamentally, our fault. Because then we would have had the power, unilaterally, to create the conditions for its cessation. Israel could have made it all better, and those of us—Lerner and myself most certainly among them—who wished we hadn't had to resort to the use of our Israel Defense Forces against militants given shelter in residential neighborhoods would then have been able to bask in the reflected glory of our pure, ultrahumane Israel. Would that it had been so. If only Abraham and Moses had set up shop in New Zealand. In fact, though, Lerner was closing his eyes to the facts and buying into the vile falsehood that depicted Palestinian terrorism as a desperate resort to violence by a people seeking only viable statehood and denied all other means to attain it. In my column, I suggested that Lerner owed us "special people" a letter of apology, and asked that he kindly remove my name from his mailing list. I haven't had the apology, but then, I haven't received any more of his e-mails, either.

. . . • . . .

On lecture tours abroad, I found that Jewish audiences tended to be overwhelmingly supportive of Israel, although concerned, depending on their personal perspectives, about either Israel's unwillingness to take more forceful measures to "wipe out" terror—like the United States in Afghanistan and Iraq—or its overreliance on military might. They were also concerned for their own well-being, increasingly worried by incidents of anti-Semitism—an airport shooting in Los Angeles, a murder in Toronto, a synagogue daubing in Britain—and fully aware of how what happens in Israel, and how it is perceived, can directly affect their lives.

It was a depressing reflection of how unrelentingly terrifying here looked from there that, especially after the conflict markedly heated up in about December 2001, the very fact of my having flown in from Israel to speak with these groups became something for which I was congratulated and applauded. "We wish we could be there with you," people told me, stroking my arm. "It's fantastic that you're doing what you're doing." All I was doing was trying to raise my family in what I wished were a safer Jewish homeland. (When I was abroad, it took me days to conquer the instinctual nausea that a wailing siren brought in Jerusalem; my office is about two hundred yards from the Red Shield of David ambulance depot, so my subconscious triggered alarms whenever there was a particularly importunate siren wail. It took me days, too, to realize that I could afford to relax and stop looking suspiciously at every bag-carrying fellow shopper in a supermarket, or every browser in a Barnes & Noble.)

A minority of Jews, from the United States and elsewhere, made second Intifada "solidarity" visits to Israel. Despite cries of alarm from anxious relatives, the participants planned these visits because they felt, quite rightly, that they were proving themselves true supporters of Israel, prepared to put their bodies in the potential line of fire, standing by Israel in bad times as well as good. Many, many more, though, stayed well away from the combat zone. All the time, people asked me about some upcoming solidarity trip: Should they go? Should they let their teenage son or daughter go? How safe was it? Was it as dangerous as it looked? I had no definitive answers for them. I told them that security for the solidarity missions was intense; that obviously the organizers would do everything to keep them away from potential danger; that you could get run over and killed, heaven forbid, crossing the road that very afternoon. But the missions were psychologically crucial both for the Israeli populace and for the visitors: making plain to Israelis that at least part of Diaspora Jewry was with them, and giving the visitors the chance to understand our reality firsthand, to form their own impressions and conclusions and to spread whatever message they thought appropriate when they got back home. Some of the members of these groups were conspicuously hardier than I am: A party of Brits in their thirties and forties asked me during a midmorning meet how, if at all, my life had changed, and whether, for instance, I'd take my kids out for pizza at the rebuilt Sbarro downtown. "No, I wouldn't," I told them candidly. "It seems like an unnecessary risk." Only later did I find out that the reference to Sbarro was not random; that was where they were scheduled to lunch. And despite my comment, they went ahead as planned.

The most unpleasant audience I tried to communicate with was at Concordia University in Montreal, which has more Palestinians in the student body than pretty much any other campus in North America. I was speaking at an Israel Day event on the campus when a sizable band of Palestinian hecklers gathered. The organizers hadn't provided me with the key tool a speaker needs to overcome such disruptions: a microphone. But after we'd shouted at one another for a while, we got to debating, which was a lot better, and a stark contrast to the violent attacks on would-be audience members there a year later during a visit by Netanyahu, who was eventually forced by local police to cancel his talk. Weeks after that, Concordia attracted still more notoriety by becoming the first campus to ban its Hillel Jewish student organization.

I was actually anxious to speak to audiences that included Palestinians. I wanted to stress that everyone was losing out in a bloody confrontation that had superseded a partnership in which we could all be winners.

At a winter 2002 event at the Hillel House at New York University in lower Manhattan, two Palestinian women asked potent, inflamed questions. The first described in harrowing detail how the Israeli army had taken over the home of friends of hers in Jenin and had left it in chaos, with human excrement all over the floor. She related another instance in which soldiers had gone to a friend's home. Looking for a resident who wasn't there and who they alleged was involved in terrorism, they had arrested his brother instead and knocked down the building, leaving the family homeless. I told her that I, too, had heard stories of soldiers looting and spoiling homes, and that such action was indefensible. I also said, as always, that the army and Israel as a whole had no desire to be back in the cities, and had been dragged back by terrorism. (A couple of days earlier, the *New York Times* had carried a nuanced, well-observed piece about Israeli reservists deployed in the newly reoccupied town of Nablus following more suicide bombings; the article had focused on the senior officer, who had been pulled away from his high-tech job. As the piece made crystal clear, that officer wanted nothing less than to be out of Nablus, a city where Israel had voluntarily relinquished control seven years earlier.) As for the second family, I said that government policy was to knock down the homes only of those alleged to have orchestrated acts of terrorism, such as suicide bombings—a policy that, for all its appalling consequences for the family, had proven effective in persuading relatives of some would-be bombers to have them rethink that decision or, failing that, to turn them in to the authorities, thus saving innocent people from a fate yet more appalling than being made homeless. "Well, I think there will never be peace," she said by way of response.

The second Palestinian woman accused me of not telling the full truth when asserting that Barak had offered to relinquish almost all of the West Bank at Camp David. "You didn't say that the Barak offer didn't give control of the border or of the airspace," she pointed out. And she was right. Barak didn't want to cede those controls, at least for the foreseeable future. And I hadn't said so. I apologized and explained why—an argument that could be summed up as "In the short term, at least, we don't trust you."

At the end of the event, I noted how stark a contrast the tenor of our evening made to the screaming intolerance I'd encountered at Concordia, or to the stories I'd been told days earlier by some of the Jewish students at Berkeley, where the head of the campus Hillel group had been ordered to leave a Palestinian meeting at which he was merely sitting in to listen, and despite his having formally registered to attend, as required.

From my experiences on American campuses, it looked like students were right back where they had been before Oslo: years of cooperation between pro-Israeli and pro-Palestinian groups at an end, and a propaganda war in progress, complete with boycott calls and divestment campaigns, at times spilling over into violence. At Berkeley, for instance, there had been several cases of Jews being attacked on or near the campus, and graffiti had been daubed on the doors of the Hillel. Several students told me they had been beaten up in the course of a "symbolic" roadblock demonstration organized by pro-Palestinian groups. The "divest from Israel" campaign was gathering pace, if not critical mass—a malicious effort to characterize Israel as the South Africa of the new millennium, a country that would be brought to its senses by the destruction of its economy. As elsewhere, Palestinian spokespeople on campus tended to be hugely more effective than their Israeli counterparts, purveying subtly false information about what had been offered by Israel for peace, and the reasons for Palestinian rejection of it. Good liberals on campuses like Berkeley apparently believed that their instinctual sympathies should be with the Palestinians and against the Israelis, rather than with the humane people on both sides and against the extremists.

On some campuses, Berkeley most definitely included, Jewish students were mounting a robust defense—merely by learning the facts of the dispute and effectively disseminating them. On others, the Jewish students had given up the struggle, or never cared enough to fight it. On some campuses where I had been invited by Jewish hosts, I encountered more anti-Israeli than pro-Israeli or even open-minded audience members. Again, that was fine by me, but it was a worrying sign of Jewish apathy.

At Guildford College in Greensboro, North Carolina, a planned discussion with Jewish and Muslim students didn't quite materialize, because the Jewish students didn't bother to, or couldn't, come. The Palestinians who attended, though, were a pleasure to meet with. Five or six of them had joined the college quite recently from the Ramallah area, and they heard me out on the Israel perception of Arafat and asked real questions about Israeli unwillingness to grant full independence to the Palestinians. One of the students, Anwar (not his real name), asked me by what right a non-Jewish Russian could get to live in his homeland, where he said Jews had never previously had a country, while his own parents, who had lived there for generations, still had no independence.

Quite a zinger, that. I acknowledged that the "Jewishness" of some of the immigrants from the former Soviet Union did not meet Orthodox halakhic standards. But if they were Jewish enough to have qualified for genocide under Hitler, I reasoned, then they were Jewish enough to merit a place in the Jewish homeland. As for the deeper question of independence, I said that he and his parents had every right to it, had always had, and would have achieved it had their leaders let them in 1948, but that it had to be independence alongside us, not at our expense. The Jews have thousands of years of history there, I told him. The Israelites were the Palestinians long before the Palestinians were.

He was gently disparaging: Don't be silly, he insisted. The Jews all arrived from Europe, and not that long ago, either.

They told me I was exaggerating the importance of Sari Nusseibeh, who they said was widely disliked and seen as egotistical. And, anyway, it wasn't for me to select their leaders. I told them I wasn't trying to, and that I'd highlighted Nusseibeh only as someone who was putting his life at risk to try to champion potentially viable peace terms. The argument was good-natured, though, and when I asked them if they could live with the Clinton bridging proposals, some of them said yes, one said it wasn't for him to decide for the refugees, but none said no. "So I guess we, in this little room, could probably make peace," I said, and they nodded their assent.

It was cold outside, but we were sitting in what was called "the Hut," an intimate, convivial campus meeting place with a log fire crackling merrily and mugs of steaming tea at hand. I imagined it was the kind of atmosphere the Oslo negotiators must have constructed for themselves, all Christmassy goodwill to all men, warmth and cheer, with the real world a long, long way away.

. . . • . . .

On Monday, December 23, 2002, our episode of *The West Wing,* "Night Five" (first shown in the States ten months earlier), was about terrorism and the Middle East again. In our real world at the time, the White House was coming under behind-the-scenes pressure to water down the essence of President Bush's address of June 24, 2002. The peacemaking quartet—the representatives of the United States, Russia, the UN and the EU—was in the process of redrafting the so-called road map to peace, a blueprint intended to end the conflict and bring the Palestinians to statehood; it had initially been accepted by Israel, but now, it was being reported, other members of the quartet wanted to water down Bush's demand for the replacement of Arafat's terrorist leadership strata as an absolutely firm precondition for progress toward Palestinian independence. The State Department was apparently encouraging some of the changes in language and emphasis. The White House was said not to be too pleased. In Jerusalem, Sharon's aides were publicly apoplectic.

Back in the fictional White House, President Bartlet's speechwriters were coincidentally coming under pressure to tone down a tough-worded presidential address to the United Nations General Assembly, a message aimed at the Arab world and designed to signal zero tolerance for terrorism. Toby Ziegler, the fictional White House director of communications, was arguing over the text, with its demand for an end to "the crushing yoke of Islamic fanaticism," with his ex-wife, Andrea Wyatt, a Democratic congresswoman. She and some colleagues wanted to add two sentences to minimize the sting: "Our goal is neither to preach nor proclaim American values," the suggested insert ran. "We have a great deal to learn from the values of tolerance and faith that are deeply held throughout the Islamic world."

But Toby wouldn't hear of it. "Guess what," he told her, "our goal *is* to proclaim American values. . . . The United States of America no longer sucks up to reactionaries, and our staunch allies will know who we mean."

"We don't have any staunch allies in the Arab world, just reluctant ones," Andrea objected, not unreasonably. "What's Egypt going to think, or Pakistan?"

Toby was still unflinching: "That freedom and democracy are coming soon to a theater near them."

Andrea tried one last time: "You have to get off your horse and just, simply put, be nice to the Arab world."

But by now, Toby was in full flow. "Be nice?" he ridiculed. The United States foolishly, he said, "instead of blowing Iraq back to the seventh century for harboring terrorists and trying to develop nuclear weapons," had merely imposed economic sanctions, and was "reviled by the Arab world" nonetheless. (This, of course, was before the spring 2003 war in Iraq.) The United States had "pushed Israel to give up land for peace," Toby said. It had sent troops to protect Saudi Arabia, "and the Arab world told us we were desecrating their holy land while ignoring the fact that we were invited." There could be no more being nice. The fanatics were coming for America now, he reminded her. "Thousands of madrasas teaching children nothing, nothing, nothing but the Koran and to hate America."

The argument was clearly won. Andrea nodded meekly. "Okay," she said. And in our living room, I said to Lisa, "Wow. The *West Wing* writers finally got it."

Then, as Andrea made to leave Toby's office, he called her back. "Let me take another look at the softer language," he said.

11.

A Way out of the Deadlock

Standing outside the B'nai Jeshurun synagogue on the Upper West Side of Manhattan on a cold night in October 2002, I felt unusually at home for an Israeli abroad. Police barriers had been set up around the entrance to the synagogue. Those going in were carefully searched by Hebrew-speaking security men, and across the street a few dozen right-wing demonstrators were angrily denouncing all entrants as "shameful." The protesters had gathered to oppose the evening's event, which saw Sari Nusseibeh in a dialogue with a leading Israeli Peace Now activist, Hebrew University professor Galia Golan. Distributing pamphlets branding Nusseibeh a supporter of suicide bombers, and loudly condemning him as a terrorist, they had formulated a catchy slogan, which they kept repeating: "Get it in your head, Sari wants you dead."

I had come because, having given a lecture earlier that day on the nearby campus of Columbia University, my evening was free and I wanted to hear what Nusseibeh would have to say to what I assumed would be a left-wing American Jewish audience. I'd interviewed Nusseibeh a couple of times and run into him over the years at demonstrations and in TV studios. And I cautiously respected him as the president of a university, Al-Quds, that had unusually maintained ties during the Intifada with Israeli institutions of higher education, as a prominent figure who had bravely taken unpopular public positions—against suicide bombings in Israel and for circumscribing the "right of return" so as not to threaten Israel's demographic balance—and as a voice of authority who had derided the Arafat-led effort to deny Jews' historical ties to Jerusalem. I say "cautiously," however, because he had also made comments at odds with his professed abhorrence for violence.

When everybody was finally checked and seated, which took a while, and the talking began, it turned out that some of the demonstrators had had the common sense to forsake the barricades and enter the auditorium, where their heckling would have more impact. Golan spoke first, and they were quite easy on her. Perhaps they were still getting themselves organized. When Nusseibeh came to the microphone, a self-effacing, bespectacled figure with gray hair and matching jacket, he accurately depicted a bleak recent past and present of hostility and hopelessness, and a future just the same—unless there was a "return to negotiation and to reason." The mistake the Oslo architects had made, he said, was to "hide the sensitive issues." This time around, those issues had to be dealt with "head-on." The settlers had to be evacuated. Jerusalem had to be shared. And then he added his clincher: Refugees had to "exercise their right of return to the Palestinian state only."

The first two of those three demands were, predictably and prolongedly, booed by the right-wingers, most of whom were gradually ejected by a colossal Israeli security guard. But they could hardly heckle Nusseibeh for the third demand—the one that was getting him death threats from Palestinian groups. By declaring that pragmatism over the "right of return" is crucial to the success of any renewed attempt at peacemaking, Nusseibeh cuts through the pro-Arafat propagandists' contention that the failure of the Camp David summit and the subsequent Intifada were primarily a consequence of Israel's refusal to end the occupation, and accurately places the refugee issue at the heart of the dispute. As he had once, months earlier, said to me: "How can we Palestinians expect Israel to think we want coexistence when our position on the refugee issue has been tantamount to a call for Israel's destruction?"

Here at B'nai Jeshurun, Nusseibeh explained his stance in the most commonsensical terms: It was not that he rejected the desire for a return by Palestinian refugees to the homes they and their ancestors had left inside sovereign Israel. It was, rather, that this return was impractical. And a second right, a right to freedom, Nusseibeh went on, was just as important. So if the Palestinians chose to go on insisting on the full right of return, he predicted disconsolately, they would be "fighting with the Israelis for generations to come. And after the blood is spilled, it will not be clear that [we] will have been able to realize that right." Whereas, he suggested, if the Palestinians opted to establish a state alongside Israel, and give all refugees their right to citizenship there, they would be realizing the right to freedom. "Far better to tell the refugee mother, who has given birth even today to a child in one of the camps, not to raise that child waiting another fifty years for a dream that will never be realized. Far better to bring that child into what is also her homeland, in freedom."

The Palestinian leadership, Nusseibeh went on, had to make the emphatic choice for freedom, waive the right to a return to Israel and do so publicly. It was not enough for leaders in private to assure the Israelis that they didn't really seek a refugee influx to Israel that would destroy the Jewish state demographically. "It has to say to the Palestinian people that it has made that choice," making clear to ordinary Palestinians that the dream of return was over, and making clear to disheartened Israelis that coexistence might be viable after all. The fact was, he observed (now enjoying an audience silence that had prevailed since the last of the hecklers was ejected), that we had long since passed the time for wheeling and dealing between negotiators. "This is a negotiation for our lives and those of our children. And rather than show cleverness, we have to be wise."

Nusseibeh ended by confronting the allegation that he supported suicide bombers, insisting that he had "always been against any kind of violence, against any kind of civilian"—a declaration that brought ringing applause. In the question-and-answer session, he was asked how much support his views had among Palestinians, and he responded candidly that he didn't know. He wasn't the only one advocating such policies, but there wasn't exactly a crowd.

In a speech at Hebrew University in the fall of 2001, Nusseibeh had spoken out even more strongly against the armed Intifada, declaring rightly that its violence had "alienated even moderate Israelis. . . . We're telling the Israelis that we're going to kick you out: It's not that we want liberation, freedom and independence in the West Bank and Gaza; we want to kick you out of your home," he said of the Palestinians. "And in order to make sure that the Israelis get the message, people go out to a disco or a restaurant and blow themselves up. The whole thing is just crazy, ugly, totally counterproductive."

And in that speech and in other comments, prominently reported in the

Palestinian media, he had made even plainer his belief that the Arafat stance on the refugees had to change. "The Palestinians have to realize that if we are to reach an agreement on two states," he said, "then those two states will have to be one for the Israelis and one for the Palestinians, not one for the Palestinians and the other also for the Palestinians."

I should stress that for many Israelis, Nusseibeh does not offer comfortable terms for a solution. He is adamant that Israel must return to its 1967 borders, including in Jerusalem, allowing only for the possibility of minor border modifications. And appallingly, even though he chose not to highlight this in his B'nai Jeshurun address, he has expressed a degree of sympathy for suicide bombers and even implied endorsement for bombings and other attacks on Israeli soldiers. According to literature disseminated not by his opponents, but by Peace Now, in his defense, to participants at his B'nai Jeshurun appearance, he told an Al-Jazeera interviewer in July 2002 that every Palestinian feels respect "for every resistance fighter and every jihad fighter and everyone who believes that there is no life possible under occupation . . . and no life other than independence and honor." And that "one must also distinguish between the martyrdom seeker who targets military targets and one who targets civilian targets."

I suppose that my problem with Nusseibeh is the very problem that he acknowledged in his Hebrew University speech: that the uprising has alienated me, rendered a potential ally mistrustful. The last purportedly moderate PLO official in Jerusalem, Faisal Husseini, died on May 31, 2001, having given a controversial "final interview" to Arab journalist Shafiq Ahmad Ali, in which he appeared to reveal that he had been fooling Israel down the years with his embrace of coexistence and really saw the Oslo process as a "Trojan Horse," used to make the first inroads through Israel's defenses in order to facilitate our eventual downfall. "We are ambushing the Israelis and cheating them," Husseini was quoted as saying. "If we agree to declare our state over what is now 22 percent of Palestine, meaning the West Bank and Gaza, our ultimate goal is the liberation of all historic Palestine from the river to the sea."

I had been a tentative admirer of Husseini's, and I still don't know quite what to make of that so-called final interview, whose authenticity has always been denied by his defenders. And I won't let myself be swept away by Nusseibeh. Why did he make those Al-Jazeera comments of his, as he sat alongside a Hamas spokesman and a suicide bomber's mother, defending a petition he had initiated calling for an end to attacks on civilians inside Israel? Was Nusseibeh trying to win over a dubious Palestinian public by trying not to alienate it? Or did his remarks show his condemnation of violence to be halfhearted? Likewise, that petition itself: Was he pragmatically tempering his message to appeal to a hostile Palestinian target audience by basing his demand for a halt to the killing of Israelis on the damage being done to the Palestinian cause? Was that why he failed to condemn suicide bombings bluntly in general? Was that why he issued no call for an end to attacks on Israelis in the West Bank and Gaza Strip? Or was the petition deliberately worded to imply a pernicious subtext—that killing soldiers and settlers was admirable, and that other violence against civilians in Israel was fine, too, in principle, but merely had to be suspended temporarily because it was alienating supporters of the Palestinian cause and thereby delaying rather than advancing their goals?

I don't have definitive answers to these questions. But I do feel, definitively, that people like Nusseibeh should be put to the test, for Israel's sake. Nusseibeh was manifestly not Arafat's lackey: Even as he served as Arafat's diplomatic point man in Jerusalem through most of 2002, Arafat was ridiculing him behind his back. "Sari who?" he would scoff in interviews, going on to declare that he, Arafat, certainly wouldn't be giving up on the refugees. And in late 2002, Arafat shifted Nusseibeh aside as the PLO's Jerusalem representative. Nusseibeh had been struggling to get money from the PA for his university. He was said to have known that he put his life in danger when he set foot in the Old City, and that in Jenin, too, there was a price on his head. It would be a shame, to put it mildly, if Israel were to recognize the potential for a path back to sanity offered by the likes of Nusseibeh only after such threats were realized.

Yet the Sharon government's response to Nusseibeh was to close down his university intermittently and take him into custody—including briefly, of all absurdities, on the day in December 2001 that he was hosting a reception at a Jerusalem hotel to mark the Muslim feast of Eid al-Fitr, at the end of the holy month of Ramadan.

. . . • . . .

Sharon's attitude to figures of potential change like Nusseibeh underlined what I consider to have been the central failure of his first term as prime minister, between 2001 and 2003—the refusal to encourage the very moderate Palestinian leadership that he claimed to seek as an alternative to the reviled Arafat.

Sharon remained resolute in demanding more of the unsuccessful same—pressing for "complete military victory" before so much as talking about resuming peace negotiations. This despite the fact that "complete military victory" was a bloodily demonstrable oxymoron: For every "wanted" man Israel killed off, for every bomber stopped en route, another two, three or four were added to the ever-widening circle of violence. Almost three-quarters of the most dangerous terrorists were said by the army to have been captured or killed during Operation Defensive Shield in April 2002; their places evidently were not too hard to fill. The more draconian the measures Israel imposed to try to thwart terrorism—from house demolitions, to targeted strikes and curfews and closures, and finally to full reoccupation of the West Bank—the more Palestinians were motivated to join the "resistance." No one would argue with Sharon about the need to do everything to prevent terrorism, but that "everything" had to include offering what might be termed a *political horizon.* As it confronts terror, in other words, Israel, for its own sake, must provide incentives for Palestinian moderation—concrete evidence of its desire for peace on viable terms. As an official at the Defense Ministry complex in Tel Aviv put it to me in late 2002: "There is no military solution, we know. Our tragedy is that, at present, there is no political solution, either. A different Palestinian leadership is required, to take responsibility, confront the Islamic extremists. That means no Arafat. And they need some incentive. Today we say, 'If you continue with the terrorism, we'll do this, that,' all sorts of terrible things. That's the stick. But there's no carrot for 'If you halt the terror. If you sit with us . . .' "

Sharon did everything but provide carrots. He said, proudly, that he did not intend to dismantle a single settlement. Indeed, he described Netzarim, a small enclave where thirty Jewish families live in the heart of the Gaza Strip, as being as important to him as Tel Aviv. While he said that he would grudgingly accede to independence for the Palestinians, he indicated that the state he had in mind for them would cover barely 50 percent of the West Bank, if that. With all the settlements still in place, this was a "solution" no Palestinian would ever accept. Nor was it fair or just. And if that was the best to which they could aspire through peaceful negotiation, why would moderate Palestinians risk their lives and challenge the extremists for an end to Intifada killing?

And yet Israelis forgave Sharon this failure—this central failure to create conditions for life to get better here—even as they indicated in poll after poll, through 2001, 2002 and into 2003, that they were determined to get back to the negotiating table and formulate terms for a peace accord. For much of 2002, indeed, a majority of Israelis were telling the opinion surveyors that they favored negotiations even on the basis of the Saudi peace initiative—which provides for a return to the 1967 borders and a just solution for the refugees—an initiative Sharon cold-shouldered. They forgave Sharon for one simple reason: Yasser Arafat. Arafat is why Sharon got elected in 2001. It's why Sharon got reelected in 2003. Israelis were desperate for peace. Most were committed to territorial compromise. They just didn't believe it was viable so long as Arafat was calling the shots, literally, on the Palestinian side. And no political leader rose to offer an alternative political path to that of Sharon, the appropriate path: confronting terrorism while simultaneously providing encouragement for the likes of Nusseibeh to risk their lives in the cause of a nonviolent future. It was hellish living here after September 2000, but for me and many like me, that was compounded by the sense that our leaders did not offer us any path out of it. We were desperately trying to keep our families safe, while our political masters, maddeningly, were promising us only more of the same, or worse.

In February 2001, Sharon ran for election as Israel's prime minister with a slogan that claimed "Only Sharon can bring peace." When asked during the campaign how he would do so, he dodged the question. "Count on me," he said; "I have a plan." Few people believed it, but they voted for him anyway, 62 to 37 percent, by far the widest victory margin in any Israeli election. Sharon was probably the Israeli politician most reviled in the Arab world—a legacy of his stewardship of the 1982 invasion of Lebanon and the massacres in the Sabra and Shatilla refugee camps. But that war had made Sharon controversial, to put it mildly, inside Israel as well. Having ruled that Sharon should have realized what might occur when the Christian Phalangist gunmen were sent into the camps, and taken steps to prevent this, Israel's Kahan Commission ordered him stripped of the Defense Ministry portfolio. A large, probably overwhelming, proportion of the Israeli public regards that war as having been an appalling mistake, a bound-to-fail endeavor to install a more convenient government in Beirut, an invasion initiated through hubris and arrogance and a certain amount of deception, and one that wasted hundreds of young lives. If Sharon could no longer serve as minister of defense after the commission had issued its report, it was widely thought inconceivable that he might ever go one better and become prime minister.

He won in 2001, and won so by such a huge majority, not because the Israeli public had suddenly changed its mind about him and come to regard him as a savior. He won, rather, because Israelis so loathed the man in the khaki fatigues and the black-and-white kaffiyeh. Sharon's triumph in 2001 was not an Israeli endorsement of his policies. He barely presented any. Nor was it a vote against Barak, the humiliated incumbent, who had inaccurately described the elections as "a referendum on peace." (A Tel Aviv University survey at the time showed 77 percent of Israelis "somewhat" or "greatly" supportive of the peace process. That wasn't the point.) It was, most of all, a vote against Arafat—Israelis saying, essentially, that they had tried everything they knew to make peace with the Palestinian leader. Their last prime minister had offered as much, if not more, than Israel could ever offer in the quest for coexistence, and he had been slapped in the face. They could hardly reelect him, only to have him slapped down again. And the only other candidate they were offered was Sharon. Abu Mazen was to acknowledge precisely this a year and a half later, as Sharon campaigned, successfully, for reelection: "Some of these people said at the beginning that the Intifada would bring down Sharon. . . . Actually, Sharon did not fall because the Intifada deviated from its proper path. I think that Sharon today is the most important leader the Zionist movement has known since Herzl. Even he did not have the 80 percent support that Sharon does."

Sharon maintained his popularity by working within the national consensus. He faced pressure from the right to ratchet up the degree of military force used against the Palestinians, and from the left to restrain the army. But survey after survey showed a vast majority of Israelis approving the responses he oversaw to terrorist attacks, even the destruction of ministries and other, non-military-related installations, as part of the deliberate neutering of the entire Palestinian Authority. Few Israelis held Sharon primarily responsible for shattering intermittent cease-fire hopes, even when the Israeli assassination of a Palestinian activist prompted further bombings and an end to one brief lull or another. That is because few

Israelis believed that Arafat sought an end to the conflict, and no Israelis believed that Hamas and Islamic Jihad wanted anything but to keep on killing Jews. "We cannot recognize Israel ever," Hamas spokesman Abdel Aziz Rantisi confirmed for all our benefit in the winter of 2002. The main goal of the current conflict was "to liberate the West Bank, Gaza and Jerusalem," Rantisi added, only because, temporarily, "we haven't the force to destroy Israel." But they'd get there in the end, he was confident, and he added, "It is forbidden in our religion to give up part of the land."

The bombers' own strategy was probably the most important factor in the sense of unity that flourished under Sharon. They chose to target Israelis everywhere, not just soldiers and settlers in disputed territory. And in doing so, they managed to render the political differences between Israelis—between champions and opponents of settlement, rightists and leftists—which remained as profound as ever, irrelevant for the time being. Since everybody was under attack, everybody had to stand together. As the PA's own deputy planning minister, Adli Sadeq, stated in the *Al-Hayat Al-Jadida* newspaper, in a post–Israeli election lament, "The Palestinian position today would not have met the terms even of the defeated [leftist] Meretz [party]. . . . Any government that can come to power in the Hebrew state will demand from us a clear-cut strategy, which must include at least that the Palestinians are not targeting all Israelis." (The reference to Meretz, the Zionist political party that had most passionately championed a dialogue with Arafat long before the Oslo process began, was significant: Meretz crashed from ten Knesset seats to six in the 2003 elections. Asked why so many Israelis had abandoned it, the Meretz leader, Yossi Sarid, said that his mistake had been not to renounce Arafat the moment the second Intifada erupted.)

Heaven forbid that this be misconstrued as encouragement of violence on my part, but it is unarguable that had they focused their attacks solely on the West Bank, Gaza and East Jerusalem, the bombers would not only have gained yet more international sympathy; they would also have fueled far greater divides within Israel—with the parents of soldiers opposed to the settlement enterprise furiously objecting to the deployment of their children to protect Jews living in areas where they did not think Jews should be, and parents from the settlements demanding protection, and claiming that if they were abandoned, all of Israel would fall. Crucially, if the Palestinian gunmen and bombers had set themselves a narrower goal, even a purportedly narrower goal, and concentrated their attacks on the territories, they might well have pushed Israel into a unilateral withdrawal. And, quite possibly, they would have so divided Israel as to tear the fabric of our society apart.

But such internal debate was muted as the armed Intifada raged, because Israelis felt that no matter how much they compromised territorially, it would not be enough—nothing would—to satisfy our enemies' ambition. The bombers and gunmen were telling us, in bloodred capital letters, in Haifa and Jerusalem, Beersheba and Hadera and Afula, that their aggression, and their ambition, did not stop at the Green Line. And their leadership, as even Palestinian commentators eventually acknowledged, was doing nothing to stop them. Why had the same Israeli public that voted overwhelmingly for Barak in 1999 now elected Sharon for a second time? asked Palestinian columnist Taufiq Abu Bakr in the *Al-Ayyam* daily a week after Sharon's reelection. "It was because of the policies of the Palestinian extremists and because the moderates in the Palestinian leadership wavered regarding curbing them . . . ," he answered. "The Palestinian extremists escalated their operations. . . . The question that should be thoroughly explored is why the Palestinian leadership has allowed them to do this."

Those behind the armed Intifada may have pleaded to the international community that this was only about ending the occupation, but on the ground they were plainly bent on terrorizing us all. In which case, most Israelis, right and left, felt they had better remain firm and united. Although the number of lives taken in terrorist attacks had never been higher, therefore, the climate of internal political debate on the Palestinian issue was relatively gentlemanly—and certainly nothing remotely paralleling the hysterical arguments that had raged in the Rabin years.

Sharon also adroitly constructed a firm relationship with President George Bush. He flew four, five, six times to meet with the new president at the White House, hammering home the same fundamental argument: The terrorism had to stop. And that had to be a precondition for any diplomatic progress. Anything else would be rewarding terror, and if you reward terror, it redoubles. As of June 2002, with Bush on his side, Sharon could tell the Israeli public that, under his stewardship, Israel and the United States were fighting shoulder-to-shoulder against the common enemy, and that no other Israeli leader could have effected such a partnership.

By January 2003, when Israel went to the polls again, there was little for which Sharon could claim credit. He had never come through with that promised 2001 plan to "bring peace." The armed Intifada was still raging. The commander of Israeli troops in Gaza had just estimated that the Palestinians there attempted a shooting or bombing every two hours. Death tolls continued to mount inexorably on both sides. Israel's economy was in free fall, its credit rating starting to slide, joblessness at 10 percent and rising. His own Likud party was embroiled in one of the most troubling political scandals in Israeli history, with allegations that criminals, using bribery and intimidation as well as more legitimate methods, had played a significant role in the process by which the Likud had selected its incoming roster of Knesset members, and the consequent fear that these politicians would be influenced by pressures from a sinister underworld. And Sharon was personally under a corruption cloud as well, over illegal campaign contributions.

Yet his Likud, though weakened, still came out on top, and Sharon won his second term. Arafat was a prime factor, but so, too, was Sharon's defeated electoral opponent, Labor leader Amram Mitzna, yet another ex-general turned politician, who came across, most unfortunately for him, as Barak with a beard and without the arrogance. A soft-spoken and successful mayor for the past decade in Haifa, a mixed Jewish-Muslim city, where he had proved that coexistence could flourish even in the tensest days at the start of the second Intifada, Mitzna is a conviction politician. But his convictions did not resonate with Israelis. Broadly, he spoke of returning to the Oslo process, reengaging with Arafat if necessary and opting for unilateral action, including the dismantling of settlements first in Gaza, then in the West Bank, if the diplomatic path proved impossible.

To my mind, Mitzna was as guilty as Sharon in offering an unrealistic blueprint. He said he would rather not talk to Arafat, but he would have done so if he had to. Well, what reason was he then offering to reform-minded Palestinians to risk their lives and challenge their autocratic leader? Why would Arafat have felt any pressure to step down or delegate some of his authority, or why would his people have pushed for him to do so, if, despite all the evidence tying him to terrorism, this Israeli leader would have rehabilitated him? I've heard compelling arguments in favor of Mitzna's talk of unilateral action—that it was a short- to medium-term means of reducing friction at a time when there was no prospect for substantive negotiations. But my feeling is that the very prospect of unilateral action would have guaranteed the collapse of any negotiations, even assuming they had ever resumed. Why would the Palestinians discuss compromise if you've told them you're ready to withdraw unilaterally if the discussions fail?

And what a victory for the bombers, and the argument so energetically purveyed by Hezbollah in south Lebanon: that if you hit the Israelis hard enough for long enough, they will break and run away. It worked for the guerrilla forces in south Lebanon, where Israel, having maintained the "security zone" as a buffer against Hezbollah and other armed groups, was losing two dozen soldiers a year on average through the 1990s. These losses prompted the foundation of the Four Mothers group, led by parents of soldiers serving in the zone—a narrow strip of south Lebanese territory extending all the way along the border—who demanded proof that the army's presence there was saving Israelis' lives on sovereign territory to the south. Their campaign won support from left and right, and in May 2000, honoring a campaign pledge to get out of Lebanon with or without an agreement, Prime Minister Barak brought the boys back home. It was an undignified withdrawal under fire, leaving behind great quantities of equipment and thousands of abandoned members of the South Lebanon Army, the Israeli-funded and -armed militia that had fought with the army in the zone. Hezbollah, delighted, vindicated and emboldened, promptly redeployed right up against the border fence, and told Palestinian groups that they now had a precedent to follow.

While far fewer lives have been lost since the withdrawal on the Lebanese frontier, Hezbollah's "success" there constituted phenomenal encouragement to Palestinian extremists, and thus the unilateral pullback contributed to the upsurge in Intifada attacks on Israel. Barak had hoped his withdrawal might be seen as evidence of a pragmatic readiness for compromise, and might even prompt peace moves from Syria and the Palestinians. But it was seen as capitulation, as weakness, and provoked more of the very violence, from Palestinian extremists, he had hoped to avoid. I put this to Mitzna a month before the January 2003 election. "So we shouldn't have pulled out of Lebanon?" he challenged me—a fair point, but hardly a full answer.

Mitzna said that if there could be no negotiated agreement, Israel should unilaterally withdraw from the loathed Gaza Strip, where seven thousand Jews in about twenty settlements require vast army resources for protection amid well over a million hostile Palestinians. And if no accord was forthcoming on the West Bank, either, he said, Israel should withdraw to a defensible line there, too, dismantling however many settlements that necessitated. It looked to me like the worst of all worlds: A large-scale pullback, of the order envisaged by Mitzna, leaving perhaps 15 or 20 percent of the West Bank in Israeli hands, would not have satisfied Palestinian territorial demands, but neither would the prospect of gaining the remaining West Bank territory have constituted sufficient incentive for a return to the diplomatic process. What a unilateral pullback would have constituted, however, was an invitation for the Palestinian terror groups to redouble their activities, and openly set up shop in Tulkarm and Kalkilya, with missiles ready to fire into sovereign Israel, ready for the final push.

Mitzna was the leading face of moderate Israel, but his positions were anything but moderate. To advocate unilateral withdrawal was to embrace the right-wing assertion that we can never make peace with the Palestinians, never find a Rabin or a Begin, a Sadat or a King Hussein, among their ranks; that we'll never have a partner and must therefore build the wall and resign ourselves to infinite generations of enmity and cross-border warfare. And it was a self-fulfilling defeatism, too, because the minute you declare that you'll pull out unilaterally if necessary, you've dealt a fatal blow to any faint hope of moderation. If unilateralism became Israeli government policy, any would-be Palestinian leader who stood up and argued passionately to his own people that terrorism was not only inhumane but counterproductive, and that the only way forward was nonviolence and negotiation, would be laughed out of town: If the Israelis were readying to pull out precisely because of the bombings and the shootings, the people would jeer, only an idiot would counsel a halt in favor of yet more unproductive negotiating sessions.

With Sharon on one side and Mitzna on the other, the elections of 2003 saw no one to champion the pragmatic political center. No wonder so many Israelis—almost one voter in six—cast their ballots for the Shinui party. Shinui was led by a canny ex-journalist, Yosef Lapid, who rose to prominence on a wave of public anger at ultra-Orthodox draft dodging. But he cannily projected himself as both a Mr. Clean and a Mr. Center by evading every effort to pin him down on his attitude to Palestinians, to confronting terror and to making peace.

. . . • . . .

Mitzna's unilateral pullback recipe was only one of several false panaceas created and advanced by Israelis desperate for a dramatic end to the deadlock—any end, as long as it came soon. It was up there with "transfer," the fanciful yet sometimes widely supported notion that Israel might somehow be able to rid itself of the Palestinians without paying a territorial price, by encouraging or forcing them to relocate to Jordan or another Arab host country. Morally deplorable, the idea is also unworkable: The Palestinians aren't about to up and leave. And nobody would take them in if they did. I'd like to believe that the overwhelming majority of Israelis recognize this: Herut, the only political party explicitly advocating transfer in the 2003 elections, failed to win a single Knesset seat, even though a spring 2002 Tel Aviv University survey had found a horrifying 46 percent of Israeli Jews expressing support for the policy. (The precedent says it all: In 1992, Prime Minister Rabin came up with the idea of deporting more than four hundred alleged Hamas ringleaders to Lebanon; I happened to be doing reserve duty as a guard in a Gaza jail on the night the orders came through to wake up some of the inmates for their unexpected bus journey north. But Rabin's hopes that these men would never darken our doorways again were dashed by the Lebanese authorities, who employed the simple expedient of refusing them entry. So they sat for a full winter in a tent village in no-man's-land, attracting international sympathy and forging a deeper community, intensifying their radical Islamic commitment in preparation for their return home. And home they eventually came, many of them to become kingpins of terror in the coming years.)

Another purported panacea, the West Bank "security fence," which was to become a source of controversy as its construction proceeded after Sharon's reelection, does offer a heightened degree of protection against bombers. But it is flawed, too: There is no possible demarcation that does not leave either Jews on the wrong, "unsafe" side of the fence, or Palestinians on the "safe" side. To be reasonably effective, the fence would have to stick fairly close to the old 1967 border, excluding most of the Palestinians—the physical expression of the right-wing bumper sticker du jour, circa fall 2002, NO ARABS, NO ATTACKS. But that would leave most of the 200,000 settlers beyond its protection. And relocating them would require the kind of unilateral action that seems so counterproductive, and would lead to bitter internal Israeli tensions as Jews were asked to leave their homes without the sacrifice advancing an agreed peace.

On the far right, in the search for a quick fix to the armed Intifada, they clamored for the government to "let the army off the leash" and "finish the job"—a demand heard most loudly when Labor was deemed to be restraining its Likud coalition partner. After Labor bolted in late 2002, such restraint was presumably removed, and yet the bombers kept coming.

On the other side of the spectrum, meanwhile, among the 1.2 million Israeli Arabs, a sense of alienation set in that was far more profound, I think, than most Israelis realize. To some extent, Israel has only itself to blame. Israeli Arabs share Israeli Jews' high life expectancy (mid-seventies for men and women, compared to late sixties in, say, Egypt); they benefit from the same low infant mortality rate (9 percent, compared to 25, 29 and 41 percent in Syria, Jordan and Egypt, respectively); and they enjoy high adult literacy (95 percent for men, 88 for women, compared to 66 and 43 percent, respectively, in Egypt). But Israel has paid lip service to the idea of equal citizenship in many areas down the decades: Financially, it has allocated woefully disproportionate funding to Arab local councils; psychologically, Israeli Arabs are not seen by the Jews as having an equal stake in the future of a state in which they are tolerated rather than embraced.

At the start of the 2001–2002 school year, Arab schools went on strike, in protest over the government's failure to build promised new classrooms and improve existing facilities. The standoff saw children sent to study, instead, in the mosques, in many of which posters of the recently slain PFLP leader Mustafa were on prominent display. I cannot conceive of a more self-destructive chain of events. We alienated the community still further in the first days of this Intifada, when police fatally shot thirteen Israeli Arabs in rioting that spread through much of Israel—deaths in the kinds of confrontations where, one suspects, had it been Jews facing off against cops, nonlethal ammunition might have been used.

But there's more than enough guilt to go around, and the Israeli Arab leadership did its fair bit to alienate Israeli Jews, too. In the fall of 2002, I attended a dialogue convened by President Moshe Katsav at his home, in which he sought to find a formula, as he put it, to reverse the rising incidence of Israeli Arab involvement in Palestinian terrorism. Convening, coincidentally, on the day after the bombing at the Karkur Junction, it marked the first time in Israeli history that this kind of grouping of Arab local council heads, Arab journalists and Jewish journalists had met to try to find ways to heal the rift. Thirty of us gathered around a large table in the high-ceilinged, stained glass–windowed room in which new governments are traditionally photographed when being received by the president on their first evening in office.

In his opening remarks, Katsav, a sad-eyed former Likud minister, said he could readily understand the Israeli Arab need to raise humanitarian aid for the Palestinians. He could understand the effort to press, legitimately, for Palestinian statehood. And he could understand the desire to voice pain at the suffering of the Palestinians. But he was "absolutely not prepared to condone efforts, albeit by a minority, but growing more and more hostile, to ideologically and actively harm the security of the state," he said. And he hoped the day's discussion might offer a pathway to prevent this.

To my horror and abiding amazement, the man whom Katsav had nominated as his cohost for the occasion, sitting alongside him, Shawki al-Khatib, the head of the Committee of Arab Local Councils, immediately knocked the initiative stone dead: "We condemn the bombings," he said in his opening remarks, but then he added in the next breath, "We see the occupation as the cause of all the bombings. We have adopted as a basic principle the effort to try to end the occupation."

Equally horrified, the editor of an ultra-Orthodox Jewish newspaper would later ask al-Khatib why he and his colleagues didn't make their goal the mutual cessation of violence, since that would boost moderation on both sides of the conflict and presumably accelerate the end-of-occupation outcome they sought. He received no constructive response.

The next day, I happened to run into one of Katsav's aides, who said the president had come away from the session more depressed than ever. And the Arab leaders present, he noted, were the moderates, the local council heads who truly represented the Israeli Arab public, not the grandstanding demagogues from the Arab political parties, some of whom had publicly expressed support for Osama bin Laden and Hezbollah from behind the protection afforded by their parliamentary immunity. It seems to me that Israeli Arabs were engaging in a gradual process of secession from the state, and the Intifada was accelerating the trend.

I think that plenty of other Israelis, hard pressed to cope, struggling economically (we have the widest discrepancy between the richest and poorest tenths of the population anywhere except the United States, and the gap is widening faster than in the United States) and weary of failed panaceas, turned to God—or at least a heavier than previous degree of fatalism, a "What will be will be" kind of attitude.

Lots of Israelis became incredibly cynical, and that includes many of our leaders, who have put self-interest above national interest to an unprecedented degree in recent years. I'm talking here about the likes of Yossi Ginossar, a former senior Shin Bet officer who was contentedly raking in commissions as the coordinator of Yasser Arafat's foreign bank accounts even as unequivocal evidence was emerging of Arafat's direct sponsorship of terrorism. In a massive exposé of the "Ginossar File," in the daily *Ma'ariv,* I was struck by a casual remark made by Mohammad Rashid, Arafat's financial sidekick, to Ginossar's partner, Ezrad Lev, as they motored through Tel Aviv. "One day, thanks to you, all this will be ours," said Rashid, casting his gaze over the luxury beachside hotels. Even hearing so casual a contemplation of the eventual overthrow of Israel was not sufficient cause for the Israeli pair to end their lucrative financial partnership with Arafat.

There was apparently even wider cynicism and self-interest in the behind-the-scenes shenanigans as the Likud selected its Knesset slate for the 2003 elections, a sordid process that was still being investigated when the new Knesset, allegedly corrupted members and all, was sworn in. That scandal went to the heart of our democracy, and took us a large step closer to the methods of a banana republic. And our democracy was also threatened by the obdurate resistance by settlers at illegal outposts to soldiers sent to remove them. We saw violent clashes at some such sites—young thugs with arrogant hatred in their eyes, beholden to no one, confronting Israelis of the same age sent to enforce the law. It will be Arafat's victory if, as we struggle to defend our country against his terrorism, we lose sight of what kind of country, with what values, we ought to be trying to preserve.

. . . • . . .

Not only is there is no quick fix; there is also, I fear, no prospect of a negotiated solution even in the medium term. But there is a middle path that might gradually advance that solution—and between the overreliance on military might represented by Sharon and Mitzna's, forgive me, defeatism: The army has to do its utmost to thwart the bombers, but the politicians must also do their utmost to encourage the emergence of a new Palestinian leadership, one that teaches mutual respect and tolerance, and one that will ultimately challenge and thwart terrorism, too. We can help catalyze a gradual change of mind-set on the Palestinian side by making clear that viable terms for Palestinian statehood—not Sharon's grudging 50 percent of the West Bank—will be offered when we get back to the talks, and that we can't wait to get back to the talks, but that the bombs and the anti-Israeli agitation have to stop first. We have to make clear that, just like Mitzna, we will dismantle all the Gaza settlements, but as part of an accord that provides for calm on the Israel-Gaza border. We have to make clear that, just like Mitzna, we will dismantle West Bank settlements, too, not in a panicked retreat from the bombers, but as part of a permanent peace accord. Stop the bombings and the incitement, we need to say, teach your people that the Jews, too, have every right to sovereignty in the Middle East, and you'll find Israel a willing, enthusiastic peace partner.

As of early 2003, most Palestinians did not believe that was the case. It was in our absolute interest to persuade them it was. Only then would more people like Sari Nusseibeh stick out their necks and campaign, with some prospect of winning support. Only then would more people like Abu Mazen declare, as he finally did in November 2002, that the Palestinians' goals could not be "realized by use of force"; that "we should have taken the opportunity of September 11" to put a halt to terrorism; that it is "the obligation of a new [Palestinian] government to determine the way forward [peacefully] . . . and use force if it becomes necessary" against those who "deviate from the Palestinian consensus. . . . We need to say clearly and with determination: 'No more, enough!' Did we build the homeland to start a war? . . . We can hold a demonstration or a march. But I do not like the word bloodshed. Shedding whose blood? The blood of our children, of your children?"

Only then would more voices be encouraged to speak confidently in refugee camps and on Palestinian university campuses about the profound mistake of this armed Intifada, how it had alienated moderate Israelis, and how dramatic could be the benefits of a radical change of course. Only then would the false dawn of the partnership with Arafat give way to renewed hope of a partnership with protagonists genuinely committed to reconciliation.

As of the 2003 elections, Israel had done far too little to get across its desire for reconciliation to the Palestinian public over the heads of Arafat's dishonest leadership and media. Sharon, scandalously, prevented both President Katsav and Avraham Burg, a former would-be Labor leader and speaker of the Knesset, from accepting invitations to address the Palestine National Council in Ramallah—scandalously because, no matter what use Arafat might have tried to make of their presence, these were rare opportunities for credible Israeli voices to be heard, undiluted, by the Palestinian public, voices that would have reflected our nation's yearning for peace. Similarly, while we had proved proficient, as Radwan Abu Ayyash's pamphlet so effectively reminded its readers, in silencing the Palestinian media when we so chose, blowing up transmitters on occasion as well as his TV center, why did we invest so little effort in transmitting our own broadcasts to Palestinian homes? Where was the properly funded Israeli cable and satellite station sending out a mixture of entertainment and political moderation to disarm the Arab world? Were we incapable of producing radio programming that might have mixed good music with a little subtle peace advocacy, beamed out on a clear wavelength to the West Bank and Gaza? The foreign ministry should have been training Arabic-speaking representatives for regular spots on Al-Jazeera, which claimed it was happy to have Israeli guests. (Al-Jazeera was once set to interview Sharon, in March 2002, but even that broadcast was canceled in a silly dispute over whether it would be filmed in a studio or at the prime minister's office.) And since the Palestinians had been told by their leaders that we dropped poison candy for their children, why didn't we take the hint and drop something much more incendiary, like pro-peace leaflets?

We need to reach out at every possible personal level, too. It is so rare, and so refreshing, to spend time with the likes of Rabbi Melchior, a man resolutely determined to foster dialogue among the devout—Jewish, Christian and Muslim—and undeterred even by the ceaseless struggle to build bridges to Muslim clerics who must defy death threats to so much as speak with the Jews. It is such a fillip to bump into a man like Professor Avi Rivkind, the head of trauma at Hadassah Hospital at Ein Karem in Jerusalem, as I did at a dinner, and hear him enthuse about how even Palestinian terrorists are not irredeemable. Eyes blazing under his frizzy gray curls, he asserted that he has built up relationships with Palestinians injured in the Intifada and brought to his hospital for treatment, who came in with no real concept of Jews as potentially normal people, and who left as more rounded human beings. Having been exposed for the first time to Jews who treat them unremarkably, they will never, he swears, go back to attacking Jews again.

And we need help from overseas with this as well. With the astute distribution of just a few million dollars, handed out to the families of suicide bombers and others at the forefront of the renewed armed struggle between 2000 and the abrupt demise of his regime in early 2003, Saddam Hussein deepened his appeal for much of the Palestinian public. Iranian funding helped Hamas widen its support base, through a thriving social and educational network, creating fertile soil for the recruitment of bombers. And Arafat managed to maintain his status for a long time via the discreetly murderous use of funding. (These funds, by the way, were often distributed via Israeli banks. Hamas, for instance, relied primarily on the Israeli banking system to get the money to the right recipients; I've seen Hamas officials, in their offices in Gaza, rifling through piles of checks drawn on Israel's Mercantile Bank. And emissaries of Saddam were known to have paid calls on Palestinians in Israeli hospitals as they established whom to favor with "martyrdom" stipends. These were tentacles of terror funding that Israel should have been able to sever easily.)

The United States, by contrast, continued to pour hundreds of millions of dollars into this region, with consequences often entirely counterproductive to its interests and ours. While the Bush administration did regulate the money it made available to the Palestinians, in order to avoid the direct financing of terrorism, it sold arms to our enemies elsewhere in the region and provided civilian assistance, too, to regimes, such as that in Egypt, in places that had become hotbeds of anti-Zionism and anti-Semitism. (The government-regulated media there, with its relentless vilification of Israel and Jews—reaching its height in late 2002 with the forty-one-episode *Horseman Without a Horse* series, based on the notorious *Protocols of the Elders of Zion*—was at the forefront of a campaign blatantly designed to delegitimize the Jews' right to statehood in the Middle East.) As for the Europeans, they were still stubbornly refusing to read the evidence before their eyes of Arafat's duplicity, and so insisted on sustaining a patently amoral regime. Sophisticated alternate use of these vast sums could create programs that educate for peace, and fund schools that teach reconciliation and nonviolence and cleave to democratic values. Monies could be allocated to set up independent broadcasting operations that do the same, providing belated competition for such state instruments of incitement as Arafat's Palestinian Broadcasting Corporation.

Our alliance with the United States is crucial to our prevailing in this conflict and finding a way to peace, however long it takes, and I don't think we can afford to take it for granted. On the afternoon of 9/11, as my sister-in-law watched the smoke rise in Manhattan from the roof of her apartment house, a neighbor snarled, "Ariel Sharon started all of this." As a friend's mother, a Holocaust survivor, walked that day in Riverdale, in the Bronx, a passerby spat out, "It's all the Jews' fault." I'd like to think that only the willfully self-delusional or the deeply anti-Semitic would readily fall prey to arguments like those. I'd like to think, similarly, that most Americans would incline to reject the assertion that their country would be spared the terrorists' murderous attentions were it to sever itself from all Middle Eastern involvement or scale back its support for Israel. But I'm relieved that Al-Qaeda did not put that theorizing to the test, that it did not portray 9/11 more specifically and prominently as a revenge act for Israel's "aggression against the Palestinians" and that Bin Laden so frequently stated his revulsion for the presence of all "infidels" anywhere in the "lands of Muhammad." And I am concerned that Al-Qaeda's depiction of the November 2002 terrorism in Mombasa in precisely those terms was no aberration, but the beginning of a trend, and one that Saddam tried to harness. The potential to stir up anti-Israeli hatreds, by terrorists citing Israel's behavior as their motivation, I fear, is far from exhausted in Europe and the United States. Were Al-Qaeda and groups like it to refocus their assault on civilization as a battle on behalf of the Palestinians, they would immensely complicate the vital antiterror assault being led by the United States. And they would complicate the Israeli-American relationship, on which Israel existentially depends.

. . . • . . .

At the same time as he vowed not to dismantle settlements, Sharon also promised repeatedly that he'd make "painful compromises" for peace if we got back to the negotiating table. I don't know what he meant by that, nor, I suspect, does anybody else. I do know that if there were a perception among Israelis that an opportunity was going begging, were there a new Palestinian leadership in place that genuinely sought moderation, and were our prime minister, whoever he might be, not meeting them halfway, the electorate would dump him. That's precisely what we did with Netanyahu in 1999. In Israel, change can come from below, forcing new leadership.

It's immensely harder for the Palestinians, under their largely autocratic leadership. But I do believe that the Palestinian masses are there to be won over, to be convinced that, despite what they've been force-fed on their TV and in their papers, bloodshed is not the only way forward. Khalil Shikaki, the most credible Palestinian pollster (whose brother Fathi, incidentally, was the Islamic Jihad leader assassinated by the Mossad in Malta in 1995), was tracking a gradual rise throughout 2002 in Palestinian support for a "mutual cessation of violence"—with a high of 76 percent in favor of such a cessation in a survey at year's end. That same survey found 56 percent of Palestinians supporting PA measures to "prevent armed attacks against Israeli civilians inside Israel" were such a cease-fire to be reached, even though 82 percent realized that such a crackdown "may lead to internal Palestinian strife." Findings like those, even though the same survey still found majority backing for attacks on Israeli civilians in Israel, and overwhelming support for attacks on soldiers and settlers, did suggest that there was at least something to try to build on.

But as things stood, Shikaki cautioned, the very nature of what would constitute the success of the Intifada had changed: Whereas statehood for Palestine would once have been deemed victory, he said, winning was now a function of how much pain could be imposed on the Israelis. In the run-up to the 2003 elections, Palestinian academics were acknowledging, the dilemma among Intifada leaders was not over whether or not to stop attacks on Israeli targets. That was unthinkable. It would have represented an intolerable victory for the intolerable Sharon. So the question was, rather, which Israelis to kill where, so as to avoid boosting Sharon while helping Mitzna: Would it be best to concentrate solely on attacks in the territories, or to continue bombings inside Israel as well? The challenge the Intifada leaders were addressing, I was told, was to find a formula for "acceptable resistance." (In the event, the bombers and gunmen continued to attack Israelis everywhere.) Moving from that kind of chilling, pragmatically murderous mind-set to a constructive one will be anything but rapid and straightforward.

But that is the transition the Palestinians have to make, and we Israelis couldn't have more of a stake in its being made sooner rather than later.

An accommodation with the Palestinians is a prime Israeli interest. Perhaps Burg, as parliamentary speaker, put it best in late 2001, when delivering a Knesset address on the sixth anniversary of the Rabin assassination. He spoke of three aspirations Jewish Israelis would like to maximize in an ideal world: We'd want control of as much of the biblical Land of Israel as possible. We'd want a state with as strongly Jewish a character as possible. And we'd want as pure a democracy as possible. As he went on to explain, however, there's a problem: In the absence of a multimillion-strong influx of American Jews, these three aspirations are mutually exclusive. You can have any two, but not all three. If we were to annex the West Bank and Gaza, for instance, we'd appropriate control over more of biblical Israel. But that larger country would be a lot less Jewish in nature, with its 5 million Jews and its 4.5 million Arabs. And pretty soon, the Jews would be a minority. And the only way to preserve Israel, albeit artificially, as a Jewish state in those circumstances would be to deny those millions of Arabs equal voting and other rights, and so destroy our democracy.

There is only one avenue, then, to maintaining Israel as both a Jewish state and a democratic one: finding the negotiated terms for territorial separation from Palestinians; and we can do that only when they have a leadership in place that honestly seeks coexistence, encouraged by the knowledge that we are again ready to offer viable terms. Their future depends on it. So, too, does ours. Yitzhak Frankenthal, whose own nineteen-year-old son, Arik, was murdered by Hamas abductors in 1994, and who set up a peace movement and insisted to me, as late as 2002, that Arafat was serious about wanting peace, cut straight to the chase: "Unless we are willing to give up being a Jewish state," he said, "we need a Palestinian state."

There is a cult of death that flourishes among Islamic extremists—the lust for murder that enabled 9/11 and that produces dozens of suicide bombers. Our interest lies in encouraging the moderates wherever and whenever possible, reaching out to them—those who do not agitate for violence and hatred, those who would change the textbooks and the mind-set—giving them the motivation to make themselves heard, however long it takes.

I won't capitulate to the extremists, but neither will I be dragged down by the belligerent rightists who mock our search for Palestinian moderation. Lisa says she'd love to think I'm right but fears I'm wrong. She sees the situation as hopeless, believes that the Palestinians will never agree to

Afterword

A perfect small gray bird is lying dead on the doorstep when I open the front door on December 20, 2002. That's how ferocious the wind has been overnight—harsh enough to fling the birds out of the trees, more than sixty miles an hour in places. Broken branches are blocking roads all over the country; streets are flooding; it's snowing up north and the waves have smashed apart breakwaters along the beaches. But I am going out to find Yasmin Abu Ramila nonetheless.

Yasmin was the seven-year-old recipient of one of Yoni Jesner's kidneys, an unwitting beneficiary of his murder. In reports immediately after his death and her transplant, the Hebrew press had her living vaguely in East Jerusalem, which could mean anywhere from the northern outskirts of Bethlehem, to near the Old City, to the southern edge of Ramallah. The telephone directory provided no assistance, but Schneider Children's Hospital in Tel Aviv, where the transplant operation was carried out, came through with her grandfather's cell-phone number. I phoned him day after day after day, and finally got an answer. I tried to explain, in Hebrew, that I wanted to visit Yasmin, just to say hello really, to complete some kind of circle. "I'm a sort of friend of Ari Jesner's—from the family who donated the kidney," I said, "and I'm writing a book, and, well, do you mind if I come and see her?"

He seemed perfectly friendly but hesitant, and he told me to call Shaare

Zedek Hospital, where he said Yasmin and her mother, Dina, were right then, undergoing a routine checkup. I called, but the hospital staff said I'd missed them. When I phoned Grandpa back, he said he was on his way to their house now, and that I should call in an hour. An hour later, he told me there was no one home. Weekdays were not really very good, he said, because his son, Fuad, was out at work. Perhaps, he suggested, I could visit on Friday, when it was more likely everyone would be at home. "That sounds great," I said. "Where do you live?"

"Kafr Akab," he said, then paused. "It will be hard for you to get here, you know. It's past the Kalandiya roadblock. You won't be allowed through. It's dangerous."

"Oh, don't worry," I told him airily. "I'll be fine. I'm a journalist. I've got all the right permits."

So we settled on Friday at 11:00 a.m. I was to call him from the Abu Ramila grocery store, owned by distant relatives of his, on the main road just past the Kalandiya roadblock, and he'd come meet me and take me to the family home.

I don't know why I professed such confidence that I would get to my destination. Probably, I think, because I'd just been reading about Kafr Akab in the Hebrew dailies. There was some discussion in the Defense Ministry about whether the Israel–West Bank anti-suicide-bomber fence was going to run north or south of this area, which, officially at least, is regarded as part of municipal Jerusalem, sovereign Israeli territory. So I guess I didn't really take in that bit about it being on the wrong side of the Kalandiya checkpoint, in the anarchic twilight zone between Israeli Jerusalem and Palestinian Ramallah.

By Friday, though, the slightly worrying reality of the location has registered. Since soldiers at the checkpoints are routinely turning back Israeli citizens, I take my British passport with me when I leave home. I also check that I have my worry beads—picked up on a visit to the Gaza Strip—as a possible defense against a drive-by shooting: My car has those yellow Israeli registration plates, and it doesn't have bulletproof windows. The sight of worry beads hanging from the rearview mirror, I like to figure, might just be enough to give a Palestinian gunman pause.

Windshield wipers swishing frantically, I drive along Road One past Jaffa Gate, the Damascus Gate, and north to French Hill, following the route of the old, pre-1967 border. Now I'm into the Arab neighborhoods—Shuafat, Beit Hanina, A-Ram, the areas of which Ehud Barak, trying to sell a Jerusalem compromise to the people, would remark: "When our ancestors dreamed about returning to Jerusalem, they were not thinking of Shuafat refugee camp." Indeed they were not. I zip through the first, unmanned roadblock near Atarot, once the site of a thriving Israeli airport and industrial zone, now a shooting gallery where several Israelis have been murdered since 2001. Atarot is so far beyond the sensible Israeli's motoring limits these days that the animal refuge here, which used to draw dozens of excited families looking to adopt a stray, is urgently seeking alternative premises and meanwhile making house calls, assembling a selection of suitable pets and driving them to the homes of the potential new parents.

Almost immediately, I come to the Kalandiya crossing, where the road is separated incomprehensibly into several narrow lanes, all of them now flooded, at the approach to the sandbagged little kiosk where a pair of soldiers are checking the vehicles coming in and out. I proffer my British passport and tell one of the soldiers I'm a journalist; he's entirely disinterested and waves me through. The line of vehicles coming the other way, waiting to enter Jerusalem, runs into the dozens, and it's barely moving.

I slip the worry beads over the rearview mirror and call Abu Ramila to confirm our meeting. There is no answer. I can't say I'm overly surprised, but neither am I about to give up and go home. I stop at a pharmacy and then at a gas station to ask for directions, which are pleasantly given, although in both cases my helpers look at me askance, apparently worried for my safety, and ask me whether I'm aware that I'm in "Area B," a section of the West Bank where the Palestinian Authority theoretically runs civilian affairs. Officially, I'm sure that's not the case, but I'd be lying if I didn't say the warnings are slightly unnerving. Eventually, I find the grocery store, still, theoretically, inside what Israel would like to call Israel. But whatever the Israeli maps say, this is now unmistakably Palestine. The cars bear Palestinian plates. The street and store signs are only in Arabic. Various offices of the Palestine National Authority are dotted about. And Kalandiya refugee camp is just around the corner, home to some ten thousand Palestinians, walled and wired in.

The two men in the grocery say helpfully that they're cousins of the Abu Ramila strand I'm after, but add, less helpfully, that Yasmin's family doesn't like to speak to reporters. I tell them I'd made an appointment with the grandfather, who's still not answering his cell phone. They make some calls, then report that he's stuck back in the direction I've come from, in Beit Hanina, doing some shopping. And then they shrug apologetically.

I'm speaking English and doing my best to look relaxed, but I am now distinctly nervous. The yellow plates on my car outside scream "Jew" to anyone who might happen along, in an area where mere Jewishness can prove fatal, albeit rarely, I tell myself. As young men troop in to buy cigarettes and more cigarettes, I press myself deeper into the shadow along the ceiling-high display stand of chocolates and cookies. I'm thinking of how quickly the word spread among young Palestinians in Tulkarm last year that a couple of Israelis were having a snack in a local café. Al-Aqsa Brigades chief Raed Karmi heard the news, and minutes later he was dragging the pair off to their deaths. I'm thinking of a line I once heard from an Israeli who's spent years reporting from the territories: about how everything is always okay until, just sometimes, it isn't.

Relief arrives in the slim, handsome, camel hair–coated form of Hamdi, who stops in for some cigarettes en route, he tells us all, to his friend's engagement party. The second-best English speaker in the store, he hears me out and, peering perplexedly into the teeming downpour, announces to no one in particular, "It's not right. He's come all this way, in this weather." His first suggestion is that another accidental shopper, who looks thoroughly underwhelmed by the idea, escort me to the Abu Ramila house. A lengthy process of extremely complicated direction giving ensues, during which my sullen-looking designated escort becomes progressively glummer. Ultimately, he remembers that he's due at the mosque, and hotfoots it. At my request, Hamdi now agrees that he will accompany me himself, but only if we're quick, because it's his best friend who's getting engaged, and they've arranged to meet here at the grocery, and the groom-to-be can't be late to his own party.

"So this is Kalandiya refugee camp," he tells me cheerfully as we wend our way along the narrow streets past the breeze-block walls with the barbed wire and the death's-head notices bearing the word DANGER. "You wouldn't want to go in there in this car," he adds. "You wouldn't get out alive." I smile tightly, aware of the fact.

Three minutes later, we pull up at the Abu Ramila home. Hamdi presses a buzzer, and a mother with a young girl under a blanket emerges from an upper floor into the downpour. I hope that's not Yasmin, I think to myself. It wouldn't be too clever if she caught pneumonia on my account. It isn't. The Abu Ramilas are a sizable dynasty, several nuclear units of which occupy various parts of this building. And their head, Farouq Abu Ramila, the grandfather with the cell phone, is here to greet me, not shopping in Beit Hanina after all. Yasmin, though, is not. She *is* in Beit Hanina, with her two brothers and her mother, Dina. That's where they've all been staying lately, Farouq explains, so as to be on the "kosher" side of the Kalandiya roadblock, in case Yasmin or her younger brother, Fadhi, also unwell, needs urgent hospital treatment.

The spacious stone entrance hall to the home is extravagantly furnished—sofas along every patch of wall—and as Hamdi's phone rings with ever-greater frequency, the three of us sit there, drink coffee and chat in a mixture of English, Hebrew and Arabic. Farouq is warm and welcoming, a likable, broad-shouldered man of, I guess, sixty, with a mustache discolored by a heavy smoking habit. He tells me that the transplant operation was a great success. He says Yasmin has made a terrific recovery. He also says they want to meet the Jesner family, to thank them, to say they are grateful for the "miracle that saved Yasmin," and that they are sorry for Yoni's death. "These things are decided by Allah," Farouq says, raising his eyes. "I didn't do it. You didn't do it. We all want peace. I know that this boy's family all want peace."

Yasmin was not at death's door when the doctors called that night to tell them to get to the hospital fast, he goes on. "She was on dialysis. She could have waited weeks, months, more, and she would have been okay. Actually, we had no idea that the donor was a Jew, or how the kidney became available, until after the operation. They didn't tell us anything about that. They just asked us to sign the form, so we signed." But it was a transplant operation in an Israeli hospital: Didn't they assume the donor was Jewish? I ask. "No, not at all. It could have been flown in from abroad. Anywhere. But we are so grateful. It was a fine thing that family did."

Hamdi is positively itching to get back by now. Why don't I drive him to the grocery, and then return to talk some more, he suggests. But I won't do that because I don't fancy getting lost in the side roads around Kalandiya. I ask Farouq for the address where I can find Dina and Yasmin in Beit Hanina and get ready to leave, but Farouq decides he'll come with me—show me the way, see his grandchildren, get some air.

So back we go, dropping off Hamdi to meet his understandably impatient friend, then heading south toward the checkpoint. The rain is still pounding down, and I have to drive on the sidewalk to avoid flooding the car. The waiting line to go into Jerusalem is shorter now—it's past noon, and both quasi-Palestine and Israel are winding down for the weekend. As we sit behind two or three cars, though, I watch dozens of Palestinians walking toward us, homeward bound across this confusing divide: from one part of what Israel says is Jerusalem to another; practically, from Israel to Palestine. Permits to cross are in short supply these Intifada days. Permits to bring in cars are even scarcer. So they walk—schoolchildren with satchels on their backs, attuned to the routine and impervious to the rain; elderly men wearing kaffiyehs and using canes, their feet disappearing into the mud as they slowly traverse the few hundred yards to where the yellow Palestinian taxis are waiting; laborers wheeling who knows what on blue pushcarts; businessmen in well-tailored suits and ties, briefcases in hand, some pulling suitcases on wheels. "Crappy, isn't it?" says Farouq, seeing the direction of my gaze. "And at nine every night, they close it. Doesn't matter who you are, there's no going in or out."

Farouq gets his ID paperwork ready as we wait, and pulls out some other documentation, too. "Look at that," he urges, passing over a typed note from the Jerusalem City Hall setting out his city tax debts. It shows him to be 9,789.98 shekels (about two thousand dollars) in arrears, including fines and interest charges. It says that a lien has been placed on his bank account and demands that he present himself to the relevant department to agree on a payment schedule.

"Wait a minute," I ask, incredulous. "You have to pay city taxes to the Jerusalem municipality for your home in Kafr Akab, as though they were still providing you with refuse collection and road-maintenance services?" Kafr Akab, where Jewish Israelis fear to tread and are generally barred from treading?

"Good, isn't it?" he says. "I went to that office and told them to do whatever they had to do. They've closed my bank account? Fine. I suppose they may come and seize the TV from my home, but what can I do? I've spent most of the past two years taking Yasmin to and from the hospital, across the roadblock. Believe me, I have no money."

We're at the front of the line now. I show my press card to the soldier; Farouq, Jerusalem-born, shows his Israeli ID card. We're waved through. I catch a glimpse of Farouq's ID picture; it shows a man of about forty. The photo must be at least twenty years old, I reckon, looking across at

Farouq, with his gray hair and wrinkled forehead. "How old are you, by the way?" I ask him. "Fifty," he says.

On the drive to Beit Hanina, Farouq relates the family history. His grandfather was born in Hebron, he says. He himself used to live in the Old City and work all over Israel, something to do with boilers. But there's been hardly anything in his line for years. He thinks peace is possible. Of course peace is possible. He thought Barak and Arafat were going to make it. "Nobody wants this killing. It's helping nobody. Let the Jews live where the Jews live and the Arabs live where the Arabs live." And in Jerusalem? "In Jerusalem, too—the Western Wall for the Jews, the mosques for the Muslims, the churches for the Christians." And formal control, sovereignty, security? He waves the formalities away: "Let them all have policemen. The Jews, the Muslims, the Christians. They can all police it together."

He says Yasmin was unwell from birth—apparently, the doctors said, because there had been too much intrafamily marriage, cousins wedding cousins, playing havoc with the genes. Yasmin's kidneys barely functioned from the start, but her condition deteriorated two years ago. She'd swell up alarmingly in between dialysis sessions. Yoni Jesner has saved her from that now. Her brother Fadhi, who's five, seems to be suffering from the same ailment, although it's not as serious yet. Farouq sings the praises of the Israeli doctors, all of them, who've treated the family. "Fantastic people," he says. "If I spent the rest of my life saying thank you to them, it wouldn't be enough."

Deep in Beit Hanina, we hit a small hiccup: two cars stopped in the middle of the road, blocking it. The trunk of the front car is open, and I tell Farouq I think I see a young man loading a machine gun into it. He is delighted by my paranoia. "It's a jack," he says, chortling. "They were fixing a puncture." It is. They were.

We park and climb three flights up an outdoor staircase, slippery in the rain. Farouq rings the bell, and Dina, Yasmin's mother, a full-cheeked but slender woman with olive skin and brown hair pulled back from her face, opens the door. The children scuffle to be first to hug their grandfather.

Yasmin Abu Ramila is smiling but shy, reluctantly complying with her mother's request that she shake hands with me. Her long hair is in a ponytail. She is wearing a white sweater with pink roses, and open-toed sandals, despite the weather. I show her some really special colored pencils

I've brought for her, with multihued lead that gives you a rainbow effect when you sketch, turning a clod into an artist. She couldn't be less impressed. "I've got a satchelful of them," she says dismissively, relating this through her grandfather, who translates.

She and her brothers take Farouq's phone and, confirming his indulgence, start calling various relatives. Farouq and I sit on blue couches in the living room, along with a microwave. Through a high archway is the children's bedroom, where there are three yellow foam mattresses in a row beneath a flaking ceiling and, incongruously, two huge posters of HFIVE, a defunct Israeli pop band. "They don't usually live here," Farouq reminds me. "They're just sleeping here so that they can get to the hospital in an emergency."

Dina insists on making tea for me, and then submits, with obvious unease, to the ordeal of conversation. Farouq cautions me: "She only went to school through fourth grade. She got married at eighteen, and had Yasmin a year later. Her husband, my son, works as a waiter at an East Jerusalem café, earning maybe fifty shekels [barely ten dollars] a day. Her children have not been well. Life has been hard on her."

I want to talk to her about the lessons all Jews and Muslims might learn from the interaction between the Jesner family and hers. I want to talk to her about stereotypes and preconceptions, the futility of violence and the preciousness of life. But translated from Hebrew to Arabic by Farouq, my attempts at the most gentle questioning—about the well-being of her children, the circumstances that led to Yasmin's transplant—elicit apologetic shrugs, the briefest of answers. My predictable "Does she think Jews and Arabs can make peace?" yields the equally predictable *"Inshallah."*

After a few minutes of this, I thank her for letting me meet her children, and for the tea, and wish her and the family well. When we leave—Farouq is going to guide me back to the main road and on into central Jerusalem, where he'll stop by his son's café—Dina comes to the front door, Yasmin clinging to her leg, and I make one final, rambling attempt at conversation: "What are your hopes, your dreams?" I ask her. "In an ideal world, what would you like to do with your life? What would you wish for your children?" Dina shrugs helplessly at Farouq, smiles and nods a gracious farewell, then closes the door.

"Honestly, David," Farouq chides me gently as we walk downstairs in the rain, "how could you expect her to answer questions like that?"

. . . • . . .

In the Gaza Strip that same day, Rabbi Yitzhak Arameh, forty, a father of six, is fatally shot in his car by a gunman from Islamic Jihad. Troops in Nablus find a bomb factory in a home in the Askar refugee camp, with five bombs ready for planting and piles of the kinds of ball bearings and metal pellets that killed Yoni Jesner. A bomb is defused at a bus stop in Netanya. And Palestinian officials protest that America's pro-Israel bias "knows no limits" after the U.S. government vetoes a Syrian-drafted United Nations resolution that would have condemned Israel for its "excessive and disproportionate use of force in the Occupied Palestinian territories."

Acknowledgments

Thank you, first and foremost, to my wife and kids, for giving me the time to write this, and not complaining too much about my consequent domestic delinquency. Thanks to Lisa as well for reading the manuscript and putting me straight where necessary.

Thanks to my wise and supportive editor at Knopf, Jonathan Segal. And to Bennett Ashley, my agent, for his counsel and commitment.

Thanks to all my colleagues at *The Jerusalem Report,* who constantly reassess their attitudes to what unfolds around us with admirable journalistic candor, and whose insights and analyses consistently challenge my own. Thanks especially to Sharon Ashley, the magazine's deputy editor and creative powerhouse, who closely read this manuscript and, to her surprise and my relief, found a little less to critique this time than in the past.

I used source material from local and international newspapers, as well as radio and TV. I am grateful to Tom Gross for his monitoring of the print media with regard to coverage of Jenin. I also referred to material compiled by Ethan Casey and Paul Hilder, editors of *Peace Fire: Fragments from the Israel-Palestine Story* (London: Free Association Books Ltd., 2002), and by Human Rights Watch in its November 2002 report, "Erased in a Moment: Suicide Bombings Against Israeli Citizens."

Other source books included *The End of Days: Fundamentalism and the Struggle for the Temple Mount* by Gershom Gorenberg (New York: Free Press, 2000); *Shalom, Friend: The Life and Legacy of Yitzhak Rabin* by *The Jerusalem Report* staff (New York: Newmarket Press, 1996); *Harakiri* (English title: *Ehud Barak: The Failure*) by Raviv Drucker (Tel Aviv: Yedioth Ahronoth Books, 2002); *My Jerusalem* by Teddy Kollek (New York: Summit Books, 1990); and *The Natural: The Misunderstood Presidency of Bill Clinton* by Joe Klein (New York: Doubleday, 2002).

Finally, my thanks to those people in these pages who graciously allowed me to write about them or in their name, however sensitive and painful the subject matter.

Index

A Note About the Author

David Horovitz is the editor of *The Jerusalem Report* and a frequent commentator on Israeli current affairs for BBC television, CNN and other outlets. He is the author of *A Little Too Close to God: The Thrills and Panic of a Life in Israel,* and he edited and cowrote, together with other members of *The Jerusalem Report,* a biography of Yitzhak Rabin, *Shalom, Friend,* which won the National Jewish Book Award for non-fiction. Born in London, he emigrated to Israel in 1983, and lives in Jerusalem with his wife, Lisa, and their three children.

A Note on the Type

The text of this book was set in a typeface called Times New Roman, designed by Stanley Morison for *The Times* (London) and introduced by that newspaper in 1932.

Among typographers and designers of the twentieth century, Stanley Morison was a strong forming influence, as typographical adviser to the Monotype Corporation of London, as a director of two distinguished English publishing houses, and as a writer of sensibility, erudition and keen practical sense.

In 1930 Morison wrote: "Type design moves at the pace of the most conservative reader. The good type-designer therefore realizes that, for a new font to be successful, it has to be so good that only very few recognize its novelty. If readers do not notice the consummate reticence and rare discipline of a new type, it is probably a good letter." It is now generally recognized that in the creation of Times Roman, Morison successfully met the qualifications of his theoretical doctrine.

Composed by Stratford Publishing Services,
Brattleboro, Vermont

Printed and bound by Berryville Graphics,
Berryville, Virginia

Designed by Iris Weinstein